Future
Talk

OTHER BOOKS BY LARRY KING

Larry King, with Emily Yoffe

Tell It to the King, with Peter Occhiogrosso

Tell Me More, with Peter Occhiogrosso

Mr. King, You're Having a Heart Attack, with B. D. Colen

When You're from Brooklyn, Everything Else Is Tokyo,
with Marty Appel

On the Line: The New Road to the White House,
with Mark Stencil

*How to Talk to Anyone, Anytime, Anywhere:
The Secrets of Good Communication*, with Bill Gilbert

Future Talk

CONVERSATIONS

ABOUT TOMORROW

WITH TODAY'S

MOST PROVOCATIVE

PERSONALITIES

Larry <u>King</u>

with Pat Piper

HarperCollins*Publishers*

HarperCollins books may be purchased for educational, business, or sales promotional use. For information please write: Special Markets Department, HarperCollins Publishers, Inc., 10 East 53rd Street, New York, NY 10022.

FIRST EDITION

Designed by Joseph Rutt

Library of Congress Cataloging-in-Publication Data

King, Larry, 1933–
    Future talk : conversations about tomorrow with today's most
provocative personalities / Larry King, with Pat Piper.
      p. cm.
    ISBN 0-06-017457-9
    1. Twenty-first century—Forecasts. 2. Interviews—United States.
I. Piper, Pat. II. Title.
CB161.K544   1998
303.49'09'05—dc21   97-39091

---

98 99 00 01 02 ❖/RRD 10 9 8 7 6 5 4 3 2 1

To my great grandchildren not yet born and
to grandchildren everywhere.
To children not yet born.
And to the children who have grown up.
This century is yours.
But you have to keep each other in sight.

Contents

CONTENTS
•
x

Introduction

The first issue we will face in the twenty-first century is when it actually begins. Already there is debate between those who want to ring in both a new year and a new century on December 31, 1999, and those who insist we must wait until December 31, 2000. This challenging and emotional controversy is solved within these pages. (Hey, I brought Al Gore and Ross Perot together on the NAFTA debate, so a minor issue like when the hell we celebrate isn't that big a deal.) Besides, this same argument was going on at the beginning of this century, whenever that was. . . .

Back on the corner in Brooklyn during the 1930s, we never talked about the twenty-first century. Our focus instead was inside Maltz's Candy Store, where we'd read yesterday's baseball scores from the newspapers and then have heated debates on someone's stoop about the Dodgers or the Yankees being the better team. But I still remember the talk whenever an airplane passed above because we'd always look up and remark to one another what it must be like to fly and how fast do you think it's going and where do you think it came from, and now that I think about it, maybe that was the same thing as thinking about the future. You had to go looking for it.

The thought occurred to me only a few years ago that I was probably going to experience this chronological changing of the guard, and quite frankly, the notion was unsettling. I didn't want to look up and see spaceships landing, I didn't want to push a button to read a newspaper, I didn't want to talk to a plastic screen and say, "Let's watch the Orioles game where Cal Ripken breaks Lou Gehrig's record, and if possible, I'd like to view it from behind home plate." I prefer real mail to faxes and looking things up in a book to a CD-ROM, whatever that is. The idea of the future, much less a new century, is scary.

And, for the most part, I'm not alone feeling this way. That's why I asked each person during these interviews what it is out there in the future that causes the most worry, even if he or she won't be around to experience the resulting horror, were it to occur. Maybe if we know our fears in advance we can then see their beginnings on the horizon and set in motion a defense or, better yet, an offense.

Similarly, I asked each of the forty-three people who sat down with me to offer advice to the rest of us who are going to wake up one morning in a new century (whenever you choose to celebrate the arrival). To a person, the words I heard most often were "change" and "learn." A year ago these ideas took me to the Library of Congress, where I visited a number of century-old newspapers to compare advice from across ten decades. Indeed, I found the same words there, as well as something else. The *Cleveland Plain Dealer* made the following observation of where its readers had been and where they were about to go:

> The age of surprises is but beginning but men have almost lost the capacity of being surprised.
>
> . . . the newspaper of a hundred years from now if newspapers themselves have not been superseded by some other device more thoroughly up to date may look back to the last year of the 19th Century as a time of darkness and ignorance or at best of mere groping towards the light that shone brightly on the 20th Century.

The twentieth century has brought us the car, the ability to fly to the moon and back, a cure for polio, the ability to talk across continents, an obligation to treat other human beings with equality, and, while not absolute, a disintegration of totalitarian political structures.

Each of these, and the thousands of other events I haven't room to mention, has surprised us. Today, one hundred years since those words were written, I think our capacity is just fine and we're ready for the next one hundred.

One more note about change. I can report from firsthand experience in doing this book that change isn't something waiting on the horizon. It's happening as you are reading this. From the time I completed the first draft of the manuscript, follow-up interviews had to be scheduled with about half of the participants because things (Dow Jones measurements, television ratings, cigarette industry litigation, discovery of ice on a moon of Jupiter, to name a few) had changed.

I know the time is coming when I will be an old man sitting in a chair in Miami going off about the good old days to someone younger. And if I'm still able to hear that supersonic whatever-it-is flying across the Florida sky, I'm going to look up and wonder aloud what it must be like to fly in it and how fast the thing is going, and if I haven't forgotten what I'm doing by then, where it came from.

—1998

Us

Our destination is based not so much on where we are going as on where we are coming from. Consequently, I decided to talk with three individuals, each with a unique ability to look inside and, maybe more important, explain in clear language what they see. All these people have passed through Harvard, though I don't think that is a prerequisite for the ability to hold a mirror to ourselves and arrive at working definitions of who we are.

Stephen Jay Gould is the popular Harvard paleontologist who writes about the complex subjects of evolution and natural history so even I understand what he's talking about. Our interviews took place over a period of months, and the experience brought back fond memories of late nights in the radio studio as Stephen Jay Gould answered questions from callers across North America about who we are with a healthy combination of fact and wit. He never had to think about an answer then and he never paused during this series of questions either. I have come away from these sessions with Stephen knowing we are best measured by what we do off the clock rather than on the clock.

Farai Chideya is familiar as a political reporter to those who watched MTV during the 1996 presidential campaign. She was a regular on CNN's *Early Edition* every Monday morning. Readers know Farai from her essays in *Time* magazine, her writing for *Vibe* magazine, and her reporting in *Newsweek*. She was a 1996 Research Fellow at the

Freedom Forum Media Studies Center, where she examined why people younger than thirty watch less television news than any other demographic. But her focus has always been on race relations, and as a result, she wrote the well-received *Don't Believe the Hype*, which explored how misinformation is used by one race against another, and is finishing a second book about the racial makeup of America. Now a correspondent for ABC News, Farai Chideya is definitely a voice to be heeded both now and in the next century.

Who we are can be defined by how we treat our children and families. The twentieth century comes to an end with the phenomenon of both parents working, an activity never before seen (except during the world wars) in our society. We are still seeking ways to care for children while parents are away from the home, and the first solution has always been the public school. This is changing. The workplace is becoming more and more family-friendly, as is government. A driving force in this direction is Marian Wright Edelman, founder and president of the Children's Defense Fund, an important and—dare I say?—loud voice for children and family. Its logo contains the words, "The sea is so wide and my boat is so small," but I can tell you that with Marian around, the waves don't seem quite as threatening.

STEPHEN JAY GOULD

PALEONTOLOGIST AT HARVARD UNIVERSITY

I don't believe in prediction, prophecy, or punditry, but no one has ever improved on the old biblical injunction (Micah 6:8): Do justly, love mercy, and walk humbly.

LK: Okay, since you're the expert on when we began, when does the twenty-first century begin?

GOULD: I'm going to celebrate on December 31, 1999 and on December 31, 2000. Each one is legitimate.

LK: Let me understand this: There was no year 0, correct?

GOULD: That's exactly why technically, if you believe all centuries need to have one hundred years, as we usually do, and because there was no year 0, every hundredth year has to go with the previous century. 1900 goes with the eighteen-hundred years and 1700 goes with the sixteen-hundred years, so by that calculation, 2000 goes with the nineteen-hundred years to form the last year of the twentieth century, and the millennium starts in the year 2001. This is why both Arthur Clarke and Stanley Kubrick named their book and film the way they did.

LK: So I should follow that idea and not do anything special on December 31, 1999?

GOULD: No. It's arbitrary anyway. The system that gave rise to this dilemma didn't even begin until the seventh century, and nobody living in the year 1 knew that it was year 1. I think people feel the year 2000 looks like a better year for a celebration because of their car odometer. When it moves from "1999" to "2000," that's more interesting than when it moves from "2000" to "2001." So to justify this, we're going to have to proclaim the first century just had ninety-nine years.

This issue comes up every century, but in the past, when there really was a pop culture—high culture distinction, official century celebrations were always in '01. But in this century, pop and high culture have amalgamated and pop culture has won, so we're just going to celebrate it in the year 2000.

LK: We're not a patient people.

GOULD: No, we all have car odometers.

LK: We are about to enter a time that others in these pages say will have a lot of change and a lot of speed, and it makes me wonder if this will change us as human beings somehow.

GOULD: If you think of human history in geological terms we've only had civilization for 10,000 years, which can't be measured when you consider the history of life is three and one-half billion years old. It's a geological eye blink. Cultural change and cultural evolution are so rapid relative to biological evolution because it has such different properties of inheritance. We invent things and pass them on to the next generation, and we accumulate, and each generation makes improvements. Biological change doesn't work that way because anything you do in your lifetime doesn't mean a damn thing because you're only passing on the genes that you had, and which your ancestors had.

LK: Technically we can do more things than we've ever been able to do, all at the same time. Does that potential overload do anything to us biologically?

GOULD: I don't know what our biologic limits are.

LK: Let's talk about sports. Will more records be broken or have we reached those limits?

GOULD: We won't see them being broken with the abandon we've seen this century. There are limits to what we can do based on the design of our bodies, but what happens is, the training will improve or more participants are included in the sample or the rules change. In 1900 only white guys could play baseball, and nobody trained for maximal musculature. Today men of all races can play and training is so good, and for those reasons you are bound to get improvement. Horse racing records have varied by just a few seconds over the past one hundred years, but that's because all thoroughbred horses are bred from a uniform stock which has been improved as much as it can be and nobody figured out any better techniques of jockeying, so you won't see anything other than minor changes. You are seeing the same pattern with several men's records. Records are broken less frequently and with less of a decrease. But this is not the case with the marathon. More people are getting into it and we are still learning new ways to train, so the records are improving. Women's records are being broken in most sports much more frequently than in men's sports and with larger percentage increments. Some will mistakenly extrapolate this to mean women will eventually reach, or outperform, men in the same sport. That's only going to occur in a few activities like long distance swimming, which favors the body form and musculature of women over men. The one exception is when a technique is improved, as we've seen in pole vaulting. They invented the fiberglass pole and saw amazing improvements.

LK: Culturally, we are moving toward what?

GOULD: I have no idea. There are trends, but that can change with a war. There is the population trend, which is now beginning to slow down, but one would presume something will happen before we have global famines.

LK: We are coming out of the most violent century on earth. What does that say about us and our direction?

GOULD: The irony is that we are, globally, a much nicer people than we ever were. There are more people with compassion for and understanding of cultural differences. We don't have public beheadings in the town square, we don't have ownership of women, and we have social support of the elderly no matter how much we argue about it. But the weapons of destruction have increased so immensely in magnitude and capability of use that when you get a madman, he is capable of doing things on a worldwide scale. I'll bet if you went back to the first Crusade there were twenty Hitlers operating in the name of Jesus, but they could only do it with stones and swords. The problem now is, when you do get a Hitler, he's got bombs and weapons despite the improvements we've made in our morality. The greatly declining number of horrible people has been balanced by such an increase in the capacity to do harm that the net amount of harm is increased even while the net amount of goodness has also increased. It is ironic. Our mentality is the greatest threat to survival as a species.

LK: You then are going on record saying no asteroids will wipe us out in the next one hundred years?

GOULD: Nobody can say that in any hundred-year period about an event that occurs once every 50 million to 100 million years.

LK: Do you think by the end of the next century we will know for sure if we are not alone?

GOULD: I certainly hope so. The problem here is negative evidence. If you do find evidence, then we know we're not, but if you don't find evidence, then we just don't know if we've even looked in the right places.

LK: Do you think with new technologies available in the next century that we might answer once and for all and with greater specificity when man separated from the ape?

GOULD: I think it's pretty well pinpointed now. The human and chimpanzee split somewhere around 6 million years ago, give or take a million or two. But it could change with biochemical evidence. Scientists are always ready for surprises.

LK: Is there any piece of the puzzle in the fossil record you'd like to see solved in this coming century?

GOULD: There is one missing piece, and that is the chemical evidence I was just talking about. The oldest human fossil is 4.4 million years old, and it's already an upright creature, so we don't know anything about the first million and a half years, which includes the transition to upright fossils. I'd love to see that. We were a pretty small population back then so it's kind of chancy.

LK: Will dinosaurs continue to fascinate us as they do now?

GOULD: I think they're overexposed myself, but they have enormous staying power when you think that the word "dinosaur" was only invented in 1840, and by 1850 there were full-scale models of them being built. But I think they will remain the biggest, the fiercest, the ugliest, and the weirdest creatures of our past.

LK: Which brings me to the *Jurassic Park* question.

GOULD: Oh, not that again.

LK: Could it happen?

GOULD: I don't think so. We will have techniques to get dinosaur DNA but I don't think there's enough DNA out there because it's a very unstable compound and it breaks down. But even if you had little bits and pieces of dinosaur DNA you couldn't make an organism because you don't have the whole program, and even if you have the whole program, there has to be an embryology, a mother's cell genetic structure. So if there is no dinosaur DNA preserved anywhere then you just can't do it.

LK: So it will continue to be the stuff of movies?

GOULD: That is the one thing I'm willing to say with reasonable certainty.

LK: What scares you?

GOULD: I do think we have the capacity to save ourselves and the question is, if we do it at all, do we do it in the wise way, recognizing the problems before they engulf us? Or do we do it the way that is usually done, which is the bumbling way, when a tragic war or famine envelops us and then we make the move. The things I fear are the extrapolation of the weapons of destruction, and the other thing is the engulfing standardization. I bought my daily Tube ticket in London a few days ago, and on the back of it was advertising for The Gap. Everything is becoming commercialized, and when that happens, everything becomes simplified. There is no separate civic dignity when that happens. Variety is the essence of things. It's low- and high-end. There's a McDonald's everywhere but there's also Armani everywhere. There's also a soul problem here because it's only one way and the local creativity is stifled.

LK: We've never been faced with having to worry about, to use your words, "having to save ourselves" at any other time in history. What does that do to us?

GOULD: We've always been able to foul things up locally but never have we been able to unleash global effects. The ozone hole is an interesting example because it is clearly a global effect. We are now on the verge of producing things like that. We need to pay attention to this.

LK: In the big picture human beings don't really make a lot of sense, do they?

GOULD: In the larger picture we are just one more species, and I wouldn't make a whole lot of fuss about what we've done in some tiny little fraction of the earth's history. On the other hand, we are the first conscious creature on this planet, and that gives us enormous potential power.

LK: Do you think more animals will become extinct?

GOULD: The answer is yes. It's hard to predict because it's not a biological question as much as it's a cultural question. It's awfully hard to expect impoverished nations not to exploit resources for the immediate benefit of their people because, after all, we did it, and what right do we have now to turn around and say, "You can't"? Nevertheless, it's the only wilderness we have left.

LK: What are the ramifications of genetic technology?

GOULD: We now have a cultural feedback that allows us, in principle, to screw around with our own genetics. I hope we won't do it except in a limited way for obvious medical benefits. In defense of technology, it's too powerful to abandon just because you see it has potential misuses. But if we use it benevolently and in a limited way in the cure of diseases and the alleviation of mental and physical conditions, then more power to us.

LK: Medical ethics will be a good business to be in next century.

GOULD: It's a good business now. But how about this: Suppose you are in the insurance business and you've spent years studying actuarial statistics because, after all, living is random. But you know how much to charge a fifty-year-old man. Now what happens if you have enough genetic knowledge that you can say, "This person applying for insurance only has X amount of years left"? Now what do you do? Only insure those you know will live until eighty? That's not fair.

We will face the issues: To what extent can a company compel genetic testing of its employees? To what extent does one's genetic information remain a private domain? To what extent do you allow two parents you know carry the gene for a terrible disease to have a child, and do you have any right to intervene? I'm not sure I even like the idea of having a field of medical and genetic ethicists.

LK: Would you like to spend some time in the twenty-first century?

GOULD: I have every intention of doing so. My chorus is singing Haydn's *Creation* on January 1, 2000. But consider this: There are very few people who have ever been privileged to live through a millennial transition, and we'll be among them.

FARAI CHIDEYA

NATIONAL AFFAIRS EDITOR, *VIBE* MAGAZINE;
EDITOR OF POP & POLITICS WEB SITE
(HTTP://WWW.POPANDPOLITICS.COM);
AUTHOR OF *THE COLOR OF AMERICA*

*Shed the useless nostalgia and try to learn what we can in the
time that we have. Then we'll be in a good position to evaluate
if the changes we're going through are positive or negative, not
based on fear but rather on some sense of opportunity.*

LK: How would you describe American society in the next twenty
years?

CHIDEYA: The people who are young today have been exposed to
ethnic diversity, unlike their parents, so I think one of the major characteristics is going to be a familiarity with other cultures and races that
doesn't exist now. This isn't to say they will associate with other ethnic
groups, and I don't think you can put a toggle on it as "better" or
"worse." Ultimately though, it's up to the individuals in American society to make what they will out of it. Immigrants can be embraced or
rejected, for example. In the long run, diversity will produce a better
understanding and a more open society. We will achieve some sort of
progress on the race issue but it doesn't mean we won't fight like hell
in the next twenty years.

LK: Do you think ethnic diversity will be taught in the schools?
Sort of a how-to-get-along kind of class?

CHIDEYA: We're just starting to teach people about differences
but there are a lot of people who consider it absolutely artificial. It's
that "feel-good ethnic diversity crap," and some of it is crap. There's
been a lot of mythmaking about who is American and what is
American. Right now you aren't seeing many constructive ways of
teaching about diversity but you do have the familiarity on a child-to-
child basis. Kids are going to have to figure out by themselves because
there isn't much of a top-down effort.

LK: Will there be more or less racial division?

CHIDEYA: We've done a lot of the hard work simply going through a lot of the legal mechanisms such as desegregation. Those tools are in place although some of the drug laws are very biased against African Americans and we haven't been able to deal with that. But as far as jobs are concerned we have made the step where legally we aren't supposed to discriminate. Now what we need to do is get over the idea that laws are enough. Anything we really want in this society, we have to put an effort into it, be it nuclear disarmament or building a space shuttle. But racial equality is something we never put any effort into. It's the chicken-egg thing. In societal change the chicken is the government's effort and the egg is the public willingness. During the civil rights era you had a few leaders like President Kennedy, but nothing happened until after he was killed. That's when you had the public support, and you can't have one without the other. Right now we have neither. America's increasing diversity could produce a groundswell of public support. If you have an affinity for your next door neighbor who is someone that is nonwhite, you may feel the issue is more important than you would have otherwise. For many, many years America will be majority white, and public opinion is going to be dictated by what mainstream white America thinks. The issue is how much will mainstream white America actively pursue equality.

LK: And the answer is?

CHIDEYA: It depends on whether or not we view the chances of every American to succeed as a realistic goal. It's human nature to want to succeed, and success is too often perceived as trumping someone else. That's a real impediment to any true pursuit of equality. People are disinterested in putting themselves on the line to change the status quo.

LK: Young people should keep their eyes on what as they cross this line between the centuries?

CHIDEYA: In terms of race relations, they need to keep their eyes on what is constructive competitiveness and what is just being churlish. You can say, "I need to do the best that I can," and that entails being better than some people. But is it necessary to undermine another's opportunity, to block his chance at life, liberty, and the pursuit of happiness, in order to achieve your own? That has got to be a litmus test, and I think sometimes people are consciously or subconsciously feeling they do have to undermine other people's ability to succeed. As you come to the millennium, it becomes a question of thinking beyond your own self-interest. Maybe we can head off a crisis rather than react to it? That would change American society immeasurably because it would be forward thinking, and that's something we've always had problems with.

LK: You've talked of "comfortable laziness" among TV viewers. Is that good or bad?

CHIDEYA: TV is a lazy medium because you consume passively. You don't have to turn the page.

LK: Are we angry now, and do you think we'll be angry in the future?

CHIDEYA: Certain people are angry about certain things, but I don't think we're angry. As long as we're economically comfortable and as long as there's a fairly good slate of programs on NBC, ABC, and CBS, nobody's going to have any major beef with society. We as Americans are very bad at incremental social change; we're much more comfortable with periodic revolution but not with putting in the hard work to make sure things get improved over an extended period of time.

LK: Are we going through incremental social change now?

CHIDEYA: We are in terms of diversity. People are still fearful, as we've seen with Proposition 187 and Proposition 209; there's still a lot of very heated debate, mostly at the regional and statewide level, on issues of diversity like affirmative action, but we're adjusting. We have to. We have no choice. Our society has fundamentally changed, and even if we cut off all immigration into the United States, as some have suggested, we would still be a diverse nation and we would still continue to be more diverse because of the differences in birth rates among races and ethnicities, so we've reached the point of no return. Some people see that as a fatal moment while others see it as wonderful. Regardless of whether you are pro or con, it's reality. We see it in women's roles in American society. Women got the right to vote in 1922 and now you have pundits wishing that right had never been invented.

LK: How soon before there's a woman president?

CHIDEYA: There will be someday, just as there will be a black president and a Jewish president, but there's also the grandfathering of power. California is 60 percent white, but the electorate is 80 percent white. The same thing happens with race and religion, so in terms of a woman president, I wouldn't bet it would happen in the next ten years.

LK: Do you think we'll reach a point where we will no longer talk of "the first woman whatever" or "the first African-American whatever"?

CHIDEYA: We will stop saying "the first" when the arena becomes "all whatever." At one point there was the first black professional basketball player, and now the NBA is filled with blacks. I do wonder what will happen in the future if certain professions we can't even envision today become more heavily filled with groups of one ethnicity or one gender. I think as we meet certain milestones other arenas will become desegregated in different ways we can't anticipate.

LK: Will we see cultures in the future coexist peacefully?

CHIDEYA: It has always been a process of thesis-antithesis-synthesis, but you never reach a synthesis although you keep moving toward it. I can document times where the mainstream media have used misinformation against African-Americans and against issues which are stereotyped, which sometimes are or aren't, as "African-American" issues. For example, the media assumed the rhetoric of affirmative action's opponents during the debate. That's bad journalism, but in headline after headline we saw words like "bias" and "preference," which were words originally used by opponents of affirmative action, popping up as neutral signifiers.

LK: What groups do you see using misinformation against each other in the future?

CHIDEYA: All groups use misinformation, but the question is what message is being picked up and replicated by the mainstream media. It happens with antimulticultural messages, antiblack messages on some levels, and on some levels antiwoman messages. For instance, a study shows women on television are more likely to be shown talking about their romantic lives and their families than talking about jobs.

That's a marked difference from the way men are portrayed. Perhaps men should complain they are always shown talking about their jobs rather than romance.

LK: Who will be the mainstream media in the future?

CHIDEYA: For the next twenty-five or fifty years it will continue to be white dominated and to a lesser degree white male dominated. We've seen a lot faster gender integration than we've seen racial integration. The Glass Ceiling Report which came out a few years ago showed 95 percent of CEOs, vice presidents, and presidents in the business world are white men, and that's what I meant earlier by the grandfathering of power. Regardless of what the demographics are for America at this time, the demographics of power are still lagging behind, and that will continue for some time.

LK: Will we become smarter in how we interpret information from the media, or will media have to get better at being more accurate?

CHIDEYA: I think the media need to be overhauled quite a bit. People will say they hate the way the media have become so tabloid and then they'll watch the O. J. Simpson trial for three years, so don't rely on the public outcry to change the media.

LK: You've said people under age thirty don't watch television news. Is that something we should worry about?

CHIDEYA: Definitely. I wouldn't be so worried if I thought the exodus from television news was people going to different mediums. But we're talking about people who are watching and people who are not watching rather than people spreading out and that is a real problem. You have to know what's going on and if you don't, that's going to restrict your options for knowing the world around you.

LK: What are the ramifications?

CHIDEYA: The idea of American democracy is we have an informed citizenry that can influence what happens in Washington. If you don't have an informed citizenry, then you have an oligarchy within the Beltway. There has to be some sort of funneling up to set the agenda for policymakers.

LK: Do these people just not care, or are they so turned off they can't care?

CHIDEYA: There's a different way to think about it. You can only care about so many things at once, and if an issue is presented as being remote to your life, you may care about it but won't reach into your wallet and write a check. National debate has got to become immediate. That's the challenge for the news business. It has to be presented as how it can change a person's life. If the issue is not going to change people's lives and they have kids to raise or if it's like here in New York where there's too much garbage and that's what's bugging you, you have to take care of it. Those who are under age thirty don't have the self-interest of sending children to school or have an aging parent to deal with. That makes you less likely to focus on the debate. But the trend suggests these people won't plug into the news. There's no news habit with these people so they won't make watching news a part of their daily routine. I just hope news organizations don't decide to go more tabloid to get these people's attention.

LK: Will the distance between haves and have-nots grow larger?

CHIDEYA: On one level I would say yes and on another I would say no. There certainly is an enormous gap in opportunity. If you are a kid born in a housing project you cannot in any way, shape, or form have the opportunity for a chance of success as does an equally intelligent child born on Park Avenue. That is a reality that we as a nation don't like to talk about. But when you talk about the distance between the haves and the have-nots, we consume the same pop culture more so now than at any other time in history. A Park Avenue kid is going to listen to the same Snoop album or the same Tupac album as the kid living in the housing project. So there is a distance of opportunity and there's a distance of income, but there may or may not be a distance in culture that's as profound as it used to be.

LK: To what do you see culture evolving?

CHIDEYA: I don't think it evolves. Certainly it changes. We assume culture is constantly becoming degraded but we've always had high culture and low culture and middle-ground culture, and I don't think that will change. The fact you can have Ellen coming out on national TV is an element of pop culture that would have been considered taboo years earlier. Every generation wants to shock its parents so it's just a question of finding the hot buttons and knowing how to push them. You are always going to have a youth culture that is going to shock the previous generation, and you are always going to have a middle-ground culture that most people are comfortable with. High culture is always going to be assumed to be what we should aspire to and what we don't necessarily enjoy terribly much and what is in decline. Even though there are good numbers for the ballet and opera audience, there is this idea it is a dying art form and if more people could shut off the MTV crap, they'd come watch opera and life would be better. But that's the nature of high culture. It's always going to be stratified and it's never going to be mass market.

LK: How will parents in the next century be shocked by their children?

CHIDEYA: Some say people who are young today shock in a superficial way, such as "I'm going to pierce my eyebrows," but also shock in other ways, such as "I'm traditional and I want to marry young and I don't want to go on the pill." You can shock by putting the car in reverse and going backwards down the highway.

LK: What scares you?

CHIDEYA: I'm pragmatic. There will continue to be racial division and gender strife and economic warfare, but I think we're becoming used to these struggles. For those who aren't, then that's probably pretty frightening.

LK: Do you think men and women will ever become comfortable working together in an environment like the armed services?

CHIDEYA: Nothing is ever resolved without issues and tensions. The post–World War II integration of the army was painful. There was tension and people were yelling and screaming about being forced to serve with people of different color and morale would be lowered, and they got through it. Doesn't mean there isn't racial tension now, but it's diminished. They've made a huge effort and have been able to overcome it. We are going through the kicking and screaming now and it will fade.

MARIAN WRIGHT EDELMAN

FOUNDER AND PRESIDENT, CHILDREN'S DEFENSE FUND

Try hard to figure out what is important.

LK: We're coming to the end of the twentieth century. Both parents work. The traditional family structure seems pulled and stressed. Where do you think we're going?

EDELMAN: A nation that doesn't stand up for its children is a nation that is falling. I think we're going to hell because a child drops out of school every nine seconds, a child is arrested every fourteen seconds, every twenty-five seconds a child is born to an unmarried mother, and in the richest nation on earth the economy is booming and we let a child be born into poverty every thirty-two seconds. And the worst thing of all is, we have become numb.

LK: Is there a country now that does a good job?

EDELMAN: There are many countries doing far, far better. Japan, England, Canada, and the Scandinavian countries are just a few. In many countries health coverage for children is a given. The United States is eighteenth in the gap between rich and poor children but we're also the country leading the world in the number of millionaires and billionaires. That says something.

LK: What legislation would you like to see in place in the next century to make this country better for children?

EDELMAN: First priority is health coverage for 10 million uninsured children, nine out of ten of whom live with parents who work every day. I want to see implementation of the tobacco tax of 43 cents per pack of cigarettes, which will deter 800,000 children from even beginning to smoke because of the cost. I want to see a high-quality comprehensive child care system in place which includes parental support from business, such as policies on parental leave. I want to see parent support groups which allow children the opportunity to go to after-school and weekend summer programs so they don't come home to an empty house. Congregations are going to have to get involved in mentoring and tutoring and homework centers and, in general, show that adults can be there. We have wonderful models working right now but we lack the resources to bring them to scale and quality.

LK: What do you say to those in the next century who want to bring children into the world? What questions should they be asking themselves?

EDELMAN: Everybody needs to ask, "Am I prepared to put this child first in my life for the rest of my lifetime?" Parenting, in many ways, never ends. Another question would be, "Do we recognize this is the most important decision that we're going to make?" I would urge them to ask, "Are we ready and able to provide this child with a stable life, and are we prepared to be good role models?" Each person thinking about children should say, "What kind of values am I trying to transmit to these children and to their children and to the future?" And then parents should ask, "If I want this child to grow up and not be a racist, or intolerant of people who are different, or violent, or a drug user, am I going to be able to reflect that value in my household?" Our children do what we do. If we don't vote, they won't. It's the most important role in a society.

LK: Do you see us moving toward a time when we might require classes for people who are going to have a child?

EDELMAN: I don't know if we need it to be required. I think it should be universally available to people, like the parents' resource centers which are developing all over the country now. It will be cultural and social and community values rather than the government getting involved.

LK: There is talk of having a ninety-day waiting period before a couple can get married. Think that will happen?

EDELMAN: I hate to say we have to "require" things, but somebody ought to sit couples down before marriage and before a divorce and say, "What does this mean for children?" I am reticent to say, "Mandate it," but I really have to think there's got to be a conscious process of some sort. I hope there will be some manner of awareness for couples thinking about marriage to really begin to consider the seriousness of this lifetime commitment.

LK: How come we don't do it now?

EDELMAN: We have a great distrust of government interference in family life, that's why.

LK: What will new parents face in the next century?

EDELMAN: We need to redefine success. We need to teach our children that it is not about things. We need to focus on heroes rather than celebrities. We need to focus on spiritual values rather than material values. Parents are going to need to think anew and decide what it is they want this country to stand for. I think we have lost our way.

LK: Will business become more family-friendly?

EDELMAN: It will happen, but it depends on a critical mass of citizens demanding it. Business will look at its bottom line. The demand will come for the public sector to do it, and once that happens the private sector will do it. They have been slow in my view, and it's going to require a different atmosphere before it happens.

LK: Will parental leave policies be in place in the next century?

EDELMAN: It would be desirable but business in large part opposes parental leave. I'd hope business will become a leader rather than an opposer. It will happen.

LK: Will employees have a choice between comp time or overtime?

EDELMAN: We're at a pivotal point right now so I can't answer the question. It has to come from the bottom up. I hope we have these policies and I'm seeing more and more people saying we need them. I will tell you it isn't going to happen without a struggle.

LK: Will there be more regulation of day care?

EDELMAN: First of all, there will be more day care because there has to be more day care. Quality then becomes the critical question.

LK: Well, are we moving toward more federal regulation of the industry, or do you see fifty different standards based on each state's rules?

EDELMAN: The ball is in the states' court right now. We have failed, with the exception of Head Start, to have federal quality standards for children in day care. So you will see fifty states making decisions, and it will filter right on down to the county level, which adds even more diversity in day care standards.

LK: Will there be standards for everyone in the future?

EDELMAN: It's too early to tell. If there is an incident of unsafe child care there will be a backlash. But in the next fifteen years, yes, I think we will begin to see a new role for the national government in protecting children, and I hope it will come a lot sooner than that.

LK: Will schools be involved in day care?

EDELMAN: They will. Prior to the school day and after the school day. We need a variety of activities to make sure our children are ready for school. Schools are a community institution just as churches and synagogues are. But it's going to be difficult to use the site without having the school control it. So we are going to have to talk about how we are going to put it all together. I'm seeing this happen now. There has to be a collaborative effort between educators and religious leaders and community leaders and parents.

LK: You've talked about the role of the religious community throughout this interview. Is it going to become more visible and active?

EDELMAN: Absolutely. The religious community needs to be the moral locomotive rather than the moral caboose. It's beginning. And we should all know they can't do it alone.

LK: We hear of the pendulum swinging one way and then another. Do you see it swinging toward a parent staying home with children again in the next century?

EDELMAN: There is deep concern in America about what has happened to the family. Keep in mind, taking care of children at home is a lot cheaper than putting children in day care. I hope parents will have a choice. Let's not call it welfare. Let's call it parental support until those children go to school. Other industrialized countries do it. We'll save an awful lot in future prison costs because we either invest in children right now or we invest in them later in far more negative ways.

LK: What scares you about the next century?

EDELMAN: We have lost our sense of what is important as a nation. We are a nation that says all men, and I include women in that, are created equal, and yet we are so far away from that in the practices we see. There is racial division. We don't need to go back and refight the Civil War, and we don't need another postwar Reconstruction era. But we can see the division between the haves and have-nots grow. In the past twenty-five years we have seen children killed by guns and drugs and a breakdown in parental and community responsibility. I worry we will value things and not people. If we can't give this value to our children we can't give it to the rest of the world, which is so desperately in need of a leader.

LK: Where did we lose our sense of what is important?

EDELMAN: In the early 1980s we started to see a fundamental structural change in our economy where people with the most get the most in tax breaks or capital gains or estate taxes, while those with the least who need the most will suffer disproportionately. In this move from a service to a manufacturing to an information economy, we never thought what it all means for families. Is it about more, or can we develop a concept of enough? It's a very simple question: What are we doing here?

LK: Are you optimistic or pessimistic, because this sure seems like a dark interview.

EDELMAN: I am disturbed by the trend but I am determined. I believe in this country and I believe the citizens will come together and say, "Enough." In 1997, without a celebrity, 250,000 people came from every state in America to Washington, D.C., to stand for children. So the answer is I'm optimistic.

Politics

In one of his first news conferences as America's new president, John F. Kennedy was confronted with a question that, I continue to believe, marked the beginning of a substantive change in the coverage of politics. A newspaper reporter stood and said his editors at the paper back home had noticed a bandage on the president's hand and proceeded to ask, "What happened?" Kennedy responded that he had sliced a finger cutting bread in the White House kitchen. Television had arrived.

Since that time we have seen an industry created by the mix of the tube and the campaign. Every newsroom has a Rolodex of pundits and pollsters, and every campaign has a file of spinners and image-makers, and television is the reason. None of this has anything to do with saving Medicare or being able to fight two wars simultaneously in different parts of the world. So, while it's a good thing this century has made available technology for a message to reach every voter, it's a bad thing the message has to be framed-produced-scripted-timed-targeted, because once all that is done, the door is often deadbolted.

I talked with four people about the coverage, direction, and potential of politics. You are familiar with them all, and that's because of, you guessed it, television.

Tim Russert is host of *Meet the Press* on NBC, which is a must-do for any politician wanting to get a message to America. He is a regular on *Nightly News* covering things political and contributes daily to the e-mail/cable/Internet news channel called MSNBC. Tim was directly involved in setting up network coverage of the 1996 presidential campaign and, as you are reading this, he's at work on the 2000 coverage, and after I interviewed him for this book I think he's at work on 2004 and 2008 as well.

The biggest criticism of contemporary television news, among the 253 other beefs, is that ideas are packed into thirty seconds and then it's on to the next issue. Not so at *Newshour with Jim Lehrer* on PBS. There you have discussions and disagreements delivered in complete sentences. That's why I chose to speak with presidential historian Doris Kearns Goodwin, a *Newshour* regular, who always teaches me something about the people who have gotten into and tried to get into the White House. One thing about interviewing a historian when the topic is the future: The answers begin decades earlier in order to get there. Trust me, you're going to learn from her interview.

And then we come to Ross Perot. He and I have joked about going on the road together, but neither of us can get away from our jobs to do it. He has run for president twice and forced Republicans and Democrats to face the political music, or dirge, of budgets. And he does it again in this discussion. But I wanted to talk with Ross about an idea he first launched on my CNN show in 1992: the electronic town hall. The centuries-old idea of democracy is about to enter the twenty-first century, and Ross is going to take us there . . . and a few other places along the way.

In 1993 Congresswoman Marjorie Margoles Mezvinsky, Democrat from Pennsylvania, cast the deciding vote on the controversial Clinton budget. In 1994 she was out of a job. Before running for Congress in 1992 she had been a five-time Emmy Award–winning television reporter. Today she is president of the Women's Campaign Fund, which is changing the face of Congress. She talked with me about changes we might see in the House and Senate. But more to the point, she has some tough words for the American public.

TIM RUSSERT

WASHINGTON BUREAU CHIEF, NBC NEWS; HOST, *MEET THE PRESS*

First: Be literate before you become computer literate. Reading and writing will be central to any success. Technical nerds will fail. Second: Learn Spanish.

LK: How do you see news coverage of people wanting to be president of the United States changing in the next century?

RUSSERT: It's going to be almost overwhelming in that the number of outlets will probably be twice what they are now. So when you see the president, or the candidates, walking through the snows of New Hampshire or Iowa every successive four-year cycle, a swarm, a beehive of cameras becomes larger and larger and larger. And more global. And that's only going to increase because every local station, every local affiliate, every cable outlet, every local access cable, and every American will have its own video camera and it's going to become almost impossible for any candidate to walk anywhere.

LK: Does that bother you, being the Washington Bureau chief of a network, to see all the affiliates with their own camera crews covering the story you're covering?

RUSSERT: Well, what we're going to have to do out of simply a logistical sense is what is now done at the White House, and that is pool. You'll designate one camera or two cameras at every campaign stop and pool the event and share the tape. Otherwise you have more cameras than voters in the room.

LK: Is it healthy to have the same picture of the same event coming out of so many channels?

RUSSERT: The pictures are similar now, and as long as you can capture the Q-and-A that goes back and forth you usually don't miss much. There will of course continue to be unilateral enterprise reporting on the candidates' positions and character. But I also think the candidates will be doing less and less retail campaigning and more and more wholesale campaigning.

LK: What's that mean?

RUSSERT: It means they're going to campaign in front of TV sets in sterile studios, call-ins to radio, while the Internet is going to explode. Johannes Gutenberg is going to be rolling in his grave in the year 2000. His dream of everyone having a printing press will have been realized, only it's going to be a computer. People will go on-line and immediately sign a petition for a candidate, immediately send a question into the TV studio to be asked. Everything will become immediate.

LK: Will it become less meaningful then?

RUSSERT: It's a possibility, and we haven't come to grips with that yet. If we now think four news cycles a day are overwhelming, what's going to happen when there are, say, nonstop twenty-four-hour-a-day news cycles? We are a country with multi time zones and that's what the Internet is going to bring.

LK: And what's the answer to that?

RUSSERT: I honestly don't know.

LK: Does this mean less face-to-face and one-on-one campaigning?

RUSSERT: Absolutely.

LK: Is that good or bad?

RUSSERT: I think bad. One of the advantages of New Hampshire and Iowa is real people have an opportunity to actually see these candidates and ask them questions. But as these states become more and more inundated with commercials and negative tactics it's going to accelerate, so as the politics becomes more remote and more cynical, so do the voters. If it becomes impersonal, I think people begin to lose interest. They want a personal stake in their leader because they have a personal stake in their future. People will become more and more alienated and disenfranchised if they can only vent themselves on talk radio and the Internet but don't see any tangible solutions. If everything is instantaneous and simply a form of protest, it's going to be much more difficult for us to develop any sense of what is the common good. Where is the commonweal? Where do we go? If everyone's a free spirit, independent contractor, lone ranger, who is going to bring all these elements together? That's the ultimate challenge for a candidate in the year 2000. You are going to have to communicate on television, on the Internet, on radio, and it's very difficult when people are grabbing you in snippets and watching you for a moment. Everything becomes quick and fast, and the result is you lose context.

LK: Do you blame the populace for not participating, or do you blame the media for creating the disillusionment, or do you blame the candidates?

RUSSERT: We all share in the blame. We cover the campaign presented to us but we gravitate to the extremes and the loudmouths and the faux pas. The candidates know something must be done with entitlements and Medicare and Social Security, and yet when someone proposes something there's a thirty-second commercial saying, "You're going to throw people in wheelchairs out on the street." The voters say, "Don't touch my Medicare and my Social Security and my pension and give me the best schools and the best parks and the cleanest rivers and the cleanest air, but don't even dare suggest an increase in taxes." So everybody shares in this, and my concern in looking at the year 2000 is the cycle of cynicism is just going to grow. But the wonderful thing about our country is that we have been able to unite and rally ourselves to deal with every crisis, whether it's fascism or Communism, smoking, drunk driving, cholesterol. We are amazing when we decide something is important to be dealt with, and I think as we begin to deal with television more and computers more and talk radio more, people begin to understand the strengths and the weaknesses of the media resources available. Just as TV commercials were extremely effective five years ago, they are less and less so now in terms of the positive ones. The negative ones are peaking. They have an impact, but the source of the negative ones pays a price. The next step, I hope, in all of this is people begin to discount, immediately, any negative commercial. Not only its source but its content.

LK: Are you saying there won't be any negative commercials?

RUSSERT: I think we'll see a dramatic decrease in them in the next century. The tolerance level is low. I'm hopeful people will say, "That's an old gimmick," or "That's foolish," or "That's stupid," or "That went out in the nineties." But let me shift here and tell you about coverage. We've got MSNBC and you have *Larry King Live* on CNN, and the other nets will be starting their own cable things. More and more you'll see *The Today Show* and political analysis, and our little political panel will talk and then we'll say, "If you want more on this issue, look here on the Internet," and we'll put up the address on the screen. On *Meet the Press* we'll have a discussion about drugs or the budget and then we'll say, "More can be found on the Internet," and you'll find the position papers of all the guests you just saw on *Meet the Press*, you can have sample Q-and-A's, people will stay around after the show and do live hits following up on what they've just seen on the screen, and it will all be integrated in a way that will be so democratized the average person will be able to talk to the candidates on the Internet, talk to his senators and governors directly. That will be a wonderful tool. And this is where you will neutralize the negative ad because you can't be negative in your response to someone. This means people will have to be computer literate, but my response is "Make sure you're literate first." I hope in the next century we place just as high a premium on being literate as we do on being computer literate.

LK: Are there going to be more news talk shows?

RUSSERT: Sure. But other than Sunday morning you're not going to find them on the networks because the networks will become more entertainment vehicles, and more news will be found more and more on the cable. The average viewer will have a menu of about two hundred channels, and that includes the satellite dishes.

LK: And that will come off the satellite or just off the cable?

RUSSERT: I'm not sure if it will be telephone cable or satellite but there will be two hundred channels. The network share is going to bottom out in the next century to about 40 percent of viewership.

LK: If there are going to be two hundred channels on television, does that mean we'll see a "Candidate A" channel and a "Candidate B" channel and an "Independent Candidate C" channel during election years?

RUSSERT: Absolutely. You already have the GOP channel. Every candidate will have his or her own channel, they'll buy complete access. You know how you go to a hotel room and they keep showing the same infomercial over and over again? Well, same thing. It can't miss.

LK: But each will be produced by that particular candidate, right?

RUSSERT: Sure. Video news releases will become an hourly occurrence, audio news releases every hour too. The candidates are going to be pumping those out for the hourly newscasts, and more and more, TV stations are going to have to be on guard about taking one of these. Just as a newspaper wouldn't take a news release and print it on the front page of the paper, will radio and TV stations take a video or audio news release and put it on the air? This is going to be a major challenge to journalism.

LK: But if they do broadcast it then they have to label the piece as being supplied by such-and-such a candidate, right?

RUSSERT: Well, I hope so. That's where standards are going to come in.

LK: Is it going to be tougher to be a reporter in the next century than it is now?

RUSSERT: Sure. You're going to be less certain and there's going to be more niche reporting, which will have its strengths and weaknesses. There will be an environment channel and there will be a foreign policy channel. There will be lots of experts in those areas, and I wonder how much opportunity there will be for generalists. The strength of network television, when there were just three channels, was that people had no choice but to watch the evening newscasts at the same hour of the day. They had a very strong uniting force on the country. That's not going to be the case in the next century. People will pick and choose when they get their information and what kind of information. You will be able to go through life never having to watch a newscast. You can simply devote your life to MTV or the Food Channel, anything you want because the information spectrum will be so broad. So then, how do you get to the country? How do you unite the country?

LK: And that brings up the issueof free TV for candidates prior to an election. Going to happen?

RUSSERT: On a very limited basis, but I think the voter will be suspicious of canned speeches. I think the alternative will be to provide time to the candidates in an interview setting by just turning over, say, ten minutes of free time and have the network anchor interview a candidate for ten minutes on live TV.

LK: Will campaigns continue to begin in New Hampshire and Iowa?

RUSSERT: Yes, in the year 2000, but by the year 2004 there will be serious consideration given to four regional primaries on a rotating basis: One time the East will go first and then the West and then the Midwest and then the South. Stretch out the nominating period over four months, and each month have a regional primary. Now, having said that, the permanent campaign is here to stay. With the broadening of the communication spectrum and the explosion of the Internet, the campaign will never stop. Every day the White House will be putting out its message and every day the opposition will be putting out its message.

LK: Do you expect fewer prime time White House news conferences?

RUSSERT: They are a thing of the past. It was something that was done to grab the attention of the country and dramatize the importance of the event. The large entertainment stations will behave the way the nonnews cable stations have behaved in the nineties. When John Kennedy was shot, the whole country watched nothing but. And what would happen today? The networks would obviously all go to wall-to-wall coverage, but what about all the other outlets? What would Nickelodeon, ESPN do? They'd keep going with their own programming. And if there are two hundred outlets and only the news stations are carrying a news conference, it's going to be a different world and a different society. In many ways it's going to be one that is more difficult to communicate to. But if people are able to access things on the Internet and develop an interest, or at least have their appetite whetted by something they see on TV and then get on the Internet, the cross-pollination between television, radio, and Internet will be inseparable.

LK: Do you expect pundits to be used in the new century?

RUSSERT: I think people are searching for honest questioning of our leaders but they also are asking for interpretation, not because they want to know what to think, but they're curious as to what others are thinking. And in many ways the Sunday shows and talk radio and communication on the Internet will be the next-century equivalent to the backyard fence. Rather than talking over the fence, which very few people do anymore because they don't know their neighbors, they watch the people talk over the fence on Sunday morning, listen to them on the radio, and do it themselves on the Internet. That's the next century.

LK: Television news uses a lot of "bullets," as they're called in the industry, in which a graphic comes outlining the major points of, say, a presidential speech. Are we going to see more of this?

RUSSERT: Absolutely. Communicating in simplicity is what we'll see. Ross Perot's charts are a precursor of the future. Yes, there are going to be a lot of simple graphics. You will see things on the TV screen that can be expanded on the Internet.

LK: You sure use the word "Internet" a lot.

RUSSERT: In terms of what people will have access to, the next century is going to be unprecedented in our lifetime. People talk about the op-ed page of the *New York Times*, well, it's all going to be there. They'll be able to read the editorial page of any paper in the country, they'll be able to call up any TV show in the country—local, network, or cable—and they'll have unlimited access to information, and the question is, how well are they going to utilize it in their roles as citizens?

DORIS KEARNS GOODWIN

PRESIDENTIAL HISTORIAN;

PANELIST, *NEWSHOUR WITH JIM LEHRER*;

AUTHOR OF *NO ORDINARY TIME,* WHICH WON

THE 1995 PULITZER PRIZE FOR HISTORY

We can return to a time when public life is valued, when the vocation of politics is respected, when a political movement can capture energy and you are fighting for something larger than yourself. The problems which seem intractable today (ghettos, education, health care) were all created by human beings, so remember, that means they can be solved by human beings. They didn't come from outer space.

LARRY
KING

•

30

LK: What is a president going to need to do the job in the next century?

GOODWIN: The most important thing needed is that which has always been needed, although the form might be somewhat different, which is the ability to communicate to the American people a sense of direction, a sense of who he is and where he wants to bring the country, and an ability to carry the country to the goals he sees the country has to reach. It's just the form of that communication which changes. Lincoln used letters he'd write to newspaper editors or Congress, and then those long thoughtful letters would get published. Roosevelt used the fireside chats and radio to let everyone know who he was and what he wanted to do to handle the Depression and move the country from being isolationist to interventionalist to support the Allied cause even before Pearl Harbor. By the time John Kennedy became president he used television and he used press conferences and speeches to move the country toward goals. That's the era we've still been in, essentially, since that time. The difference now is the fragmentation of the television market. Recent State of the Union messages have been listened to by less than half the people because they had more choices. Now there is speculation that computers and the Internet will be a new form of that communication. Already you can get detailed biographies and issue platforms of every candidate, but that's only if you're a consumer who wants to find that. Will it become so common in the twenty-first century that it will become a substitute or a replacement for television? I don't know the answer to that. It sounds absurd at this moment, but that may be what was said about television replacing radio or radio replacing newspapers. But candidates will be able to communicate on the Internet and we can just add that into the mix.

LK: Where is the country going to have to move in the twenty-first century?

GOODWIN: I still think one of the major goals that has always been a part of the American mythology or dream is economic justice. At certain times in our history that goal becomes more or less important. What we've seen in the seventies-eighties-nineties is a move away from middle-class stability and toward a greater gap in the distance between the rich and the poor. In order for the country to be productive with an economy that's doing well, the resources and rewards need to be distributed around the society so there's a spirit we are all part of this great enterprise. And one of the major chores in front of the leaders in the next century is how, without diminishing the entrepreneurial spirit of the country, we can strengthen the labor movement, how to get corporations more responsible in distributing profits and resources of corporate success and for government to have a role in this antigovernment world in helping to make the process work more fairly.

LK: How is the presidency going to change?

GOODWIN: One of the ironies in the modern communications world is that presidents tend to get overexposed. Cameras follow them wherever they go. They appear too willingly on the evening news, go on talk shows, go on MTV, and as a result when they need to go before the public at an important moment, we've already seen them and it doesn't have the dramatic impact that it had in the past. Roosevelt only held his fireside chats two or three times a year, holding himself back, knowing he could only go before the public so many times or it would lose a majesty and a mystery in a sense of the office of the presidency. One of the things that has to be recaptured by presidents of the future is how to preserve the majesty when everybody is so overexposed.

Reagan seemed to do okay but all the recent presidents seem too involved in having every thought of theirs recorded. They have to figure out how to preserve the presence of the office. They have to understand the modern communications world which can be used to their advantage. They can reach people much better than could Lincoln, who had to wait for people to read his speeches recorded in newspapers.

LK: So it's hard being presidential in a multimedia outlet?

GOODWIN: That's right. The community is more fragmented. Leadership depends upon building a sense of community, and right now at the end of this century it's a lot more fragmented, partly because of the many media outlets, partly because the society has become more of a spectator type of society because television ads become more a part of their means of entertainment and information, which is essentially a passive device.

LK: Do you think presidents will continue to do Saturday radio addresses?

GOODWIN: I hope not. What's wrong is that nobody sits around their radios and listens. It's just another talk the president gives, and it diminishes the importance of the ones he really wants us to rally around. I would prefer the president use the powers of his publicity to really make sure to saturate the country with the fact the president is about to give an important speech.

LK: So the State of the Union address might be delivered on a January afternoon rather than a January evening in the future?

GOODWIN: I could see that happening, yes.

LK: Will campaigns continue to begin the day after the last election?

GOODWIN: You know, just as we used to talk about the nuclear arms race, about unilateral disarmament being an impossibility and that's why the arms race could never end, you just keep hoping somewhere along the line some candidates will band together and promise they won't start their campaigns until, say, three months before the convention. Britain manages to get by with a shorter time span. The problem with the permanent campaign we're now experiencing is that it dissolves the attention, and by the time candidates go through it, they're not learning anymore. When Truman was going around the country on the train he could feel what people were thinking and feeling. Now so much of it is projecting an image onto the country. I used to think what would happen is the candidates would go nowhere and sit in a satellite place and project a picture of the city behind them every twenty minutes and they could appear to be elsewhere when they were only in one place. I think we're moving more toward that but I doubt it will fully happen. They can use television to reach out to the large markets and don't even have to go to the small places, except for maybe a photo opportunity in a small place. So much of a campaign now is projecting an image onto the country rather than going someplace and absorbing the country.

LK: You are saying candidates could make a lot of points if they would wait three months before the convention before saying "I'm in"?

GOODWIN: I am. If not three months, then six months is sufficient time. February through July. But you need the commitment from each one of them. The country would say amen and feel absolutely in agreement and maybe even pay more attention to the race.

LK: So you think candidates are doing less face-to-face as a result of technology? And is that good or bad?

GOODWIN: I have no doubt they are doing less. New Hampshire is retail politics. You are viewed by video everywhere you go face-to-face so it's hard to imagine when your campaign is being covered every moment that you're really natural when talking to somebody. Public opinion polls never tell you the intensity of what people feel but the people's voices tell it much better than any statistical analysis. You look at their face, you see the expressions, you hear their voices, and you learn. Nobody, except experienced television people, is natural when they're talking to people and a camera is rolling behind them and probably the people themselves know they're in a scene so it's not clear they are even being straightforward. They might appear more confrontational just to look that way or they might be unable to tell the truth because they know they're on camera.

LK: You have spoken about free television for candidates. How would it work?

GOODWIN: Figuring it out isn't that difficult. I can't do it sitting here but a commission of people who know television and the campaign processes could figure out whether it's a separate channel, or do you take a piece of time on the channels that are watched most often. There's a way to relieve the candidates of this need to buy time. Assuming television networks are still a public trust, somehow that's a responsibility they have for having a part of the public airwaves.

LK: So it would work in whatever state in which the primary is coming up? That's where the free time would occur and then a few weeks before the general election the time would be available nationwide?

GOODWIN: That's right. It makes sense. Obviously, we're not going to force the people of Wyoming to listen to the candidates running in New Hampshire because every time one of these guys came on they'd turn it off. Television is going to be free in the next century, there's no question about that. It's hard to see any other way out of this bind and there will be a lot of kicking and screaming, but it will work itself out. Had this been done ten years ago when there was public television and the three networks it would have been easier. Now, with cable and MSNBC and everything else, it's going to be much harder because the proliferation of channels has occurred before any precedent was set. It may become a legislative act. But now that I think about it, this may be an answer for yesterday's problem. But unless it's shaped to the state of the media at the time it may not be an answer. People may still not watch.

LK: We've done a good thing because we know nobody was watching and now that we've done it, nobody is watching.

GOODWIN: Exactly.

LK: Are New Hampshire and Iowa still relevant?

GOODWIN: De Tocqueville a long time ago talked about the American psyche and the fact that people were happy in their neighborhoods until somebody built a bigger home than they had before, so the next person built an even bigger home, and what we have now is this sense of the other states trying to push back the timing to have the first primary to compete with New Hampshire, then it was Iowa and now it could be someone else. I don't know how long the power of New Hampshire and Iowa's caucus can prevent other states from doing this. Obviously if it goes back further in time the whole thing becomes absurd. The first straw polls will be taken the day after the election. Given the reach of television and the national capacity of the media today, it does seem somewhat anachronistic to have these small states be so important in creating momentum. If I truly believed the candidates were face-to-face and learning in the retail politics, I'd probably argue there is a lot of benefit to be had from these smaller states, but I'm not sure that's what's going on anymore with New Hampshire and Iowa. Candidates walk around only to be seen walking around.

LK: So where would the first primary be held?

GOODWIN: The only thing that might take its place, and this could be a blessing or a curse, would be regional primaries. We seem to be moving toward that anyway. New England may have the first primary just to keep the tradition of New Hampshire. But on one hand you get the mix of states, which is a good thing, but on the other hand you do lose the retail politics side of a small state.

LK: Do you think a candidate will say, "I had an affair" or "I used drugs" and still be elected?

GOODWIN: Yes. I think in so many ways that what the people are looking for is someone with the presence and the confidence to be truthful. As long as the candidate has come to terms with whatever it is we are talking about (why the affair took place, what kind of hurt it brought to the family) and say we've gotten over that, I think the country would come to terms with it. We underestimate the American public, and the problem with most leaders is spending so much energy hiding the flaws or mistakes. History seems to show when a president admits a mistake, his stock goes up. John Kennedy, when he took responsibility for the Bay of Pigs fiasco, his opinion poll numbers went up. When Cleveland admitted he had fathered a child out of wedlock in that earlier campaign in the nineteenth century he won the election in part because people still instinctively think your public morality is more important than your private one. I remember when Bill Clinton's Gennifer Flowers press conference took place, I was with a group of reporters and all of us said, "Well, that's the end of his campaign and he'll be out within twenty-four hours," and he stayed in and the country got over that. There are qualities in presidents that are far more important than whether or not they had an affair twenty years before, and those would be what kind of confidence do they have, what empathy do they have for other people, do they have a sense of timing, do they have political skills, do they have public values that matter.

LK: Will Americans continue to elect a president of one party and a Congress of another?

GOODWIN: I don't think so. There's this conventional thought to split it on the part of the American public and I'm not sure it's as calculating as that. It's just happened that way. Maybe it's happened this way more recently because people just tend to distrust government more and they feel it's a certain check and balance by splitting their votes.

LK: Will presidents be driven by polling as they are now?

GOODWIN: Bill Clinton is doing polling and he's not even running again, so that shows you how it's become a part of the way the White House looks at the world. It can be a potentially positive tool to have a sense of where the people are at, but then you have to put that aside and use that as a means of how to move people to an idea you have. But if you don't think about how to move them forward to what you want, then you have lost all meaning of leadership. It's almost like too much knowledge can be a very bad thing in this case. It may reach a point where we are polling every minute and somebody realizes how idiotic it has become. It would be very healthy for a leader in the future—almost like refraining from smoking or drinking—to just deliberately say the pulse of the country will be taken every now and then but not every day. Great leaders have always had intuition, not something scientific like a poll, as to what people are feeling and thinking. That's where the art of public leadership comes in. You can trust in that more than you can a poll because it's filtered through that person's (the leader's) own emotions.

LK: Do you see the third party being a major player in the next century?

GOODWIN: I think it is more likely third parties will flow in and out of elections even more than in the past because the hold the two major parties have on the electorate is so much diminished.

LK: Is there any going back for Republicans and Democrats? Can they regain a hold?

GOODWIN: It's hard when people have fallen out of the habit of identifying strongly with something. It's not simply the numbers that are no longer Republicans and Democrats, the much deeper loss for either party is that in the past being a member was in a large part an identity with the self, it was like are you a Catholic or a Jew, or are you a Southerner or a Northerner? You passed it on to your children. In today's world there are few people who feel that way, and this is part of the fragmentation of community I was talking about earlier.

LK: Are we still going to elect a president with the Electoral College, or is it going to be done by popular vote?

GOODWIN: The Electoral College will still remain. Americans have a hesitancy toward changing the constitutional structure of the country. You see it every time one of these amendments gets proposed. Even though there is a certain anachronism to the Electoral College and even though people could argue the popular vote is what matters, I think it would take a real crisis like someone getting a huge popular vote and still losing the Electoral College to bring about any fundamental change.

LK: What worries you about the new century?

GOODWIN: My most intense worry is Americans in the past have felt they were part of the American story. They had a sense of the history from which they had come. Historical memories were so much a part of the binding tide of the American people that it helped them have confidence. It sustained us in the sixties, was shattered in Vietnam, and now is continuously shattered by a lack of direction. The Cold War is over and we don't have the Communist enemy to fight anymore, and so what worries me is if a crisis occurs and requires a pulling together we won't have the habit of mind to do it like we've had before. And will there be a leader who can mobilize both the energy and the spirit of sacrifice in the American people?

LK: Future presidents will come from where?

GOODWIN: I think it is more likely future leaders will have more of a shot at getting into public office at the higher levels without having been in it before. I think in part, because of the current situation we're in, the cynicism about politicians also makes it attractive to look at someone coming in from the outside. So people will be able to move across from celebrity and other fields, whether it's business or education or even sports or . . . movie stars. I don't think there was a door closed because Ross Perot wasn't a public figure. He just needed a different temperament. He showed that the lockhold we've had, except for generals, isn't absolute.

LK: There going to be a woman president in the next century?

GOODWIN: Definitely.

Future presidents of the United States should pay attention to these former presidents of the United States. Each brought a sense of confidence internally inside himself and knew what had to be done rather than what people were telling him to do, an ability to communicate with the country, a sense of timing, a sense of dignity and respect for the office, and an understanding of the challenges he was facing and an ability to mobilize the resources of his nation to meet those challenges.

1. George Washington. He was creating the republic and everything he did was a precedent.

2. Abraham Lincoln. He had the ability to mobilize the North for a war on the basis of an ideal vision of what democracy is good for, in terms of the abolition of slavery, and knew how to time the move toward emancipation perfectly, so he kept his support of the North without losing the border states.

3. Franklin Roosevelt. He faced the Great Depression and the war and mobilized the spirit of the country behind the positive actions that he took to deal with these challenges.

ROSS PEROT

CHAIRMAN, PEROT REFORM PARTY;

1992 PRESIDENTIAL CANDIDATE;

CHAIRMAN, PEROT SYSTEMS, DALLAS

We are the owners and custodians of this country, and we need to do what every other generation has done until this moment, and that is to pass on to our children a better country than was handed to us. Either we will or we'll be involved in self-indulgence. Freedom is very fragile.

LK: What do you see as the biggest problem facing America in the next century?

PEROT: It's right here and it's as fundamental as who are we as a people: Are we going to come together as a united team in the twenty-first century, or are we going to be divided and have some of the problems that we have today. Government can't do a thing about it. Government can punish you for being bad but it can't make you good. Our biggest challenge in determining what we are in the twenty-first century is whether or not we, as the owners of the country, will become so well informed that we can't be manipulated by propaganda and acting in the election process. So first off, let's start with the bedrock: Who are we? We have to be a kind, loving, willing, sharing people. We've got to be people who will help one another. We can't be people who hate one another, and we've got to remember united teams win and divided teams lose, and we'd better take the Three Musketeers' motto, which is "All for one and one for all."

LK: Then what?

PEROT: The next step is to look at this huge financial debt which can wreck the twenty-first century and we have a narrow window of opportunity to fix it. So we fix it now or we pay a terrible price and millions of people are going to suffer for decades in the twenty-first century.

LK: So do you think we will fix it?

PEROT: Well, we got the biggest tax increase in history in 1993 and then three years later the same people promise you a tax cut. Keep in mind there was a Scottish historian, Alexander Tytler, in 1787 who wrote that democracies have a short life and once the people understand they can vote benefits for themselves, then they go into financial collapse. He says the typical life of a democracy is two hundred years. We're a little older than that but the clock is ticking. We have a $5 trillion debt. The 1995 White House budget forecast an 82 percent tax rate in the twenty-first century. I hope I made my point.

LK: But are you optimistic we will do it?

PEROT: It's the people. The system won't do it. If we let these trends continue, with certainty we're going to have a financial collapse, which is the last thing this country needs. Let me give you numbers: We have $20 trillion in assets, $42 trillion in liabilities, which is a negative net worth of $22 trillion. We have a $5 trillion debt, and here is the end of the story and I'll get off numbers. Let's say we just round up all the currency in circulation and pay off the debt. We're all broke, we've just emptied our wallets. Well, we don't have $5 trillion in currency in print to do it. Even Forrest Gump will understand that's too much debt. Give me this problem over World War I. Give me this problem over World War II. Our ancestors have faced and dealt with far more difficult things than this. We have to be as strong and committed as they were.

LK: Are we going to have a third party in 2010?

PEROT: History teaches us that from time to time we have a third party. When 62 percent of America says it wants a third party, it is an idea whose time has come.

LK: Is this because of revolution—the Democratic and Republican parties have failed—or is this because of evolution of some sort?

PEROT: Anything that's not working is always the fault of the other party because nobody wants to take responsibility. The facts are, when you put them together, there's nobody else to blame. In 1964, 76 percent of the people trusted our government. Today only 19 percent trust our government. So the highest priority is to restore trust and confidence.

LK: And how do you do that?

PEROT: Set high ethical standards for the White House, the House, and the Senate, and they need to be laws and not rules. For example, it's absolutely wrong for former presidents to be paid $2 million for twenty-minute speeches in Asia. It's absolutely wrong for former trade negotiators to be paid a half-million dollars a year by any number of foreign countries. And there's an unbroken pattern once they leave that job of switching over to the other side. We've got to cut out the cashing in. Hardworking Americans are supporting former presidents in a regal lifestyle for the rest of their lives, so they never have to compromise their ethics and integrity, and yet they do. This has to be cleaned up to restore confidence in government.

LK: That night when you were on my CNN show and made the now-famous announcement you'd run for the presidency if you could see some sweat from the public—do you think we will ever see sweat from a disengaged electorate?

PEROT: They have to be informed. They have to understand the issues. Everyone that can vote needs to vote. Our turnout is sad commentary on the responsibility of our country's owners. The fact we're easily manipulated and don't cast an informed vote is another sad commentary on our attitude as owners. Saddest of all is, we are cynical and turned off, and that ensures the future of our country will be damaged. Too many people feel helpless and we've got to change that.

LK: How do you do that?

PEROT: We've got good people in Washington but they're trapped in a bad system, and one of the worst parts of the system is the amount of money they have to raise for a political campaign. This corrupts the process. Special interests give to both parties and they don't have ideology. They just want to protect their deal. So we've got to make sure everyone understands the vote is far more important than the campaign contribution unless the campaign money that is given can manipulate your mind. For example, the Willie Horton ad? Terrible, but it worked. These are the kinds of things the American people need to get smart enough to say, "Oh boy."

LK: Tell me about the electronic town hall you envision.

PEROT: We have the technology to do it right now. The hardest part for years was the feedback: You could get the message out by television but getting a response was difficult. With the kinds of computers that will be available in the home in the future, it's going to be easy to have a dialogue where you discuss the issues, get instant feedback across America on the issues, and get a strong consensus.

LK: Would it occur on a specific network at a specific time?

PEROT: Yes. You want it to go to the maximum number of people and everyone gets a network. Not everyone has cable. You don't want it limited to a small number of people because you want to involve everybody and literally get citizens involved like they used to get involved in little towns across the country in the town hall meeting. This is the new auditorium.

LK: So it would be on, say, Wednesday nights, and instead of watching *Larry King Live*, the president comes on, says, "Folks, Social Security is what we're talking about tonight, and I need an answer from you in the next twenty-four hours."

PEROT: On one that important, I propose it go on several weeks and really, really educate the people and then, when we've finished, let the people respond. And we'd have to go on at night, at a time when most people watch it, C-SPAN could play a huge role in this except that's limited to cable but technology is going to change over the next ten or fifteen years and, with good luck, C-SPAN will be everywhere. They'd be the natural group to handle this if they go into every home.

LK: So the president would make his case and then—

PEROT: It's not just the president. The case would be explained and the different points of view would be explained and more than anything else on important issues like Social Security you would just show people the numbers.

LK: Would we vote by mail and would we vote to our congressman and/or our senators and then he or she in turn would vote our collective response?

PEROT: Those are all good creative ways to do it. And it's a way to get the owners, the voters, involved. One of the planks in our platform is Congress will not be able to raise taxes without the approval of the voters. Let me give you the numbers: In 1920 taxes were about $20 a year per person. Today it's $5,700 per person a year. We are addicted to spending. Listen to these words: The budget must be balanced. The treasury must be refilled. The public debt must be reduced, and the arrogance of public officials must be controlled. Cicero said that 2,000 years ago. Now that people have seen our thirty-minute television show which looks at a specific issue, I think it'll become a trend. People aren't turned off by charts showing facts, and I think that's going to become a trend. We have to get past all the emotional concerns about doing things differently. One thing our platform plans, to answer your question, is to vote over the weekend, do it two days because some religions would keep you from doing it just one day. Then no exit polls until the last polling booth in Hawaii is closed. In the next twenty or thirty years I would say it'll be almost impossible to buy a television without a computer hooked into it. It's going to change shopping, so I can see voting being done this way too.

LK: Cicero was a pretty bright guy.

PEROT: It's human nature to avoid dealing with a problem until after a crisis occurs. Maintain the status quo until after you have to fix it. We can't do that this time around.

LK: Future presidents—will they come from the business community and bypass public service?

PEROT: They're going to come from across the spectrum. You need people who know how to make things happen. None of our social programs, which account for two-thirds of our budget, work. It's like designing airplanes and none of them fly and nobody is saying, "What's wrong with our program here?" In government we have all these people who have never had to deliver a product on a budget. Our number one growth industry in the United States is the U.S. government.

LK: This sounds like we could use somebody from the business community.

PEROT: Keep in mind most of our legislators have legal backgrounds, and lawyers don't have to know how to make something work.

LK: What must a president do in the next century?

PEROT: All of these things we're talking about in government fit together like pieces of a complex puzzle. They are interrelated and they must fit precisely. But we consider them one at a time. You can't create a car with one guy doing the tires and another doing the engine and another doing the fenders and then I get them all shipped to one place and realize nobody built a starter, and worse than that, they weren't designed as part of an overall system. That's the way things are done in Washington.

MARJORIE MARGOLIES-MEZVINSKY

PRESIDENT, WOMEN'S CAMPAIGN FUND;

MEMBER OF U.S. CONGRESS FROM PENNSYLVANIA, 1992–1994

Always ask, "How are the children?"

LK: Let's say it's the year 2010. What will have changed in the way issues are handled in Congress?

MEZVINSKY: We have raised the American public, whoever "we" are, to pay attention only to what it wants to hear rather than what it needs to hear. Somehow that's going to have to change. This means talking responsibly about entitlements. I think in the year 2010 we will be looking right down the barrel of a real crisis with regard to Social Security, Medicare, and any other entitlement. So I'm hoping there will be responsible people who are directing legislation that say, "This may cost me big but we have to talk very seriously about making sacrifices." We've got to talk in the future about coming together and figuring out how the next generation is going to be in the loop. I can tell you, as somebody who tried to talk about it, it's like painting a target on your chest.

LK: So the problem is, obviously, the system, which could use a little work, but the American people need a little work too.

MEZVINSKY: You turn on your television around election time and everyone is "dissing" on one another and the American public says, "I knew you were a sleazebag because all politicians are sleazebags, so the real issue is who is the least sleazy?" What has settled in is an unwillingness to really listen to what we need to listen to.

LK: How will this "unwillingness" change into a willingness? A strong leader? Use of the media? A president?

MEZVINSKY: A combination of them all, with the understanding that going through the eye of that needle is going to be very painful and may require a number of tries to do it. It's going to need a lot of explanation.

LK: A lot of explanation is achieved how?

MEZVINSKY: When I talked to the president after my vote in 1993 which resulted in his budget passing by one vote, I explained the only way we are going to get entitlements in front of the people is to get to the people outside of the Beltway so they understand what's going on. So I asked for an Entitlement Conference. You saw it last year with the Volunteer Summit in Philadelphia. The one message coming out of that was if a kid has a mentor in his or her life, it makes all the difference in the world. It's a simple recipe: Find out what resonates and what combination of things will move the public to act responsibly.

LK: Will there be more summits to move in that direction? Is that how it will be done?

MEZVINSKY: There has to be a focus. When we pass each other, we need to always ask, "How are the children?" That's what we've got to start doing. The Masai warriors of Africa, revered for their toughness and strength, are also known for always asking each other, "How are the children?" We need to keep thinking about the next generation and how we're going to pass the baton to them. I know I never stepped on the House floor to vote without thinking about my children and how the legislation would affect them.

LK: In the year 2010, let's say someone is running for Congress. How long will that campaign last and where will money come from?

MEZVINSKY: I think it is impractical to think Congress is going to change fundamentally the way members are elected, because right now the system so favors the incumbents. Yes, we may get something that resembles campaign finance reform, but I will submit there will be at least one loophole in it that you'll be able to drive a truck through. In 2010 our races will look, unfortunately, the way they do now, despite the many people out there saying they should be a lot different. Free TV time is not going to do the trick. So we are still going to have to raise a lot of money and the races will continue to be too long. I just don't see a movement toward genuine change, which we definitely need. There will be a simple message like we saw in 1994 with Newt Gingrich and the Contract with America, where we cut taxes and spend more on the military and not touch entitlements. It's what people want to hear but it's not the truth. We also need a Congress that looks more like the rest of the nation, and I'll bet you in the year 2010 we'll still have under one hundred women (we now have about fifty).

Still, the next shift in the look of Congress will happen in the year 2002 because of redistricting from the 2000 census. We know that women run as well as men in open seats. And after a census—as in '92—there were many more open seats.

LK: How will legislation change in this year 2010?

MEZVINSKY: I think we're getting more complicated rather than simpler. At some point someone is going to say, "This system needs to be streamlined and we need fewer committees, item-specific legislation, and a less-complicated, more family-friendly Congress." We are not moving in that direction. Reform has to come from within.

LK: Do you think voting will increase?

MEZVINSKY: I hope so. I look at countries all over the world where people stand in line for days trying to vote and then I look at America where some elections only have a 20 percent to 30 percent turnout. It has to come from the top and the bottom. Those who are running have to be trusted more, and from the other end, I think a key is education. Those of us who have been there need to go into the classroom and talk about it. I think voting over the weekend would attract more people, but again, I don't see a real movement for that.

LK: Isn't there an irony in that we have all these media available to us but we can't understand, or don't want to understand, the issues that are important?

MEZVINSKY: Maybe the real irony is that the people who joke about our Founding Fathers not wanting government to work except in times of crisis are right. The irony may be the complexities of this government are in fact a double-edged sword. The difficulties of making changes in the day-to-day process frustrate everyone, but keep the government running. I think the Founding Fathers wanted change to be slow and deliberate.

LK: What are some of the important changes that have occurred in Congress that the public might have missed or not paid attention to?

MEZVINSKY: The 103rd Congress voted on the Family Medical Leave Act. It took seven years to get that through, and had the women not been there, it wouldn't have happened. I think we saw a chipping away at the misguided notion the Second Amendment is absolute and everyone has the right to bear any kind of arms and it's okay to take one of our cars out of the garage and back in a nuclear armament. I don't think we would have had the automatic weapons ban had women not been in Congress.

LK: How come people missed it?

MEZVINSKY: People are human. If you open up the paper and there's an article about John Wayne Bobbitt and there's an article about taxes, most people are going to read about John Wayne Bobbitt. It's human. And we're all trying to put together our days, pick up the kids, make dinner, make sure our parents are okay. Sure there's lack of interest, and sure there's frustration involved, and sure the tax articles are just so darn complicated and dry. It's b-o-r-i-n-g. And I'm not sure of the answer.

LK: Will there be continued polling, and do you think there will be more interest groups?

MEZVINSKY: Yes. That is not going to change. I see it as growing pains. I think people will become more numb to it and more used to it.

LK: Do you think we will have term limits?

MEZVINSKY: I think term limits have been overturned enough in the courts so that it's not likely. Other than that, it's not practical. Legislators like their jobs, and they are not going to vote themselves out of their jobs. Term limits are something I have mixed feelings about: If term limits mean we are not going to have career politicians then I'm all for it. But if term limits mean—because of the extraordinary and complex system we exist in—that staff and lobbyists will be running the government, then I'm not for it.

LK: Will politics be as cutthroat as it is now?

MEZVINSKY: I don't see it changing anytime soon. I think the pendulum will swing back, but I don't think it's swung all the way out yet. I travel all across this country, and people ask me why I even put myself through it. But if we're all out there saying we're not going to do it because it's too dirty and too awful, then who are we going to get in there? My answer is I'm not sure.

LK: Will future members of Congress be people who have been divorced and do you see us moving away from the high pedestal we use for these people?

MEZVINSKY: Thirty years ago you would have never found someone who was divorced. I think people are now saying there isn't anybody out there who hasn't done something that can be written about. That's what people fear. The number of women who have said to me, "I can't run because of Nanny Gate," well, I can't begin to tell you the number of people who have talked about it.

LK: What scares you about this coming century?

MEZVINSKY: Our inability to face facts. Our willingness to seek easy answers. You talk to somebody about Social Security and they say it's a contract the government made with the people. What good is the contract if the government can't keep its part of the deal? People are living longer and requiring more support than people ever dreamed when Social Security was created. So today we hear, "The government is breaking its contract with the people," when what we really need to be saying is "Let's sit down and take a long hard look at this contract and figure out how to make it work even when the times change." I'll say it again: People need to listen to what they need to hear, not just what they want to hear.

LK: Do you see this willingness occurring?

MEZVINSKY: No I don't. People say government shouldn't come into their lives. Well, dissect your day and you will realize it does come into your life. By the time you get into your car in the morning you have had, what some people would say, government interference. It's important people understand that and I think they fundamentally don't because it's not easy to look at. I got a call when I was in office from a woman who wanted to know, "When will government stay out of my Medicare?" And the answer is "When you no longer have Medicare."

War and Peace

You are going to read the views of three intelligent men whose take on the world is, to say the least, divergent. Yet they all have the same destination, which, I can only guess, is identical to yours and mine. And aside from the occasional Hitler, this has always been the case as long as human beings have been around. We want to live in peace.

The coming years are going to test our ability to resist those who would push a button. Entire societies can now be annihilated, which suggests that those with such a capability will no longer conquer, as has been done until this moment, but destroy. I'm not sure future Hitlers will understand the difference, but those who choose to dominate will be leaders of nothingness.

And so it is appropriate in a discussion about the future of war that we also discuss the future of peace. Colman McCarthy wrote for the *Washington Post* from 1969 to 1996 and is the founder and director of the Center for Teaching Peace, which educates people about conflict resolution and mediation. This is something he was brought up with, as his father was a New York attorney helping immigrants who could pay and then helping immigrants who couldn't. As a result he saw different faces, heard different accents, and witnessed different cultures from an early age. I think that's why Colman does what he does. In addition he is an adjunct faculty member at the Georgetown Law Center and the University of Maryland. He is also a volunteer teacher at Bethesda and Chevy Chase high schools. And so that's why I went to his home just outside Georgetown to talk about the future of solving disputes.

I first met General John Shalikashvili when he was a guest on my television show shortly after being named chairman of the Joint Chiefs of Staff. He didn't join the military, like those before him, but was drafted a year after becoming an American citizen. (And his dream is to have those folks in the Publisher's Clearinghouse van come up to his door and ring the bell. So he always sends in the coupon.) General Shalikashvili completed a look at the military through the first decade of the twenty-first century, appropriately called the "Joint Vision 2010 Plan." Because of this, and because he is one of this country's greatest military minds, I spent an hour with the general in his Pentagon office to talk about how we might, God forbid, fight another war. He retired as chairman of the Joint Chiefs in 1997.

In any discussion about politics, the adjective "global" appears more and more with words like "economy" and "marketplace" and "village." And so it is appropriate to talk with a fellow who not only is a fellow New Yorker, but who has spent most of his life in foreign affairs. Richard Holbrooke was involved in the 1968 Paris Peace Talks to end the Vietnam War. He has been an assistant secretary of state for European and Canadian Affairs and assistant secretary of state for Asian and Pacific Affairs. In 1993 he served as the U.S. ambassador to Germany and recently brokered the Dayton Peace Accords for Bosnia, a negotiation that came within minutes of failing.

COLMAN MCCARTHY

FOUNDER AND DIRECTOR, CENTER FOR TEACHING PEACE

Read Gandhi, who says, "It's the law of love that rules mankind. Had violence, i.e., hate, ruled us, we should have become extinct long ago. The irony of it is that the civilized men and nations conduct themselves as if the basis of society is violence." Also read Dr. Martin Luther King, who says, "Love must be at the forefront of our movement if it is to be a successful movement. Love is our great instrument and our great weapon, and that alone."

LK: Do you believe human beings in the next century are capable of learning how not to go to war?

McCARTHY: Violence is a learned behavior, and we teach it to ourselves in countless ways. The first educators in violence are our mothers and fathers. If they treat each other with harsh language and physical violence a child learns, "Well, that's the way I should solve my conflicts." The first educators in how to deal with conflict are in the home, not the school, not the media. It starts with the family. So if a child learns from adults at home that there's another way to deal with conflicts rather than using fists, guns, or harsh language, the child will learn that. If the adults don't know how to do it, then the child isn't going to learn how to do it.

LK: So the question becomes, how do you stop after doing it forever?

McCARTHY: Nobody is born violent. Walk into the hospital labor room where all the new babies are lined up in the nursery. You can't look at one and say, "Well, this is the murderer right there and the other one, well, she's going to be a saint. The other will be a teacher, and this one over there is a rapist." We start out the same. Then we're influenced by our home environment and the media become educators. Ninety-five percent of children's TV programs have violent themes, and the violence is rarely punished.

LK: What do you say to those families and communities that have a weak education system, because you're making it sound as though they haven't a chance.

FUTURE
TALK

•

51

McCARTHY: It's very difficult to do. I don't ever want to give up hope for reform or change. But I would tell those folks to go to their local elementary school or middle school or high school and demand the curriculum be expanded. Look, there are 78,000 elementary schools in the United States, 28,000 high schools, and about 3,000 colleges. If all of those systematically, beginning in pre-K, are taught courses in mediation, conflict resolution, and peace studies the same way we teach English and math and science and physical education, you have a society committed to knowing solutions to violent conflicts and how to practice them. We don't do that, and I'll prove it to you.

LK: Prove it.

McCARTHY: I pull out a hundred-dollar bill during lectures and I say, "If you can identify these six people, this is yours." I get everyone's attention. So I say Robert E. Lee, and every hand in the room goes up. Ulysses S. Grant, and every hand goes up. Paul Revere, and every hand in the room is up. Everyone knows those three because they're generals or folks involved in war. So then I ask, Who is Jeanette Rankin? No hands. Who is Dorothy Day? No hands. Who is Jane Addams? No hands. I haven't been able to get rid of the hundred-dollar bill yet. Teachers don't know this either.

LK: So who is Jeanette Rankin?

McCARTHY: The first member of Congress who was a woman from Montana. She came here in 1917 and was one of about thirty who voted against going into the First World War. She was defeated in the next election and went to India, where she studied under Gandhi, came back here, and in 1941 got elected to Congress again, and voted against the U.S. going into the Second World War. She tells her brother, "I didn't miss a thing, the boys are still doing it." She gave the speech about how you can no more win a war than you can win an earthquake.

LK: But in the next century you're not saying, "Don't teach Paul Revere," rather teach Jeanette Rankin or Dorothy Day as well?

McCARTHY: Let's get a full-sided education is what I'm saying. But that's just part of it. Look at the Supreme Court, where nine justices committed to violent solutions by voting to execute people on death row as an answer to the murder problem. Every child who was a freshman in college last year was in first grade when Ronald Reagan became president. They've been brought up with Libya, Grenada, Panama, Somalia, the Gulf War, Haiti, and so if you have a problem, go bomb somebody. That sends a message to our culture.

LK: We're supposed to be talking about the future here but how do you handle the fact Saddam Hussein probably hasn't a clue about his country's version of Dorothy Day. And by the way, who is Dorothy Day?

MCCARTHY: Dorothy Day founded the Catholic Worker Movement in the 1930s and fed and housed and clothed people on the Lower East Side of New York. She wrote about nonviolence and matched her writing to her actions. Look at your question from an Iraqi child's point of view. He is as trapped by his government as our kids are trapped by our government. We are violent. Our government gives our military $700 million every day. That's $9,000 a second.

LK: Will peace be easier to attain in the next century?

MCCARTHY: It's likely to be harder because of the proliferation of small arms and conventional weapons and their resale, which means it will be easier for civil wars and tribal wars and regional conflicts to erupt and to continue without any of the larger nations (U.S., Germany, France, England) troubling themselves over who is being killed or why. The U.S. is the biggest supplier of the arms, and it reminds me of what Dr. King said in 1967: "A nation that spends more money on military defense than on programs of social uplift is approaching spiritual death."

LK: Does the United States have spiritual death now?

MCCARTHY: Yes it does.

LK: What must peacemakers do in the future that they haven't done yet?

MCCARTHY: Be aware the largest audience of "undecideds" are in the schoolhouses every day. That's where the peace movement needs to focus. Too often, it prefers to have a conference or seminars or issue a report describing the mess we're in, which we already know. There are two kinds of people in the peace movement: problem describers and solution makers. I've got wheelbarrows full of reports telling us how many kids are being killed by handguns and how many homicides and how many dysfunctional families there are. The numbers are all there. Why do you think the ROTC is in school? The Pentagon is smart and knows where the kids are.

LK: It's been suggested technology will make war an easier thing to do.

MCCARTHY: Western thought has always phrased the debate between good and evil, and the good people wage war on the evil people. Eastern thinking sees the debate this way: It isn't between good and evil but between ignorance and awareness. Gandhi always talked about how you can't make people good but you can create the conditions where it's easier for them to choose the good. That's education. If you educate people toward what is good, there's a better chance they're going to choose the good. Our schools don't focus on the peacemakers or the history of nonviolence or where it has worked and how it was done, so our kids graduate from school as peace illiterates.

LK: But if we want to be realists, both today and in the next century, we need to be ready when all hell breaks loose someplace in the world. How do you answer that?

MCCARTHY: I answer this way: Nonviolence doesn't mean nonaction. You react in a way that doesn't adopt your adversary's ethic of violence. If we're invited into the—to use a State Department word, "hot spot"—send in negotiators and skilled people in mediation instead of the Marine Corps.

LK: If the president in the year 2020 is faced with a crisis and missiles are pointed at the United States, what does Colman McCarthy say to him or her from this century?

MCCARTHY: You can't ask the pacifist to stop the war when the other army is marching down the street. There are all kinds of scenarios where nonviolent force looks absurd, but we rarely look at the absurdity now that violence is causing. Thirty-five thousand people are killed every month in wars around the world. So the question becomes, what are the results of killing all these people, and rarely do we ever question that. At the same time we have the scenarios that pacifists are idle dreamers. The president you speak of has to ask himself or herself, "How come schools aren't teaching alternatives to violence?" Lech Walesa is a pacifist, and look what he was able to accomplish in Poland. In 1978 Lech Walesa said, "We're going to overthrow the Leninist-Marxist government," and I remember nobody from Heritage or Brookings or Cato or any deep-thinking senator saying, "Yeah, Lech, you are going to do it." They said, "My God, you're going to go up against the Commies? Here comes World War III!" Well, it happened. Six Poles were killed by the Jaruzelski government. That was it. And Walesa at the reconciliation ceremony quoted Gandhi, "You do not want to bring the adversary to his knees but, rather, to his senses."

LK: But what does the president do in the future?

MCCARTHY: If I'm talking to the zealot who wants to blow something up, I try to appeal to him as a human being, I try to talk to him and see his goodness and say, "What common problems do we have?" and make the point, "It's *not* you against me but you and me against the problem." The problem is the problem. Look at it this way, in 75 percent of fights between husbands and wives, they are fighting separate issues. The husband did something six months ago that upset the wife and the wife did something this morning that upset the husband. Define what the fight is about. Now, if you don't frame this as you and me against the problem, then whoever loses the first round is going to say, "I want a rematch and I'm coming back with bigger bombs and bigger fists." Pacifism is never passivity.

LK: What is the common problem around which the two sides might unite?

MCCARTHY: Well, that zealot in the year 2020 is probably someone right now in high school or college. I'm trying to do things now to head off that problem in the year 2020. It's like asking the fire chief to rush over and put out the fire and saying, "By the way, my house has been burning for the past twenty years. Can you put that out too?" Same with the husband and wife I was talking about: Our divorce rate in America is approaching 60 percent. That's not bad people getting married, it's uninformed people getting married who don't know how to deal with basic conflicts that come up in a relationship any more than governments know how to deal with conflicts. It's the same dynamic.

LK: Name some peacemakers that should be studied in the next century.

McCARTHY: Jesus, Tolstoy, Einstein, Isaiah, Jane Addams, Dorothy Day—

LK: I know Dorothy Day.

McCARTHY: —Alva Myrdal, A. J. Musti, William Penn, Chief Seattle, Erasmus, Pérez Esquivel, Vincent Harding.

LK: I don't know any of those folks.

McCARTHY: That's exactly the point I've been trying to make! We have people now in the first grade and the second grade who have to be educated by saying, "There's another way to deal with your conflicts without using fists, guns, armies, and nukes." We don't educate them. I went to the big Virginia State Prison the other day and sat with the warden for a while and asked, "What's the biggest problem here?" thinking he'd say rape or drugs or guns or something like that. He said it was illiteracy. Three-fourths of the men read at the third grade level. Now, I go to Garrison Elementary School, and 95 percent of the kids come from fatherless families. The principal there tells me he starts to lose these kids, that is, they figure the game is rigged against them and they have no chance, by the third grade. Now that's not a coincidence.

LK: What scares you about the next century?

McCARTHY: That we'll keep wasting our wealth. We're a great country and a wealthy country and we spend $700 million a day on war while a company like Oxfam International reports 35,000 people a day die of malnutrition. That is economic violence. You worry about terrorism? Well, this is the picture of America and there's enormous resentment. I would resent it too if my kid was dying of hunger and I saw these folks wasting their money with weapons. We're the world's largest arms salesman.

LK: What should parents do in the future to teach their kids about peace and nonviolent conflict resolution?

McCARTHY: Parents are going to have to learn this too because nobody taught them about peace. But there's more to it. I can remember when my three boys were younger and people would come visit our house for dinner or something and they would always ask, "Well, boys, what do you want to be when you grow up?" That question always unsettled me. The question should be "How do you want to serve society when you're ready to do it?"

LK: If someone gets ticked off in the next century, what should he do?

MCCARTHY: Ask yourself what the results will be if you throw a punch.

LK: What are the threats to peace in the next century?

MCCARTHY: Ignorance.

LK: That was the threat to peace in this century.

MCCARTHY: That's right. You're catching on.

LK: You think you'll lose your hundred-dollar bill sometime in the next century?

MCCARTHY: I'm always hoping I will. Maybe it'll be one of your readers.

LK: You think there will be a World War III?

MCCARTHY: There are people in the Pentagon planning World War IV. We already have World War III when there are 35,000 people a month dying in the forty wars around the world right now. Whether you name it number three or not doesn't matter because it's happening. Peace has a lot of obstacles, but I always say if your path has no obstacles, it probably isn't leading anywhere.

GENERAL JOHN SHALIKASHVILI

CHAIRMAN, JOINT CHIEFS OF STAFF, 1993–1997

Remember the television game Name That Tune. *It's a question of how many notes you have to hear before you recognize the tune and press a button. We need people now who can name the tune after hearing only two or three notes. Whatever you do, train yourself to feel comfortable in this kind of environment where you'll hear two or three notes and you move on. If you're one who needs to have three lines played before you know the tune, then you probably have something to worry about.*

LK: Will we see a move toward designing weapons systems that can be used by all the armed services rather than, say, just a jet for the navy and another jet for the air force?

SHALIKASHVILI: I think the answer is someplace in between. We are recognizing that some key weapons systems can be designed as such so there is applicability to more than one service. This is particularly true, we are finding now, with attack aircraft. So a lot of work is being done to come up with a joint aircraft that will be applicable for the air force because it will have deep and long-range capability and also be applicable for the navy because it will be able to take repeated landings on a carrier deck. Certainly such things as rifles too. You will find more commonality but there still will be unique weapons systems. A tank will be a tank for the army.

LK: This suggests the missions of the armed services will overlap.

SHALIKASHVILI: I think some missions will overlap. As long as there's a healthy redundancy, then it's good. But when it becomes a costly redundancy, then it's bad. There's an awful lot of worry about how many air forces we have. I think the way we've evolved is just right and I don't spend sleepless nights worrying about it. I worry how many aircraft we have as opposed to other weapons systems and how the synergism on a battlefield is maintained. When one service or one type of system gets out of balance with the others, that's when I begin to worry.

LK: Do you foresee one of the branches of the military being merged into another?

SHALIKASHVILI: I don't think so. There's no great war fighting advantage, and what ought to drive us on the one hand is whether we can fight more effectively with a change and secondly whether what we have is too expensive, and by making adjustments can we accomplish the same thing, and I see neither.

LK: You have prepared the "2010 Plan," which is an idea of what the military should be like in the next century, and there is reference only to "the armed forces" but no specific reference to "the army" or "the navy." Should we read anything into that?

SHALIKASHVILI: No. I don't see a difference in how we organize ourselves in the different branches. But I do see each of the branches fighting differently than they fight today. And I see the beginning of a new approach into how we develop requirements for weapons systems. I see a promise of revolution, an electronic revolution going on in the civilian community to alter significantly the way we fight. That's not to say all of the sudden we aren't going to have ships or airplanes. The revolution is not going to be brought about because we developed a new machine gun but because it offers us opportunities to see the battlefield much much better than we did before, to be able to bring that knowledge to leaders who have to do something about it very quickly through communications systems that we could only dream about before, to display that information rapidly in ways that make sense to a commander, and he, in turn, can affect what is happening on the battlefield through smart munitions that can reach deep.

LK: One can take from this conversation that there's going to be less hands-on in war. We'll see the target of the missile through an onboard TV camera rather than actually shooting people?

SHALIKASHVILI: I think there will be, always, a need for a way to occupy land and hold it, and for that you will need to have soldiers on the ground. You can't hold land from the air. That requirement will exist but how we go about it and what tools we give the soldier and what tools we give those who support the soldiers, whether that's air forces or naval forces that support the land campaign, therein will lie the difference. And how you synchronize the whole battle.

LK: You speak of "dominant maneuvers" in the "2010 Plan" in which everyone is working together, the army and the navy and the marines and the air force. Tell me how that's going to work.

SHALIKASHVILI: If you look at war as it existed at the time of World War II, you had the ability to see very little of what the enemy was doing, and you knew some what your own forces were doing. During Desert Storm we saw the first promise of a revolution with new satellites that could see and hear and with new communication systems that could move large volumes of information very quickly and bring them to these command centers where it could all be fused together in one clear picture. You could, all of a sudden, see much better, and then you were beginning to get munitions that could strike with some precision. We saw all of that on television when a bomb would go down a chimney. Some folks estimated that we were at a point where we could see 25 percent of what was going on in the battlefield. And so they could maneuver forces in response to real knowledge they had, instead of assumptions. You could begin to dominate maneuvers because you have the vision that the enemy did not. Well since Desert Storm, we've improved vastly the ability to see, to hear, to move that information, to fuse it, to present it, and the number of aircraft and other weapons systems that can now deliver smart munitions. People now say maybe we're at the 30 percent level or so where we can really understand what's happening on the battlefield and we can do something about it in a smart way. The dominance with which we now approach the battlefield is much greater.

LK: This sounds like those on the battlefield will have some sort of earpiece so they can be told, "Go this way" or "Move right."

SHALIKASHVILI: Oh sure. I think the way we communicate soldier to soldier has vastly improved but the people who have to make decisions about how to move larger units understand now better and don't have to rely on sketchy reports they get from the front because they can see it with the various sensors, which are in fact satellites, and drones and aircraft. One listens to the enemy's communication systems while the other one gets a good picture on radar and another listens through computers, and there's another that sees in daytime and at nighttime. That's the revolution and you would not have had the same revolution occur in civilian life that you now take for granted. Our challenge is not to invent something new but to apply the electronic revolution to our business.

LK: Will war be fought quicker in the future?

SHALIKASHVILI: If wars get bogged down and are of long duration they will more rapidly degenerate to the old way of fighting. I think that wars will be of much shorter duration because the precision with which you can now strike someone is so far greater. You can degrade his capability so much faster.

LK: As you put together this 2010 plan, what were you thinking about the enemy you would be fighting?

SHALIKASHVILI: The comparative value between us will not so much be that our tank will be so much better than his, although I hope we retain a qualitative advantage, or the airplane or the ship. I'm convinced the qualitative edge will in fact be the intelligence, command and control, and communications systems that I've been talking about. After all, in civilian life that's our strength today, and how well we capture that and apply it to our business will determine for how long we can keep that advantage. I think the race will be between us applying that which we already have and those who wish us ill trying to catch up. How quickly we recognize where our strength really is and how smartly we apply it to our war-fighting business will determine how long we'll be able to stay ahead of it. Today we are clearly head and shoulders above anyone else in our ability to carry on the beginnings of that kind of a fight. Today's armed forces are in fact head and shoulders above anyone else's armed forces. Our challenge now, as we enter the next century, is to widen that gap and, at a minimum, retain that differential.

LK: Will the enemy be a country or a local faction or a group?

SHALIKASHVILI: I think we should not pretend to know that which we don't know. One of the things that has always bedeviled us in the United States if you look at our history is that we've never been very good at picking who our next enemy was going to be, and for that matter, when and where we were going to fight our next war. We don't have a good track record at all. So I'm not sure we're any smarter today. My sense is, though, that we as a global power will be challenged every bit as much in the next century as we have in this last one. We have global interests to protect and others will find it necessary to attack those interests. Whether that is Iran as it develops into the next century or whether that is some other country or group of countries, I don't know. But I do know there are some near-term phenomena that are becoming very bothersome as we end this century and will be with us in the next one.

LK: What are they?

SHALIKASHVILI: Such things as small nations with weapons of mass destruction that now, at relatively low cost, can be put on missiles that can deliver those weapons over long distances. It will certainly be terrorism because small nations feel that through the use of state-sponsored terrorism they can effectively engage someone much larger. We will face the threat of weapons of mass destruction from smaller states—

LK: Iraq, Iran?

SHALIKASHVILI: Yeah, Libya, Iraq, Iran. We will be facing state-sponsored terrorism from these groups. But we must understand because these new threats are appearing and will be with us into the next century, that doesn't mean we can now neglect our capability to fight conventional conflicts. We don't have that luxury.

LK: You think poisonous gas and chemical weapons will be used against the United States?

SHALIKASHVILI: We would be foolish if we assumed that they wouldn't. We have seen that such weapons are a cheap way for even a third world country to give it military capability that they wouldn't be able to have in a conventional way, so I think it's a possibility and we need to be prepared for it. But it's also weapons such as chemical, poison gas, and biological weapons, for that matter. We've seen it in Tokyo and it's certainly within the realm of possibility that we could face that as terrorists become more sophisticated in the next century.

LK: They're getting better.

SHALIKASHVILI: That's right. We must not think of a terrorist as somebody who uses a 2,000- or 3,000-pound bomb but also as one with an aerosol can that will spread biological or chemical agents.

LK: Is it your feeling then that these weapons will come from a terrorist or a small group rather than a country?

SHALIKASHVILI: Sure. And that makes it even more difficult to deal with. But what makes a terrorist more of a threat today is that while the terrorists might be an independent group, they do receive financial and other support from states that find it advantageous to encourage terrorist groups, particularly those that attack the United States.

LK: There going to be a missile shield of some sort above the United States in the next century?

SHALIKASHVILI: I think we will most likely have a missile defense, so if you think of that as a missile shield, certainly when we enter the next century we will have, I believe, very effective defenses against the theater ballistic missiles that threaten our forces. We are also moving out with a development of a defensive system against ballistic missiles that could hurt our country. It's just a question of how soon they are ready for fielding and how soon we need to field those because a threat is approaching.

LK: Will they be in the air or ground-based?

SHALIKASHVILI: I think initially they'll be on the ground, but what will then develop is probably hard to say. It sounds exotic and exciting to have these systems up in the air but you need to make sure you can get a significantly improved capability for the vastly greater expense of putting all of that in space.

LK: What will be done differently to ensure weapons don't fall into the wrong hands?

SHALIKASHVILI: I think as long as there are different nations that produce weapons systems, and I see absolutely nothing on the horizon that will change that, because partly it's a matter of economics and partly it's a matter of maintaining your own industrial base to produce those systems, there will be weapons systems available on the market. I think we will probably be better at developing regimes where we will cooperate and try not to create imbalances in regions. We've already done quite well in some parts of the world. In some parts we have not done well. But there's going to be a weapons market and nations regrettably will continue to push sales because it's a matter of economics.

LK: Countries buying these weapons will be where?

SHALIKASHVILI: I think they will be the third world countries that don't produce them themselves, and they will pit one of us against the other in order to be able to as cheaply as possible attain these weapons. I think the weapons market will be there and the weapons sales will continue, but hopefully we can put kind of a control regime over the whole business.

LK: Regime?

SHALIKASHVILI: I think those that sell weapons will look at it in a responsible way so that we do not introduce weapons into a region that will make it more likely for a state to attack another. So we need to keep a balance. And also responsible from the standpoint that we do not drive nations into poverty simply because they are investing all of their resources that should be invested in social programs into weapons systems. On the other hand, it's not realistic that we believe we can be the policeman of the world and say, "We can have weapons that you can't have."

LK: The military is going to do more with less?

SHALIKASHVILI: I think that's a reality.

LK: Is this because you will outsource a lot of research and development into the private sector, or is it because the army will be smaller and the navy will be smaller and so on?

SHALIKASHVILI: We will be smaller because of necessity because there will be fewer resources. We will be smaller because we will be able to have systems with vastly greater capability, therefore we will have fewer systems.

LK: So the Department of Defense budget will be smaller?

SHALIKASHVILI: I think the budget has become significantly smaller, and how much smaller it can get depends on what this nation wants its military to do. Certainly since Desert Storm we are some 40 percent smaller. We are doing, from the standpoint of day-to-day operations, a lot more than we did during the Cold War. How far can we carry it forward? Some more. As I've told you, it won't be necessary in my judgment to replace airplane for airplane. I think we will be able to get airplanes that are more capable than the ones they replace, therefore we will need fewer. And we'll need fewer people that deliver bombs to the airplane because we will use smart munitions and we'll need only one weapon per target or two per target where before we might have needed thirty or forty or fifty. So there's a natural downsizing effect that's occurring as you get more capable. In the twenty-first century will the military be smaller? Absent a vast threat that develops out there, I believe the armed forces will be smaller.

LK: Want to give me a number?

SHALIKASHVILI: No, I can't give you a number, nor can I tell you that the cost of such a military will be smaller because these technologies also cost money.

LK: Will people joining the army or the navy have to be computer wonks, have college degrees to deal with the technology?

SHALIKASHVILI: I don't think so. We are finding a surprising thing: The young men and women who come into the armed forces today are, first of all, as good as ever, bar none. Secondly, they are more than capable of operating the equipment that is already very complex. So that's not a fear of mine, but when I look at those potential adversaries out there, for them it's a fear because the kind of people they get into their forces are not the same kind that we get. We've talked a lot about how what is going to make us better is the technologies. It is also the people.

LK: Is there anything that scares you about the next century?

SHALIKASHVILI: No, I don't think so. In a broader sense the next century will have an awful lot of challenges, but it will have opportunities that far exceed the challenges. Look, we're leaving behind what probably can be characterized as the bloodiest century in our existence. If nothing else, surely the next century will be better. And if we're smart about it, it can be vastly better for our children.

Ambassador Richard C. Holbrooke

SPECIAL ENVOY FOR CYPRUS; VICE CHAIRMAN, FIRST BOSTON

*We should dream the great dreams. We should spend more of
our wealth to seek solutions to global problems. To those in other
countries, I say America can provide leadership but it can't provide all the resources. You will have to provide more of your own
resources.*

LK: What is going to change in foreign policy during the next century?

HOLBROOKE: One of the interesting things to me is what won't
change. There have been three popular books written since the end of
the Cold War with provocative titles (*The End of History, The End of the
Nation State,* and *Clash of Civilization*). Each puts forward a thesis. The
first is Western liberal democracy has triumphed and now history will
beat it out. That's categorically wrong. The transnational issues, which
include the spread of AIDS, terrorism, communications, drugs, and
environment are brought forth in the second book to transcend the
nation state. Wrong again. The nation state is transcending its role but it
remains a critical variable, as we have seen in the Middle East and
Bosnia, in Russia and China. The third book suggests it is inevitable the
great civilizations will clash. Not true. The fact is, the end of the Cold
War did not mean the end of history, but rather the resumption of history. The end of the Cold War did not mean the end of America's
involvement in the world, but rather a continued American involvement
no longer based on a single concept of containing Communism. It is
now based on balancing a variety of American interests: human rights,
environmental issues, stopping the spread of disease, but also the traditional strategic interests such as those which led us to take on Iraq in
Desert Storm. That was about oil. When the twenty-first century begins,
the American public will face a world which combines elements from
the period between the two World Wars and some uniquely new elements, which include terrorism and the environment and ignore international borders, but which require governments to band together if they

are to be solved. The growth of international trade is, and will continue to be, one of the biggest changes in the world.

In this environment where international economic policy is the key to our own economic survival, we cannot turn our backs on the traditional political issues. You can't disaggregate economic and political policy. You can no longer separate strategic and humanitarian policy. The United States public, which seems to have election after election in which foreign policy issues are never mentioned and is becoming more and more reluctant to spend money for foreign policy, is making a grievous mistake by thinking it can save money internationally while trying to grow economically based on international markets. You can't have it both ways.

LK: The suggestion is made in campaigns to reduce foreign aid—

HOLBROOKE: And it will continue to be made, but it is wrong. It has to go up. We first have to break ourselves of the myth that foreign aid is a giveaway.

LK: How is the United Nations going to change?

HOLBROOKE: First of all, the United States has to stop being a deadbeat in the United Nations and pay the billion dollars it owes. We changed quarterbacks in 1996 by throwing out Butros-Butros Gali (UN secretary-general) but that doesn't mean we can't put any air in the football.

LK: Should the assessment be lowered from its current 25 percent?

HOLBROOKE: It's already gone down from 30 percent to 25 percent, and if it goes down to 22 percent or whatever, I don't care. We can't be the biggest deadbeats in the UN now or in the next century. We can't go around and say, "Even though we have a new quarterback, we still want to not pay to see the game or, for that matter, play in it." I understand the money owed will be paid back in a phased manner but we have a divided government. It's going to take strong unambiguous leadership from the president. It can't be left to the secretary of state or second-level people regardless of how effective and skilled they are. The president must be involved personally in the fight for UN reform.

LK: How will the UN change in the next century?

HOLBROOKE: The UN messed up Bosnia because it was asked to Mission Impossible in Bosnia. That was a job for NATO from the very beginning. The UN role going forward, then, is not to do things it isn't built to do.

LK: No UN peacekeeping forces in the future?

HOLBROOKE: Of course there will be peacekeeping forces. In Bosnia, however, there was never any peace to keep. The UN forces in Bosnia had no authority to shoot, and permission to do so had to go all the way back to New York.

LK: Who will be a superpower in the twenty-first century?

HOLBROOKE: There is only one. I define superpower as a country that is dominant, like in baseball: hits, runs, home runs. You can lead in one category, but a superpower leads in them all. The United States has the strongest economy, the strongest military, the most dynamic people with new ideas, and the strongest opportunity. I also think we are the moral leader in the world, and that should be part of the superpower definition. But there are a lot of important powers at a level below the United States.

Having said that, there will be times in the next century when countries are stronger than us in one way or another temporarily. The Russians will continue to be a nuclear power, and that's an important component of world leadership. By their geographic size they will be an important political power. Furthermore, if Russia implodes, which is one of the three or four possible outcomes, that could become a crisis.

In the first third of the next century, India will surpass China in population. But China's economy is conducting one of the greatest revolutions in the history of the world. Twenty-three percent of the world's population is increasing its wealth over one generation, and that is an extraordinary event in the world. This changes international trade flows, environment, global warming, population issues. It is also a nuclear power. The direction China takes is the greatest unanswered question in Asia today. Its leadership is geriatric, and the political structure on the surface appears relatively unchanged, but, in fact, apparent stability is undergoing vast change. The intellectual roots in Communist China are bankrupt. I would guess in the first ten years of the twenty-first century there will be a major political evolution in

China. Communism will transmogrify itself into something substantially different, but it won't be democracy.

LK: What will it be?

HOLBROOKE: Maybe a Mexican-style one-party situation with greater personal freedom.

LK: You mentioned India.

HOLBROOKE: Visiting India is like visiting two countries superimposed on one another. Ninety percent of the population is living at or below the poverty line in a desperate situation. But India has a substantial second nation of 100–200–300 million people who are well-educated, skilled, and trained. It's no accident that the Bank of America has relocated its worldwide back offices to Bangular because it can get all the services it can get in the States at a tenth of the cost. India, however, has an unresolved strategic problem with its neighbors: Pakistan and Nepal and Sri Lanka and Bangladesh and Butan. As a result, I don't think the story of India is at all finished. That India stayed together as a country in a time when other countries such as Russia, Yugoslavia, Czechoslovakia disintegrated is in itself astonishing. The fact India is food self-sufficient, which it wasn't at independence when it had 300 million people, is equally astonishing. So Russia, China, and India are the big three of the future.

LK: So there's another tier of countries below those three in terms of power and influence?

HOLBROOKE: Exactly. England, France, and Germany. Their economies are stagnant but they have geographic position, very strong human infrastructures, and great traditions, along with state-of-the-art technology. Two of three are nuclear countries as well.

LK: Some predict a united Europe in the next century. You agree?

HOLBROOKE: No. They lost their moment for a united Europe. If Maastricht had come five years earlier, while the Soviet Union was still there to unify them, it might have happened. What de Gaulle called the *"Europe des Patries,"* and what Margaret Thatcher also supported, is the more likely way of the future. That's the European Union, which will be more "European" but not a union. So until you have a single national election structure for all of the countries, it can't happen.

Furthermore, as Europe increases the number of countries in the European Union, the commonality diminishes. Germany, France, Italy, the Netherlands, Belgium, and Luxembourg used to closely knit together, but today it's now fifteen countries stretching from Portugal to Helsinki and from Greece to Ireland. And in the first decade of the next century, Poland, the Czech republic, Hungary, and Slovenia will be added, and possibly Romania will be added as well. As these countries come in with less and less in common, except a common economic market, the political integration will recede, notwithstanding the effort for a common currency.

LK: What happens in Cuba?

HOLBROOKE: Communism has survived in Cuba because it's an island and therefore less vulnerable to the infectious disease in the winds of freedom. Sooner or later, those winds will cross the Caribbean and infect Cuba. It's hard for me to see how Castro's dominant charismatic leadership can be transmitted to the next generation intact.

LK: Will Communism disappear?

HOLBROOKE: Aside from Vietnam, the other so-called Communist states (North Korea is a fascist state pretending to be a Communist state, but it's a pure old military dictatorship with total control, and China is a dictatorship) have repudiated the Leninist-Marxist tenets.

LK: What's the greatest threat, then, to the United States?

HOLBROOKE: It's no longer a single threat like godless atheistic Communism. The greatest threat to the United States in the next cycle of history could come from a series of different issues: nuclear weapons in the hands of maniac terrorists from a small rogue state like Iraq or Libya. Nuclear devices can be built and stored in something the size of a suitcase. Just think what would have happened if the terrorists in Peru who seized the Japanese embassy had something like that? This isn't a Hollywood movie anymore. The world's police forces are all aware of it but there's a limit to how well we can prevent it. The second threat is the destruction of the environment, and the spread of AIDS as enormous continuing problems. On these two issues we are not spending enough resources or exercising enough national leadership. The third threat is the refugee issue. Ninety-five percent of all refugees in the world are caused by political actions, as in Rwanda and Bosnia or Cambodia, not by famines or floods. Refugees cost the world billions of dollars a year and create great dislocation and are never-ending.

LK: You don't mention fundamentalism.

HOLBROOKE: It's a euphemism for extremism. Fundamentalism in religion is not so unusual; it's been with us throughout the centuries. Look at the Crusades. I don't think it's a fundamental threat to the United States.

LK: Let's move to an area where you've spent some time: Bosnia. What will people in the next century be saying about it?

HOLBROOKE: The jury is definitely out on whether the dawn of the twenty-first century will see a Bosnia partitioned like Cyprus, a Bosnia divided into two countries like Czechoslovakia, or a Bosnia which is one country with a loose central government, as called for in the Dayton Agreements. Now, the people of Omaha and San Francisco don't need to worry because their lives aren't affected by one, two, or three countries where Bosnia is today. But the United States and NATO have invested a great deal in making sure their word means something in the world, so we have more than a small interest in the outcome.

LK: When you were in Bosnia, many here in the United States were saying they had trouble connecting with or understanding the troubles of countries with names ending in "ia." With technology and mass media and communication, might that change in the next century?

HOLBROOKE: It's a key question. All across the United States, interest in foreign policy and foreign affairs is declining. Television networks, with the sole exception of CNN, are declining in the amount of news they cover internationally. In January of 1997 *Time* ran an article about foreign film audiences in the United States now constituting 1 percent of the film-going audiences, when during the years of Truffaut, it was 5 percent. The ratings say don't give the public foreign news at the same time when we are more involved in the world economically, and every mid-size American company exports to live. More land in

Iowa is under the plow for export to Japan than for American consumption. The people of the U.S. should learn they are part of the world for their own economic and political self-interest, and that means knowing more about the world. The rest of the world follows the United States in every detail. You can be in Europe and they are watching the O.J. Simpson coverage. Even American football and basketball are now becoming international sports. That's the power of American culture. I'm all for the rest of the world knowing our culture, but we should also learn about other worlds and cultures and not pretend we can pull a cover over our heads.

LK: You think people in the future will do that?

HOLBROOKE: I am a congenital optimist. Once Americans identify a problem, and identifying a problem is 50 percent of solving it, they go out and solve it.

LK: How do we become, as you say, a part of the world?

HOLBROOKE: Look at your television show. While its internal equivalent of the Nielsens is very small, collectively the cumulative audience over a year is hundreds of times larger. If more guests were internationally oriented, they could be more educative.

LK: Might television be used to bring two sides of a conflict to the table?

HOLBROOKE: You already do that.

LK: But I'm talking about working through a solution while on the air.

HOLBROOKE: Even Larry King can't settle the Middle East in an hour. Television is an important diplomatic tool. Walter Cronkite and Barbara Walters both played key roles in getting Sadat and Begin together in 1977. I remember Marcos in 1985 using the Brinkley show to announce an election to his own people. You interviewed Karadzic. I'm sure that had a different rating number than when you interviewed Sharon Stone, and quite frankly I'd prefer to see Sharon Stone than Radovan Karadzic, but it's healthy to do this kind of thing because you and they are speaking to the world.

LK: Could a single interview with Radovan Karadzic change how later negotiations occur?

HOLBROOKE: As a negotiator I would pay very close attention to such interviews because I look for clues, and every once in a while history changes on a television show. Real diplomacy, like Dayton, is twenty-four hours a day, with the press excluded, though. So there's a time for Larry and there's a time for Dayton. I can recall sitting in the Pentagon and talk turning toward the "Christiane Amanpour effect" or the "CNN effect," which was the Mogadishu picture of the American body being dragged through the streets. The prevailing myth is that television can pressure you into instantaneous policy reactions. I don't believe it to be true. The pace of history is accelerated.

LK: Will there be a World War III?

HOLBROOKE: No.

LK: Ethnic wars?

HOLBROOKE: No. There will be more local wars than during the Cold War. Why? During the Cold War local wars had the possibility of leading, by chain reaction, to a general war. Now that constraint is off. Exhibit A? Bosnia. Exhibit B? The tensions between Greece and Turkey, where the issue was a ten-acre island in the Aegean Sea with seventy sheep and no people and we came within hours of a war. We stopped the damn thing but the issues today are not resolved and are getting worse because the Cypriots are buying Russian missiles which can reach the Turkish mainland. That is going to be a probable major crisis between Greece and Turkey, and that would have never happened during the Cold War. And it won't lead to general war because the Germans, British, French, Chinese, and Japanese are out of the general war business. The United States, as a result, must constantly work to make sure second-tier political issues like Cyprus or Bosnia do not escalate into first-tier issues. That's the essence of leadership in the world, and I don't think we've been active enough in the post–Cold War period.

LK: So we are going to have more small wars?

HOLBROOKE: Yes.

LK: Will nuclear weapons be used in the twenty-first century by one group of people against another?

HOLBROOKE: Very possibly.

LK: Will it include the nuclear powers of the world like the French or the U.S. or the Russians or the Chinese?

HOLBROOKE: No. You'll notice that leaves India.

LK: And?

HOLBROOKE: They have a very dangerous situation with the Pakistanis, and I'm not as confident the whole situation in the subcontinent can be calmed. We are not going to have a nuclear war among the nuclear powers but we could have a nuclear confrontation with terrorists. Techno-terrorism is a possibility too. Suppose someone figures out how to crash the Federal Reserve system, which moves $2 trillion worth of paper every day. We could have a worldwide financial panic, which would be more terror-provoking than weapons.

LK: Might there be an international policy in which countries speak in a single voice to terrorists rather than the disjointed way we do it now?

HOLBROOKE: A collective security effort against rogues can only be done if there's very strong leadership, and that leadership will not come from the United Nations and it will not come from Europe. The U.S. can't provide it in every circumstance, but if the U.S. does it, we have a real shot at it.

LK: Will there be more or fewer security measures in airports and public buildings in the next century?

HOLBROOKE: I'm an optimist but I don't believe progress is an inevitable event in this area of security. The White House is now a fortress. Airport check-in times keep getting longer, but I see no chance it's going to change. I hate to say this because it is one of the most marked deteriorations in the quality of our lives, but I can't imagine any optimist on that issue.

LK: Will economic sanctions continue to be used as a policy tool?

HOLBROOKE: Yes. They worked against Serbia. Many believe the sanctions against South Africa also helped. Collective leadership is important. But where there's a sieve like Cuba or Iran it hasn't much effect.

LK: You speak of collective leadership. Who?

HOLBROOKE: I mean collective action with American leadership.

LK: Will there be more Daytons, and might there be areas in the United States specifically set aside to hammer out solutions to differences between countries?

HOLBROOKE: The word "Dayton" has taken on a new meaning in diplomacy. It's no longer a city in Ohio; it's a concept for negotiations. We've been hearing calls to Dayton for Cyprus, the Mideast, Ireland, and other issues in South Asia. It's the right thing to do conceptually, but the prestige of the United States has to be behind it.

LK: But will it be done in Dayton or does it matter?

HOLBROOKE: Doesn't matter. But you need an isolated venue with the press denied access. And the people inside the compound are those with authority to make the final decision and not the ones who have to go back to their capitals. And there must be agreement to stay as long as necessary. All three of these issues must be agreed to in advance. The Turks and Greeks haven't agreed to that kind of a deal yet, so there hasn't been a "Dayton" for them.

LK: What advice do you have for future negotiators who might participate in future "Daytons"?

HOLBROOKE: Establish the parameters of "Dayton." Failure at a Dayton-style conference can be a disaster. We came within a half-hour of failure at Dayton. We had written the failure press statements and were planning for the press conference and all sides had seen them. There were eight hundred journalists reporting we had failed, and it was only when all three parties saw between eight A.M. and eight-thirty A.M. on November 21, 1995, that we were really going to announce failure that they made the final concessions. That was the greatest gamble I've ever participated in.

LK: Future secretaries of state will travel more?

HOLBROOKE: I don't think they should. There are many trips that must be done either because only the American foreign minister can represent us at an international meeting, like the NATO foreign ministers meeting, or because the American secretary of state is the negotiator. But just getting on a plane and traveling is not productive. Why? Because the number one priority of foreign policy today is building a domestic consensus. You have to work with the Congress.

LK: What changes might we see in the next century in how the State Department and Congress work together?

HOLBROOKE: I've discussed the idea many times with members of Congress that it is repetitive to go before the Senate Foreign Relations Committee and then the House Foreign Affairs Committee, plus the respective appropriations and authorizations committees. To consolidate them, and I'm told this by the leadership of the Congress, is impossible because of the political needs of the individual members. They each want their place in the sun and on C-SPAN and in the evening news.

LK: It's ego, not information?

HOLBROOKE: Yes. The entire appropriations-authorization process which was devised at the turn of the century to deal with a weird accounting problem, where you first authorized the money and then you appropriated it, and which not one American out of one hundred can explain, is an absurdity. I also believe we should have a two-year budget and each Congress should pass one two-year budget. This cuts in half the amount of time you have to spend defending the budget, and it allows for more coherent policy planning. Every member of Congress I discussed this with says, "You're right," and every member of Congress says, "It won't happen."

Science, Medicine, and Technology

The first name that comes to mind for an interview in this section is probably the first name everybody would have picked: Bill Gates. His company, Microsoft, is close to becoming a part of every computer on the planet with its software and operating systems. Bill is now America's wealthiest human being, with a fortune of almost $19 billion (in fact, there's a Web site on the Internet designed specifically to record how much money Bill made any given day). So I decided the best way to get his attention was to write an interview request in longhand and send it via the mail. It got to him, and soon we were sitting down for a discussion about the next century, except he was at a keyboard in one part of the country and I was using a keyboard somewhere else. I never even saw the guy, and for that matter, I never talked to him during those forty-five minutes. The interview was done via e-mail.

During the 1996 Democratic Convention in Chicago, I found myself on a panel about politics in the information age, and it was there I met Esther Dyson, the president of the Electronic Frontier Foundation and a guru in the computer industry (of which there are many), who is well-respected (of which there are few). Esther doesn't have a telephone in her house but is a leading voice about the ramifications of the Internet. I called her on a Sunday afternoon in her office, where, obviously, she does have a phone.

Medicine is about to undergo some incredible changes as genetic technology research continues to open more and more doors toward curing diseases. So it made sense to talk with the man in charge of making our lives healthier, Dr. David Satcher, who directs the Atlanta-based Centers for Disease Control and Prevention. The future of going to work and taking it easy is going to center around going for a walk, says Dr. Satcher.

There's another part of medicine that is fast becoming a part of any conversation inside a medical school, and that is the research under way right now about human genes. Residents of the future will be mapped and screened at birth through their DNA. That's the easy part. What happens after they leave the hospital is cause for concern as well as excitement, as Dr. Francis Collins tells me from his office at the National Human Genome Research Institute.

Whenever the twenty-first century is discussed, the matter of age comes into play. Here's the reason: In 1900 the average life expectancy was forty-eight years. Today it is seventy-six years. On one hand this is progress: Science is helping us live longer. But more and more we are hearing, if not using, the phrase "quality of life," and that is the result of what is left when you take away the science. Progress creates problems.

One person who has made a living dealing with these and other problems associated with our health is former U.S. Surgeon General C. Everett Koop. He has gone head to head with tobacco companies over advertising campaigns he claims are directed toward teenagers, while warning the rest of us about the economic as well as physical ramifications of smoking. Today Dr. Koop runs the respected Koop Institute at Dartmouth. In addition, he hosts the popular Time/Life collection of videos explaining causes and treatments of a variety of diseases. He came to the table in this interview as he always does: with experience and facts, and I came away knowing I had seen a real picture of what we are going to face.

BILL GATES

CHAIRMAN, MICROSOFT CORPORATION

Get comfortable with technology. Don't watch too much TV. Read a lot.

LK: I'm having this conversation with you on a computer, and I'm wondering if e-mail is going to replace the post office in the next century.

GATES: E-mail won't replace the post office, but it will replace a lot of paper the post office and overnight services carry around today. Take bills for example. Today it's unnecessary for a company to go to the expense of printing a bill on paper and sending it to you, which you then pay by mailing a check and sending it back through the mail, which the company then delivers to its bank, which in turn routes it back to your bank for payment. It's inefficient, time-consuming, and it doesn't offer particularly good service. Today, and certainly in the next century, a company can send an electronic bill and you can pay it all via e-mail. It's easy, it's fast, and it's efficient. Paying the bill takes a matter of seconds and delivery is virtually instantaneous (the denizens of the Internet call the post office "snail mail" because it's so slow). As people and companies switch to e-mail, the clutter of paper in our physical mailboxes will decrease, although the clutter in our electronic mailboxes, the ones that show up only on our computer screens, will increase. Still, physical mail isn't going away entirely. You might send a wedding invitation by physical mail to underscore its importance and formality. But you might send an electronic version too, just to make sure it was received. It's a lot easier to RSVP to an electronic invitation than a physical one: Just click the "yes" button.

LK: What about overnight mail like Federal Express?

GATES: The post office and delivery companies are going to see the quantity of correspondence they deliver fall, but at the same time they'll see the amount of merchandise they deliver rise. The Internet will evolve into the world's greatest marketplace because it will be such an easy way to find out information about products, including who has the very lowest prices. Quite a bit of the shopping we do in person today will be done over the Internet in the future, and whenever we buy a physical object, it will have to be delivered.

LK: What about catalogs? Are they gone?

GATES: Much of our shopping will be done from electronic catalogs, which can be more convenient than paper ones. An on-line catalog can know your tastes and emphasize items you're likely to want, the way a knowledgeable clerk would. It can have enormous depth in terms of the range of items it offers and in the information about each. You won't have to be overwhelmed with the information because you'll control how much and what kind you get. An on-line catalog can always be up-to-date, with discontinued items removed and new items added all the time. If an item is out of stock and won't be available for three weeks, the catalog can say so.

LK: Is electronic junk mail going to be a problem like physical junk mail is?

GATES: It could be a huge problem. For me, it already is. I probably get more unwanted e-mail than anyone. Fortunately, the power of the computer can be used to filter out messages from people we're not interested in corresponding with.

LK: Do you worry your child won't learn penmanship because there's always a keyboard and a printer nearby?

GATES: When I was in school I always felt it was unfair that kids who happened to have bad handwriting were penalized at grade time. Obviously, everybody needs to learn basic writing skills. We want our kids to have a full complement of basic communications skills. I'm a lot more concerned that kids who only use calculators and never learn to do multiplication and division by hand may fail to grasp the basics of mathematics.

LK: Will there be any use for pencils and paper?

GATES: People will use pencils and paper for a long time but they won't use them as much as they do now.

LK: How will the keyboard change?

GATES: The keyboard will remain important but it's going to lose the importance it now shares with the mouse as an input device. Over the next ten or twenty years computers are going to get very good at recognizing the spoken or written word, and the little video cameras that we'll use for teleconferencing also will allow computers to recognize gestures. The computer will know if you nod or shake your head, and it may even read your lips to improve the accuracy of its voice recognition.

LK: Tell me how a computer will be used in the average home thirty years from now.

GATES: You'll have lots of thin flat screens covering walls of your house and you'll carry a hand-held device around with you. The screens will feed whatever visual information you want—live video from a place in the world you like, an art reproduction, or maybe a stock ticker.

LK: This sounds like the virtual reality scene in *Disclosure*.

GATES: I'm not sure *Disclosure* got it quite right, but you will be able to interact with virtual (imaginary) tools and places. Games will still involve socialization—people meeting and trying out their skills on each other. The difference is you'll be able to do it at a distance and in some pretty amazing virtual surroundings.

LK: What happens when the power goes out?

GATES: We're very dependent today on electricity and we still will be in fifty years. If there's a power failure you won't get much work done, although battery technology will improve enough that short power failures won't necessarily shut down all of your computers.

LK: Will laptops and personal computers become antiques, and if so, what will be their replacements?

GATES: Today a five-year-old computer is considered an antique. Computers are going to continue to evolve rapidly. They'll get much smaller and faster and will fit into everyday life without calling attention to themselves.

LK: Are we still going to use modems, and how fast will they be?

GATES: There's going to be electronic circuitry that plays the role of a modem, modulating and demodulating signals so they can be transmitted from one place to another. But this circuitry will be built into our computers so we won't give it much thought. Speeds will be exceptionally fast as compared to today.

LK: Will we still call it the Internet?

GATES: Yeah, we'll still call it that. It's kind of like the term "personal computer," though. Its meaning is always changing. A PC is so much better today than five years ago, and an old one seems almost quaint. The evolution of the Internet, like the evolution of the PC, is continuous. Just in the past year we've seen it evolve from being largely text-based, to being graphical, to having pages with audio, animation, and even limited video. Whatever it's called, the interactive network will touch many parts of our lives—like electricity does today. We'll use the network to stay in touch with people, to learn about the world, and to manage many of our affairs. But we won't be as keenly conscious of it as we are today because the Internet will become integrated into our lives. The Internet will be how we get television entertainment, how we make our phone calls, how we get our news, how we choose our music, how we share documents with colleagues, and how our kids submit some of their homework. We don't think about electricity when we flip on a light now and we won't think about the Internet when we flip on a screen a few years from now.

LK: How do you envision politics being affected by the Internet?

GATES: I think there will be experimentation in many areas, including electronic democracy. I think legislators who educate themselves and make decisions and compromises on behalf of the citizens they represent provide a valuable service, and they will continue to represent us. And I'd be surprised if some political jurisdictions didn't at least experiment with direct democracy, where individual voters cast ballots on a variety of issues, because the Internet will make it practical. Candidates and incumbents are already putting political pages on the Web, and many news organizations have begun covering politics on the Internet. These trends will accelerate.

LK: There is already discussion, and debate, about security, access to pornography by minors, and First Amendment rights as a result of the Internet. Want to guess how they'll be resolved?

GATES: That's a good list and I'm sure there are even more. They'll be debated intensely on both sides both on and off the network but I can't tell you how they'll all be resolved. I can only say it's important that we discuss them widely so that decisions involve a broad cross-section of society.

LK: Are we going to get television and news and entertainment from the Internet rather than from a set hooked to cable in the house?

GATES: News and entertainment will be delivered from the Internet to cable television and telephone connections in our homes. We'll access this information using a variety of devices, some of which will resemble today's televisions.

LK: Do you expect to get the *Seattle Post Intelligencer* delivered to your home electronically, or will it be found at the doorstep every morning?

GATES: I'm sure Seattle newspapers will be delivered electronically but they may also be delivered in a pared-down form on paper to people willing to pay a premium. Electronic news will be much more interactive, which will make it pretty compelling reading compared to what is possible on paper. Reading a newspaper on a screen will be a comfortable, enjoyable experience within twenty years because screen technology will get amazingly good.

LK: Will telephone wires exist in the next century, or will they be replaced by fiber optics? And are we going to see the end of telephone poles?

GATES: Telephone wires will still exist in one form or another, although wireless services will become increasingly important. One technology called ISDN is in use now and is a way of using existing telephone wires to send data in digital rather than analog form. It's popular but it's not going to cause existing phone lines to become obsolete. Fiber optic cable allows a remarkable amount of information to be transmitted, but it's unclear how long it will be before we have fiber all the way to homes. This is really a question of more interest to phone and cable company executives than to consumers, though. What consumers care about is the quality of the service they get, and will it improve one way or another. Will we still have telephone poles? Fiber optic wires can be buried underground or carried overhead just like twisted-pair copper. Whether the wire is buried or not is an economic question, not a technical question. It is true, however, that a great deal of wiring will be replaced over the next couple of decades, and the new wiring going in will last for a long time. So if a particular community wants underground wiring, this is probably a good time to start thinking about how to make it happen.

LK: What worries you about the next century?

GATES: The world's rapidly growing population concerns me. We need to encourage people to start thinking about the consequences of having too many people on the planet—food and water shortages, pollution, too many people crammed into drug-infested and violence-filled urban centers.

LK: What problems do you think we won't have in the next century that we do have right now?

GATES: I'm not sure, but I know medical problems are going to diminish as medical technology improves. This will be driven by the biotechnology industry, which is helping scientists understand the human genome, which in turn is helping them understand specific diseases.

LK: Will a person be able to work in the next century without having any computer skills?

GATES: There will still be jobs for people without computer skills, but a smaller percentage than exist today. The proportion of the workforce that lacks computer skills will decrease as people not having those skills get retrained or retire. Most young people have computer skills or at least an enthusiasm to get them.

LK: Describe an office in the next century. Telephone? Fax machine? Conference room? Will there be an office building?

GATES: The key element of the office of the next century is that it will have lots of flat screens, just like your house will. And these screens are going to be everywhere once they get thin enough, cheap enough, and high enough in quality. You'll carry around a lightweight screen the way you carry a wallet or cell phone or newspaper today. The notion of a fax will disappear because documents will be transferred electronically without having to pass through the intermediate stage of being printed on paper. If the recipient wants to read it on paper, she'll print it. "Telephone" refers to an audio-only electronic communications link, and we'll continue to have this kind of connection. But I think audio-only communication will be the exception rather than the rule. Communications will usually involve videoconferencing, collaborative work on a document, or some other kind of data interchange beyond audio alone. We'll have conference rooms, but some of the participants in a conference may be in other places and hooked in electronically. Some will participate from home when being face-to-face isn't important. Office buildings and even cities may lose some of their importance because the Internet and corporate intranets will enable workers to communicate, share information, store data, and collaborate regardless of where they are.

ESTHER DYSON

PRESIDENT, EDVENTURE HOLDINGS;

CHAIRMAN, ELECTRONIC FRONTIER FOUNDATION

Don't lose your common sense. Everything at the end of the wire is just other people.

LK: What are some of the issues we will face in the next century as a result of the computer?

DYSON: The same issues we deal with now, but they are accentuated by the digital infrastructure available to us right now. Privacy, freedom of speech, accountability, and confidentiality are just a few which come to mind. The Internet, for example, will create conflict between countries.

LK: Between countries?

DYSON: It's easy enough to have laws and enforce them in your own country, but things that happen on the Internet are going to go on regardless of national boundaries. This is good but it's already resulting in conflict. It's possible for a country to contact our government and detail a conversation between one of its citizens and one of our citizens and ask us to shoot one of them, which, of course, we wouldn't do. But the guy in their country might be shot if they feel like it. They could close down Internet access; that could occur in China and Singapore, for example.

LK: How do you see this being resolved?

DYSON: Well, the United States could let that country know it's being stupid and if it wants to be part of the world economy and part of the Internet it's just going to have to adjust to the fact you can't control what everybody says. It's not just those countries but the potential is there. Also in the Middle East, and now the French are upset there is too little use of French language on the Internet. The Germans have closed access to certain news groups. There is concern about Holocaust revisionism; sexual stuff and so forth is a concern as well. Here in the U.S., the Food and Drug Administration is concerned about medical information on the Internet. In some cases I agree with them because there should be regulation against fraud, but not all countries' definitions of fraud are the same.

LK: How will the issue of possible inaccurate medical information be resolved in the United States?

DYSON: There are problems with uninformed people. We have the same problem in real life where certain people don't want their children operated on even though standard medical thinking suggests than an operation would save or help the child. There are other cases where most drugs have certain uses which are advertised and then there are other uses which cannot be advertised but doctors can nonetheless prescribe the medicine for them. The problem is that such information is now much more broadly spread than ever before. There's a responsibility for people to be smarter because they are going to be bombarded with a lot of information, both true and untrue. The question becomes how much can the government rely on the good sense of its citizens and to what degree should it get involved?

LK: The burden is on whom?

DYSON: That's the question. Where should the burden be? I don't know that this is something that can be resolved. Right now you can watch the *Larry King Show* and not some other show. You can rely on editors and other intermediaries to filter information for you, and as long as there are lots of these intermediaries competing in the market it's great, but when you start giving that kind of control to the government, that's when I have a problem.

LK: You speak of conflict between countries over an Internet transmission. Do you see Congress becoming involved or a trade delegation addressing the matter?

DYSON: That's already happening. But you won't and shouldn't see a Select Committee on the Internet. These issues belong in the Commerce Department and Justice Department. The Internet is a medium underlying everything. In most cases, you want to look at the effects of the Internet on existing portfolios, not so much at the Internet itself. It's sort of like a hex on the Internet but not the Internet itself.

LK: Pornography continues to be an issue on the Internet. How will it be resolved?

DYSON: This is where there's a better solution. Simply, it is giving control to the parents. Do not give it to the government. It's the job of parents to control what their kids see, and frankly, they should surf the network with their kids and talk about what they see together. It's the parents' job, but yes, there are going to be more commercial services available to help parents. You can buy magazines for your kids that in effect control what the child sees. These services will operate in a similar way. I can set my computer and say, for example, I want all the sites that are rated "clean" by the Catholic Church and "nonviolent" by the Citizens Committee on Violence, plus I want special sections of French history because I'm trying to get my little rascal to learn the language. You will define for yourself what you want your kid to receive. Not all parents have the same goal for their children, and one person's eight-year-old is as mature as someone else's child of eleven years. You can have parents' groups or religious groups or political groups doing this. And they will rate what's on the Internet so you can say, "I want things with such-and-such a rating by such-and-such a group."

LK: People will have a role rather than this thing called the Internet. Correct?

DYSON: People mistake democracy with voting and they mistake decentralization with democracy. The Internet encourages decentralization; it doesn't necessarily encourage democracy. Democracy is when 51 percent of a group wins and then it imposes its will on 100 percent. What the Net allows is for people to fragment into smaller communities where everybody voted for the same thing. It's the same as the marketplace where the people who want red ketchup get red and the people who want green ketchup get green. The problem is we all need to live by certain things in government; I can't have my own choice of how much fluorine there is in the water. The real value in the Net is not in voting electronically because that is a simple logistic issue. Rather the value is in giving people the ability to discuss these things and to participate in the decisions with ideas and proposals. They don't just choose from a set menu; they get to define the menu. For those people who do care, it gives them an opportunity to be heard. The danger is you can also get, for example, a group of right-wing nuts who never communicate outside of their own group and never hear any contradictory opinions. It puts more responsibility on people to consider various points of view and be smart.

LK: You think in another fifty years there will be a computer hooked to the Internet in every home?

DYSON: Pretty much in the United States. The rest of the world will continue to be challenged. But there will always be people who resist whatever it is. For example, I don't have a telephone in my home.

LK: You think you'll have a phone in the next century?

DYSON: I had one in this century and decided I didn't want it around. I moved in the other direction.

LK: So you don't have a phone in your car either?

DYSON: I don't because I don't know how to drive.

LK: It has been said the distance between the haves and the have-nots will grow as a result of the computer and people saying, "I'll learn it" or "I won't learn it."

DYSON: It's going to be pretty necessary for the next generation of kids who will be workers. It's similar to the ATM we have today in that you do typically learn it without even noticing. Do you remember learning how to use the telephone? Besides, computers are going to become easier to use. But you're going to have to learn how to think and how to do the knowledge work, so the issue isn't the computer but education and having intellectual skills rather than physical skills. If you look at what's happened to the economy overall, the mental jobs are increasing and the physical ones are declining. Marriott, for example, is now aware how important it is for its hotel maids to know English so they can speak to the guests.

LK: Are there ramifications from visiting the Internet or using a credit card and the issue of privacy?

DYSON: It's not just the government that will have access to this information; it's American Express, it's Spiegel's catalog, it's the FBI, it's whoever cares to find out.

LK: The minute you visit a Web site you've left your stamp, right?

DYSON: The capability is there and you should be worried about it if you care for your privacy. The answer is not specific government regulation. At the same time, there should be a legal presumption your privacy will be protected. The Electronic Frontier Foundation, where I'm chairman, is leading a program called eTRUST in which you are told what each Web site is going to do with the information. Then you make the choice of going in or not going. If they don't do what they have said they're going to do with the information, they can be sued for breach of contract. Each Web site will have an icon called a golden key which shows what they do with the information they collect. You then make the decision. It's voluntary. But I really think it would be dangerous and stupid for the government to pass a law about what to do with data in general. Frankly, I would like British Airways to know how much I fly on American Airlines because then they might treat me better. That's something I don't want to keep as a secret. But I might want to keep secret how much alcohol I bought or that I visited a particular site. This is one of the easier things to solve through market mechanisms.

LK: What's one of the difficult things?

DYSON: What do you do about hateful speech on the Internet? I believe in freedom of speech but there is stuff on the Net which is scary. And, frankly, that's why we have a court system because you do need to apply human judgment to whether or not one guy is just expressing himself while another guy is inciting people to rape and murder. In the end, you make that distinction in court.

LK: Are we going to have Internet law in the next century?

DYSON: Absolutely. But a lot of it will be the same old law just applied on the Internet. Nonetheless, U.S. attorneys and U.S. citizens in general will have to understand the Internet is not located in the United States.

LK: Where is it located?

DYSON: All over the world. And that's part of the challenge.

LK: Will there be an advisory board or an ad hoc committee from various countries that will oversee the Internet?

DYSON: There are already several and none is in charge, which is the way it should be. The Internet is not something that is divided up among countries. By and large it is a separate jurisdiction and it should be governed from within rather than a council of government types.

Moreover, within the Internet there will be a variety of jurisdictions, but they won't correspond to national borders. I'm trying to make an important point but the question prejudges the answers.

LK: I'm asking if you see a need for something to oversee this thing we call the Internet.

DYSON: Of course there should be what amounts to treaties between the jurisdictions. I see a lot of multilateral treaties about many of these issues and there's already lots of discussion from the World's Intellectual Property Organization (a formal organization that oversees patent and copyright issues) to G–7 to the Organization for Economic Cooperation and Development. All are holding conferences and trying to sort out lists of issues.

LK: So there won't be a single something running the Internet?

DYSON: There's not going to be a "government" of the Internet. There are going to be lots of communities on the Internet which will have governments of their own and there will be multilateral agreements between them and between various governments. Various governments will have their own agreements about what constitutes a "taxable event," for example, or what constitutes fraud. The Internet is not a piece of property owned by governments.

LK: So there is no representative of the Internet. It's everybody.

DYSON: It's the people who are on it.

LK: But there is not a single person or group that will be speaking for the goodness or looking out for the welfare of the Internet now or in the next century. Correct?

DYSON: There are a lot of self-styled representatives. For example, the Electronic Frontier Foundation isn't elected. We have points of view, and people who like those points of view give us funding.

LK: Are there going to be hackers in the future?

DYSON: You mean criminal hackers or noncriminal hackers? Hackers are not necessarily criminals; they are just skilled programmers. The criminal variant is called "crackers."

There will definitely be a lot of criminals roaming the Net just as they roam the regular world. Criminals use cars to make getaways and meet with one another and transport stolen goods, and they'll also use the Internet. The Internet is going to be a very important part of life for just about everyone, including criminals.

LK: I'm getting the feeling we're going to need an Internet dictionary here.

DYSON: It exists already. To answer your question, there's going to be continued improvement on both sides. There will be people getting better at breaking systems and people getting better at protecting systems.

LK: How will people conversing through e-mail know they are talking to each other and not some proxy or substitute?

DYSON: How do you know you're talking to me now on the phone?

LK: I don't.

DYSON: Touché. But to answer your question seriously: There will be technical means of authenticating that the person you are corresponding with is the same person at that address you corresponded with the last time. You can establish legal accountability, but this raises a lot of important questions about identity in the first place.

LK: We could manufacture a whole new person.

DYSON: That's right. Just as you can in the real world although with a little more difficulty.

LK: And that person could go out to violate every freedom of speech rule there is but we couldn't do anything because that person doesn't exist.

DYSON: Now you raise the issue of accountability. That person does exist because someone created him. The problem then is to go out and find the creator.

LK: How has technology changed the way you go to the office?

DYSON: It has not meant that I have to travel less. What it has meant is that I can do my office work from the road. The need to physically meet with people is never going to go away but my ability to communicate at a distance with the people in my office who already know me is getting much better. Technology does not replace the face-to-face relationship-building meetings with people you don't know well, but it does replace information-oriented meetings among colleagues.

For example, I sit in my hotel room in Poland after meetings I have to be physically present for and then I do all my e-mail and send notes to my secretary.

LK: Will there be countries that refuse to be a part of the Internet?

DYSON: There may be, and they will be really cut off.

LK: What scares you about the next century?

DYSON: Not a lot. There are lots of individual problems; one of them is how do we educate the next generation so they can use the Internet specifically, but also so that they can lead fulfilling lives and be responsible. I think the Internet is a very handy tool but there is no substitute for parents and teachers, real people who can give children a moral education. They need to know how to behave, morality and ethics as well as knowledge and fact. So I don't think the Internet is going to replace parents. Yes, it's better in some ways than books because it's alive and it lets kids talk to other kids, but it is in no way as good as teachers and parents.

LK: You think there will be books?

DYSON: Absolutely. But eventually you'll carry many books around in the form of a disk or a screen and you'll find a place or rent a screen and just download it.

LK: Do you see new forms of art as a result of the Internet?

DYSON: There is already interactive storytelling. But now you're into the issue of intellectual property rights. Either ownership is going to be determined by contract or content is going to be owned by the world. You can say anything created in this on-line community is the property of the people in the community. We're going to have to establish practices and standards for a lot of the things out there.

DR. DAVID SATCHER

DIRECTOR, NATIONAL CENTERS FOR
DISEASE CONTROL AND PREVENTION

Individuals and families and communities have major responsibilities and opportunities to improve our health. I believe it does take a village.

LK: Are we going to be healthier in the next century than we are today?

SATCHER: The answer is yes, but it depends on a few things. We will have the information that we need to be healthier. We'll have the information technology in terms of communicating that information on a timely basis to allow people to be healthier. We know more now than we've known before about the role of diet and physical activity in health. We have more vaccines than we've ever had before, so we're going to be in a position to prevent more things, and I'll give you an example: Hemophilis influenza-B averaged 20,000 cases in children until 1985. We started the immunization against that in the mid-1980s and now there's been over a 90 percent decline. But there will also be more challenges to be faced. There will be new infections like the *E. coli* 157 we struggled with a few years ago and that Japan struggled with in 1996. But I think the opportunities to improve our health will be greater than the challenges we'll face.

LK: Those challenges will come from where?

SATCHER: Our environment will be one place in terms of environmental hazards. We know about dioxin, for example, but there are a lot of other issues out there that we're researching to determine what role, if any, is played in human cancer. But we'll also face microorganisms which can survive and mutate and change in such a way that antibiotics we have won't be able to confront them. We're seeing new viruses, new parasites like cyclospora, which occurs in imported raspberries. Obviously, our struggle is to stay ahead of this, which means developing new vaccines and antibiotics. But there's another issue, and that is antibiotic resistance. This involves proper prescribing habits on the part of physicians, avoiding overprescription of drugs that aren't needed, and appropriate use of antibiotics by patients. Some will stop taking their medication because they feel better but before the infection has been eliminated. That lets the hardiest germs survive. And we need to continue isolating patients on the wards who have antibiotic-resistant organisms so they don't spread readily to other patients. We've seen changes in microorganisms just within the past year, such as more penicillin-resistant streptococci.

LK: This sounds like something Robin Cook would write.

SATCHER: Oh no. This is real. New viruses will continue to grow. Old viruses like dengue fever will continue to reemerge and find new ways to survive.

LK: You speak of research. Are you comfortable it will continue at the pace which is required to keep up with developments?

SATCHER: Yeah, I'm not comfortable with it, but if we can continue to get the support of Congress and the White House, and there's an awareness in both places now, then I will be.

LK: And that research will be in what areas?

SATCHER: In the control of emerging infectious diseases, in dealing with environmental hazards, and in prevention technology. I'll give you another example: Almost 30 percent of the Medicare budget goes to treat diabetes and its complications. Most of those complications can be prevented, but as a nation, we haven't invested in prevention, and so we're paying a lot of money to treat things that could have been prevented in the first place.

LK: And that brings me to the next question regarding prevention: How many more required shots will children have to take before entering school?

SATCHER: There will be more, but we might be able to combine vaccines so children won't have to get a separate shot for each immunization. We're doing research on that issue right now. I hope we can complete all the required vaccines by thirty-five months of age in the next century. In the future we might immunize children before they are born. It's going to take a lot of work to get there from here, to understand the immune system, but I think it will happen.

LK: Do you see a time coming when we'll take a pill rather than get a shot?

SATCHER: Well, we've been giving the oral polio vaccine since the 1960s but every case of polio that we have in this country is the result of that vaccine because it has the ability in rare cases to revert to its virulent form. As a result, every year we have eight to ten cases of polio, all related to the vaccine. So I think we're going to be recommending we go back to the shot to prevent these eight to ten cases. I don't want to make a promise, though, that we will come to a time when no shots are required because a pill can be taken instead.

LK: What diseases will be cured in the next century?

SATCHER: You have to combine "cure" and "eradicate." The only naturally occurring disease we've eradicated in our history is smallpox. We'll probably eradicate polio by 1999. Soon after that we'll eradicate measles. And maybe yellow fever as well. Vitamin A deficiency, which causes blindness in so many people throughout the world, is another one I think we'll eradicate. AIDS is interesting because it's highly likely some of the new drugs constitute not necessarily a cure in the sense it completely does away with it, but it controls the disease. I think that will happen for AIDS within the next few years. So we're talking about a "cure" in the sense that it doesn't go away, but instead is controlled. We think because of some of our genetic intervention that within the twenty-first century we will find a way to control diabetes completely, and people will not have to give themselves shots several times a day. We are making a lot of progress in cardiovascular diseases. So on the front of cure and prevention, we're going to do well.

LK: Do you see a time coming when tissue from a fetus will be used to cure another person?

SATCHER: Yes. Parkinson's disease research uses fetal tissue now. But there's controversy because some people feel that if you go in that direction too rapidly, you'll have abortions being done and being influenced by the fact the tissue can be used to treat people for diseases.

LK: How do you see this playing out?

SATCHER: We're going to have to be very careful. It's a legitimate concern. But short of that I think there will be ways to transplant fetal tissue without necessarily doing an abortion. We're seeing it now with some of the blood from the fetus that can be used to prevent disease that we haven't thought about before.

LK: Is your concern over the possibility fetal tissue could be sold?

SATCHER: We have to protect against the role of entrepreneurship, the selling of organs and tissues to treat diseases. But increasingly we will find ways to use human tissue from the fetus and other places without the destruction of that person per se to treat diseases. Given the nature of Parkinson's, Alzheimer's, and diabetes, I see the day when the transplantation of cells and tissues will play an increasing role in the control and treatment of those diseases.

LK: Fewer people on waiting lists for organs as a result of the fetal tissue or even just donations?

SATCHER: Hard to say what's going to happen on organ donations. I think we'll see an increase; however, I think some of the research we're doing is going to make whole organ donations less important in some cases, like liver transplants. We have the growth of organs and tissue culture research, and that is leading us to the point where we'll probably need less in terms of organ transplants.

LK: I've heard talk of artificial blood. Is that possible?

SATCHER: Yes. But it will be less artificial than you think because with genetics research we will have the ability to produce and develop what is actually not so artificial in terms of blood. Genetics research is leading us to the time where we can produce things that we would have called artificial in the past but is now natural blood tissue.

LK: We are a people with Thigh Masters and exercise machines and athletic clubs, and yet we are also a people consistently categorized as out of shape. How do you see these two extremes playing out?

SATCHER: At least 60 percent of the people in this country are not engaging in moderate physical activity, and another 25 percent are completely sedentary. I think we'll see progress in those areas.

LK: How do you do it?

SATCHER: Through a combination of education, motivation, and incentives. At the work site there are an increasing number of ways businesses can provide opportunities for employees to exercise on the job, and they will find it a way to decrease the cost of health care for employees. So there will be incentives for employees to become more active because it benefits the company financially.

LK: So every morning at ten the employees go for a walk?

SATCHER: I want to give the 6,000 employees here at CDC an extra half-hour for exercise every day. I'm ready to do it but I have to work it through the system. Walking is still the single most beneficial activity that people can engage in if they could do it for thirty minutes a day. We would see a 50 percent reduction in cardiovascular disease–related deaths. We would see a 30 percent reduction in hypertension and diabetes, and a significant decrease in depression and anxiety. And all this will happen if businesses just allow their employees to go for a walk. More and more businesses are going to move in the direction of work site physical activity programs. And I want to see schools get involved more because they've gotten out of the business of physical education. No state requires it for graduation.

LK: That going to change?

SATCHER: I think so. We have to get schools involved in helping to control the cost of health care in this country. It makes good sense for states to invest in physical activity for their school children because that's going to result in a better chance of having healthy people for the future.

LK: What government policies would you like to see in place that aren't in place now?

SATCHER: All states should support physical education at school. I want to see a decrease in advertising tobacco and making it less appealing to children. Eighty-five percent of people who smoke started doing it before they were old enough to know better, so there should be a government policy that would protect children from that happening. There should be policies in place that reward businesses for providing opportunities for employees to be active. Here's an example of what we're talking about: General Motors spends more on health care for its employees and retirees than it does for steel. My argument is we need to shift emphasis to prevention.

LK: In the century upon which this book is focused, we will have more of the population growing older than ever before. More people will be retiring. How will society have to change to accommodate this change?

SATCHER: As a nation, we haven't yet responded appropriately to the increasing aging of our population. It's very clear a lot of people have a lot to offer after retirement—much more than we have ever given them credit for—so we've got to find a way to take advantage of this tremendous resource. We're going to have to have programs which allow older people to be more active and involved after they stop working because we know if we do it there will be fewer long-term illnesses as a result. For example, strengthening and flexibility exercises for the elderly could prevent many of the hip fractures we have every year. Many of those could be prevented if those people were involved in some kind of program of physical activity. The government's paying for those hip fractures through Medicare. Why don't we pay to get more people involved in some kind of physical activity and reduce the hip fractures? Older people worry more about dependency than they do about death. They want to be independent for as long as they can and then die after a short illness rather than a long illness.

LK: Tell me about smoking in the next century. Are we still going to debate it?

SATCHER: We will. The difference is, in the next century the debate will be global, as will be all public health issues. Microorganisms don't respect national borders. We've seen a significant decrease in the percentage of people smoking in this country over the last twenty years but we've also seen an increase in the tobacco companies' marketing to developing countries. Today there are 3 million deaths from tobacco in the world every year. In the year 2020 that number will climb to 10 million. You'll see the CDC involved in providing prevention plans for these parts of the world.

LK: What scares you about the next century?

SATCHER: How we deal with microorganisms is one of the things that scares me. We underestimated the ability of microorganisms to change and we failed to realize the global nature of the struggle. The other thing that scares me is the trend of people to congregate in large cities, and there will be twenty-five mega-cities (populations of 20 million or more) by the year 2020, and many of those people will be poor. They won't have basic sanitation. So at the same time we develop ways to control infectious diseases, people are going to behave in such a way as to expedite the growth of infectious diseases. The ability of people to travel from one place to another, to be in one city today and somewhere else in the world tomorrow, is going to improve and increase. There will be more tourism. So we're going to have more mega-cities where problems are incubated, not just infectious diseases, but violence, because the gap between the haves and the have-nots will widen. All of these things worry me in terms of our ability to prevent and control things we think we can control. We will react because there will be things that we didn't predict, but we will be proactive as well, as is already occurring in the development of a response to emerging infectious diseases.

LK: As the population increases will more unusual diseases be found?

SATCHER: The answer is yes. But if we can control infectious diseases on a global scale, that will ameliorate the impact.

LK: Do you think we will screen people for diseases before they travel?

SATCHER: I think there are a few things we're going to do but it will depend upon what's going on at the time. For now, though, we screen for tuberculosis and malaria for anyone coming into the United States. But there are certain countries where the incidence of a particular disease is so low, there's no need to screen.

LK: The focus of the person who has your job in the next century will be what?

SATCHER: Dealing with the continuing threat of emerging infectious diseases. Working with people in modifying their behavior is another. We may have an AIDS vaccine within the next ten years, but how do we deal with people still transmitting the disease through IV drug use and unprotected sex? Behavior is something to which we're going to be paying more and more attention.

DR. FRANCIS COLLINS

DIRECTOR, NATIONAL HUMAN GENOME RESEARCH INSTITUTE,
NATIONAL INSTITUTES OF HEALTH

*Individuals are going to have to become more informed about
their own medical care. Entrusting decisions about your own
health will go better if you learn about new developments.*

LK: What tests will we take in the future when we go to the doctor's office?

COLLINS: There will be three different kinds: prenatal testing,
tests to determine a diagnosis of a particular illness, and—where there
will be the greatest growth—predictive genetic tests, which determine
the likelihood of developing an illness. Breast cancer is an example of
a disease for which we already have a predictive test. Two genes,
BRCA1 and BRCA2, are markers for some forms of cancer. Not everyone taking this test is going to be fully prepared for the consequences
of the test results. This is the leading edge of what will be a brand-new
part of medicine, which will alter the way we approach prevention and
health maintenance.

LK: Some of these diseases we will test for are what?

COLLINS: We already have tests for certain inherited forms of
colon cancer and ovarian cancer. A test for an inherited type of
prostate cancer is probably two years away. There is significant evidence that people most likely to get lung cancer from smoking are
those whose genes predispose them to that disease. We have a test for
Alzheimer's disease, but there is a concern in the medical community
about healthy people taking that test, because we don't have a cure or
an effective treatment yet. That is going to be a critical determinant of
which tests will be useful. I think the public, in general, will not be
interested in a test that says, "You have a higher than average risk of
dying from this terrible disease, but there's nothing you can do
about it."

LK: How will this be handled in the next century?

COLLINS: We increasingly will develop better means of intervention for the people at high risk. I see it happening in stages. There will be more effort toward trying to prevent the disease in the first place, and because every killer disease tends to cluster in families through some genetic component (and we'll know the genes involved in these diseases over the next ten years), we'll be able to make predictions through DNA testing as to who is at the highest risk. That information will help us learn why this person got the disease and that person didn't. So we can develop gene therapy or drug therapy that will allow us to prevent the disease from ever starting. That's what many of us get up in the morning dreaming about. But we will have to go through the phase of having diagnostic abilities more advanced than our therapeutic abilities.

LK: If a test shows a fetus has the markers for obesity, what happens?

COLLINS: That is a major ethical dilemma which will challenge us over part of the next century. Right now, we don't have the technical ability to make predictions about traits like obesity, but we will. Of course, some of these are contributed to by environmental causes such as lifestyle.

LK: But if a couple in the future ask a doctor to test the fetus for obesity or a learning disability, will the doctor be obliged to do it?

COLLINS: It's not clear. My personal view is, as a society we need to decide where we're going to draw that line and then stick to it. But there's a collision of principles between a couple wanting to make reproductive choices about their own family, and the notion that a eugenics approach is fraught with danger. We've never before had the precise tools to practice eugenics in such a specific way, although the Nazi program attempted to weed out so-called deleterious genes. Already we are having discussions about prenatal testing for breast cancer susceptibility. Should a couple be allowed to use that kind of information to terminate a pregnancy even though we're talking about a possibility of giving birth to a female who might or might not at age forty-five develop breast cancer? Most people say this should not happen.

LK: If we can't do anything about what the marker shows us, will the test even be performed?

COLLINS: Currently, we don't require couples interested in prenatal diagnosis to tell us they will terminate a pregnancy prior to getting a test for Down's syndrome or cystic fibrosis, but I would be uneasy with the concept that tests shouldn't be allowed unless some drastic action will be taken. Sometimes just knowing will help you prepare yourself and is useful.

LK: Will we walk off the street into a clinic and ask for a test to see if we have the marker for a specific disease?

COLLINS: Yes, I see it working that way. We'll have to add to this idea that the person making the request has his or her eyes open about what the benefits and risks are, as we do with any medical procedure. In the course of the next ten years it will be possible for anyone over the age of eighteen to find out what tests are available, to learn what interventions are available in the event they are at high risk, and to design a lifestyle and medical surveillance with a higher likelihood of keeping them well than if they hadn't received this information.

LK: Guidance must accompany the test?

COLLINS: Nobody should have the test without education about its meaning and without full and informed consent. Clearly, this is very private and powerful information and it shouldn't be dumped on a person.

LK: Is that information owned by the individual or can it be obtained by private industry?

COLLINS: By the individual. I hope by the beginning of the next century we will have all of those questions legislatively solved. We already have some federal legislation with the Kassebaum-Kennedy bill, which says health insurance companies can't use genetic information in any way to discriminate against those in a group plan. But we're going to need more laws that say employers can't deny anybody a job or a promotion or make any other employment decisions based on genetic information, and we need privacy legislation that protects the confidentiality of medical records. Medical records in this country are a disgrace in the way they are accessible by nearly anyone, including those with no business poking in them.

LK: If a person has one of these tests taken, will he be required to tell an insurance company he has done so?

COLLINS: No. We need legislation that says insurance companies may not request or require genetic information.

LK: Will these tests, eventually, be available in the home?

COLLINS: We are a long way from that, but technically it could eventually be done. I worry about that scenario because the technical part of the test is the easiest part. The educational and counseling step will be more difficult. That person will need a chance to ask questions prior to taking the test so he or she will understand the significance. Maybe we'll do the educational steps on the Web, but a one-on-one relationship is certainly a better way to do it.

LK: Will medicine cure more diseases in the future?

COLLINS: It will. Drugs of the future will be discovered on the basis of genetics. Gene therapy is a new idea, but the idea that we will be able to treat a disease at its most fundamental level, that of the DNA sequence, is a very appealing one. Lots of progress has been made. I think it is very probable, with a twenty- or thirty-year lead time, that many diseases currently treated with drugs or not treated at all will be treated with gene therapy, either by going in and inserting a gene into an appropriate tissue or by developing methods to go in and turn off a gene that is doing something toxic. The obvious genetic disorders such as cystic fibrosis are a target where this strategy will work sooner rather than later. For cystic fibrosis, we know the gene which is lacking, which keeps the lungs well hydrated and able to handle bacteria. Now we have to develop an efficient gene delivery system which can accomplish this. Commom diseases are on the list too. Already we are looking at gene therapy in heart disease.

LK: Might a future driver's license carry a DNA print for ID purposes?

COLLINS: I worry about that. It sounds Orwellian. I do think it's an open discussion for law enforcement to keep large files of DNA fingerprints on individuals, particularly those who have been involved in some way with the law. Clearly, that information can make all the difference in whether or not you catch somebody or, for that matter, whether you let somebody go.

LK: But it won't be recorded at birth and kept on records?

COLLINS: No, your genetic information belongs to you.

LK: We've never had to face issues like this before, have we?

COLLINS: We haven't. But we already are trying to look ahead and anticipate issues and see the potholes and fill them before we fall in. The prenatal arena is where some of the thorniest issues lie. It gets us into a discussion we, as a society, have not been particularly good at, because it involves the whole question of abortion. There will be people who will feel neither the government nor anybody else has any business telling a couple whether they can or cannot initiate or terminate a pregnancy. There will be others focusing on the consequences for society if eugenics starts to run amok. But the social-legal-ethical consequences of this technology are being considered upfront and debated in a public setting rather than waiting for a crisis. The question right now is whether or not social policy can keep up with the pace at which genetic technology is moving.

LK: How will doctors be different in the next century?

COLLINS: Every doctor and every nurse is going to have to acquire the skills of a genetic counselor. We won't have enough specialists to take care of all the questions and education needed for genetic medicine as it moves so quickly into the mainstream. Some of us right now are trying to influence medical school curricula to incorporate more of this kind of training, which presently is nonexistent in some schools. Half of the physicians already out of school and now in practice have had no training whatsoever, so we're going to have to do something about this as well.

LK: Technology forces questions, doesn't it?

COLLINS: So what else is new?

DR. C. EVERETT KOOP

UNITED STATES SURGEON GENERAL, 1981–1989;
SENIOR SCHOLAR, KOOP INSTITUTE, DARTMOUTH COLLEGE

Stay informed. There's no way of telling what you see on the Internet is true, up-to-date, or quackery. Old books have the grace to turn yellow on the pages, but everything glows with equal intensity on the Internet.

LK: We are moving into a new century with a population that is older as a result of baby boomers retiring. What is going to have to change in society to handle this?

KOOP: There will be many changes, most of which will be made incrementally as the need arises. There will never be a forward-looking sociologic plan for elderly people, although I think that would be a better way to do things. The major problem will be economic, because while we have five people working for every retiree right now, shortly after the turn of the century that ratio drops to three people working for every retiree. We've never faced that kind of situation before. The second thing that will be a tremendous economic-social-cultural issue is that as people live longer, many are just as active at eighty as they were at fifty-five. So we're going to have older experienced people competing for jobs that require judgment and expertise against a much younger population that we have always thought, and rightly so, deserves a chance at the top. So there will be a lot of adjustments.

LK: What kind of adjustments?

KOOP: They will vary from place to place. In Algeria, for example, the retirement age is around forty-five or forty-seven, so that younger people get a chance at jobs. The problem is, you create a tremendous group of idle people. Of course their life expectancy isn't as long as ours, but they've taken this concern about competition between old and young long before we have thought about it. Something that could be done here, if people continue on Social Security, is that the salary these people are paid after they become seniors and still work becomes less than before they received Social Security. I think you will find as the pinch gets tighter that there will be a deep concern on the part of thinking people about whether or not those in executive positions at major companies should make $4 million or $5 million. These will be felt as pressure points and result in some kind of change demanded by society as it moves along.

Now, from the health point of view, I think the total health care of elderly people will have to be limited in some way. Some flexibility will have to be developed into the way we deal with these folks, of which I am one. A major problem with the elderly is that of dependence. They find their way into a nursing home and these are extraordinarily expensive, and I don't see how the government can continue to fork out $45,000 or $50,000 per person of senior citizen age who isn't dependent upon somebody. You might see a return to several generations ago when the extended family took care of older people. You will see this especially where people are devoted to their parents and can't afford to put them in a nursing home. By being flexible, however, for quasi-independent elderly people who can't quite function but don't want to give up their home and move into a nursing home because they can't afford it, and because the current system requires they spend down to poverty before long-term care under Medicaid is available, I think there's a way out.

First there should be flexibility in Social Security for these people so that some of it can be siphoned off to pay nonskilled labor for home care for short periods of time. Shopping could be done for these elderly people, tops can be taken off jars for them, and chores could be done. So a home helper for three hours on Friday and two hours on the other days would create a tremendous saving to society for what would have been nursing home care. The second thing that we ought to look at is electronic surveillance. Let's say your father is quasi-independent and wants to live alone but has to take medications and is forgetful. A television set with an audio override on it can perform that service. Whether the set is on or not, a voice comes over the television which says, "Harry, it's ten o'clock. Have you been to the bathroom?" At noon it says, "Harry, it's time for your digitalis," and a machine delivers the pill. If the pill isn't taken, a phone call is made to Harry reminding him to take the pill.

LK: Would these home care workers you spoke of earlier be licensed?

KOOP: They will have to be licensed and it would provide a nice kind of employment for unskilled labor. Also, there are a lot of sixty-five-year-old people who would be happy to do some of these things for a seventy-five-year-old, especially if they got twenty bucks a week. While I don't like to call it "forced volunteerism," I think this will be expected of elderly people for themselves and others because they will be such a huge cohort.

LK: Electronic home care is a good industry from the sound of this.

KOOP: There are others. For about $7,000 a year a telephone with a television monitor on it can be adapted to independent living for older folks. A lot of these things will happen.

LK: There is a movement toward the privatization of hospitals—

KOOP: And it's not okay. Medical schools are in dire straits right now, and one of the ways they can get out of the problems is to sell the teaching hospitals. You see it at Georgetown and George Washington University in Washington, D.C. In places like Tulane and the Medical College at the University of South Carolina, the medical school has already been bought. If philanthropic companies are making money because they are cutting down on the things that made medicine so great in this country, they will start teaching that in the medical schools. It also puts the control of medical education and the control of medical hospitals into the hands of fewer and fewer people. When you have that, it becomes easier to establish monopolistic kinds of practices, and that doesn't bode well for patients.

LK: Will there be fewer hospitals?

KOOP: You are going to find a small community with two hospitals being forced to avoid duplication. One may do OB-GYN and another may do transplants but both won't do both. That's a worthwhile thing to do because while it may alter the convenience of care, it doesn't alter the quality of care. Small hospitals operating close to the edge all the time may close if their doctors aren't making any money. That's going to be tough in the rural areas.

LK: Will time spent between doctor and patient increase or decrease in the next century?

KOOP: I talk to physicians in teaching hospitals who work for a managed care company now and they say the number of patients they are forced to see, albeit only fourteen minutes per patient, makes it impossible to finish and still get to the rounds with medical students. Managed care is putting more patients on one individual and cutting down the time.

LK: It's been suggested America should get on the road of having a prevention campaign for its youth so later on the country doesn't face an older population suffering from a lifetime of smoking, drinking, and lack of exercise. You see that ever happening?

KOOP: I see it coming about but it's happening extremely slowly. I've been preaching it for twenty years, but prevention is very hard to sell. We have a population with an insatiable interest in health but it likes the glamorous things like kidney transplants, artificial hips, and baboon hearts. I wish we could make the "Just Say No" program for smoking glamorous or give credits to a society for being in that mode. Then we would have found a secret to success. I don't think it's going to take place quickly because it never has taken place quickly. Adolescents consider themselves to be immortal, they like to take risks, they don't like any admonition beginning with the word "don't," and they have no interest in health consequences that aren't immediate. The idea is great and it should be tried. There's a premise that everything we do in public health is always done too late. We tell them don't drive drunk after they kill somebody and we tell them not to be obese after they have an insatiable appetite. So I think we need to aim at the preschool child. They aren't aware, until the age of five or six, that they can say, "No I won't" and get away with it.

LK: Now does this occur in the school or the home?

KOOP: Everyplace. Kids are farmed out today so you can't leave it to homes alone.

LK: This curriculum would look like what?

KOOP: It would teach kids to say, "I will always brush my teeth, buckle up, eat the right diet, get the right amount of exercise, not smoke, not take drugs," and so on.

LK: Would this be a "Scared Straight" program?

KOOP: No, you can't impress kids that way. You say it's good for you. But you have to start in the preschool. Make it a game. Look, a lot of what goes on in preschool is just using up time. Kids get up, run around in circles, and sing funny songs. What if the song is about taking charge of their own lives? It's doable.

LK: How will cigarettes be treated in the next century?

KOOP: Cigarettes will always be around and we have a marvelous opportunity to do something as people are aware of the chicanery of the tobacco industry. If the people opposed to tobacco prevail you will see a major difference in the way cigarettes are advertised, but don't think for a minute they won't be advertised in some way. The Internet will be an amazing way for Joe Camel to appear. And if Joe doesn't sell cigarettes, he will be around as a friend and we will remember who he represents. We're on a roll right now. You would think the rest of the world, seeing what's going on here, would jump on the bandwagon. When we are saying curtail advertising here and Europe is saying as an economic community curtail advertising there and Asia is beginning to flex its muscles and say the West has pushed us around long enough on the promotion and advertising of cigarettes so let's cut it out, the entire world market is being threatened, and that leaves no escape hatch for the tobacco industry. So it may sound selfish but if you want to get smoking out of America you don't talk very much about the international angle because that would change the thinking of the tobacco world. Buying cigarettes in the future will be treated the way beer is purchased now.

LK: In another thirty years the surgeon general's warning on the side of a cigarette pack will say what?

KOOP: Smoking this product as directed can kill you, it contains a lethal drug, produces a smoker's death in at least one-third of the people who use it.

LK: That's a lot of words. Will it fit on the pack?

KOOP: I think it might be the only thing on it.

LK: Are we going to have a "drug czar" in the future?

KOOP: I never liked the name and I think we're going to have to look at other options. One is the fact we've never had enough treatment facilities for people. When I was surgeon general, we'd go out and preach about the damage drugs do to people, and surprisingly, people would respond by saying, "Okay, I want to quit." But there was no place to treat them. And then we'd have to say, "Come see us next January," and I knew that person was a goner.

LK: You think drugs will ever be legalized?

KOOP: I can't predict the way society will go because it can do such stupid things. My own feeling is making drugs legal would result in our losing a generation of teenagers. I see how it could happen, especially if marijuana is legalized. That's a gateway drug, and after a while, people will start saying, "Gee, there must be something better out there."

LK: There is discussion about having a surgeon general also be an assistant secretary of health. Good idea?

KOOP: Bad idea. We don't need an assistant secretary in the health world anymore because there is nothing for him or her to be the assistant secretary of. The Centers for Disease Control and Prevention, the National Institutes of Health, the Food and Drug Administration, Public Health Service, and Office of the Surgeon General all report directly to the secretary of health and human services.

LK: In the next century will there be a surgeon general?

KOOP: I think there always has to be somebody, a persona, in whom the people have confidence. If there isn't a surgeon general, then there will have to be somebody like it. I am absolutely convinced the reason smoking went from 26 percent to 29 percent from 1989 to 1996 was because there wasn't a voice like mine constantly reminding people about the dangers and the fact 3,000 kids start to smoke every day.

LK: What should future surgeon generals keep in mind when they get your old office?

KOOP: Put the health of the public first. Be willing to make political compromises without moral compromises, and be independent. Had Henry Foster survived his process in Congress to be confirmed, I think he would have done anything Bill Clinton said. That's not what you should have in a surgeon general. I used to tell the Domestic Policy Council, though I never said it to Mr. Reagan's face, that they could fly up a rose bush if I wasn't going to be allowed to deal with AIDS the way AIDS had to be dealt with. Nobody wanted to send me home so I got away with it. I think AIDS would be more of a problem today had I not been there when the Reagan White House was hoping I would just shut up. The president never tried to shut me up but others did. I wouldn't stop. I wish the Public Health Service could promote the surgeon general up from its ranks rather than keep this position a political appointment.

LK: Since the population is getting older, do you think government will do more for senior citizens?

KOOP: Our grandparents' generation always had an extended family. I remember people staying with my parents who I always thought were relatives. They weren't. They were down and out. That was a safety net, and it was developed by communities and friends and churches and ethnic groups. Now we seem to put Grandma and Grandpa out to pasture. And you are seeing it in places like Japan where age has always been respected and revered. Nursing homes are springing up all over Japan. But it will be a draw. The elderly can influence elections, but on the other hand you run out of money eventually or there has to be a willingness of others to spend money for the elderly. Children and the elderly people are the dependent ages right now, each competing for a shrinking piece of the pie.

LK: What's going to happen with Medicare and Medicaid in the next century?

KOOP: Both are out of control. On the present plottings they could take over 100 percent of the budget long before the middle of the next century, so something has to happen. First, you will see a commission appointed to study Medicare, which is still a federal program rather than being pushed off on the states. If Medicare is saved, then it has to be reduced, because there is no way we can continue to do the things we're doing now as the number of eligible people increases over the years.

LK: So will there be a Medicare price for a heart procedure and then some other price, the Medicare price being lower than the other?

KOOP: I think something like that could happen. I also see that after a certain age or under certain circumstances, and I hate to say this because I've watched it happen in other countries, there just may be things that aren't done for older people. We spend $3 billion a year in this country for renal dialysis. At age fifty-five in the United Kingdom, they shut it off. I was quadriplegic in 1986 from an old broken neck injury and I was restored by some very competent, quick, and fancy surgery, and I'm now neurologically intact. But I was nine years too old to have had that done for me had I lived in Great Britain. So you have to be awfully careful when you say, "After a certain age you can't have this procedure because you might be depriving the younger society of a lot of benefits." There is going to have to be a means test.

There is no reason why people who make enough money to care for themselves should be getting Medicare. If that happens, it might be a sliding scale: Some people pay nothing, some people pay half, and so on. And there has to be adequate insurance which doesn't cost $50,000 a year. All of these things will have to be considered by the commission I mentioned earlier. In addition, I think people who smoke or drink should pay more than those who don't because they cost the government $90 billion a year. But we're not quite there yet where we can say, "You can't have this because you don't have enough money." Somebody then is going to say, "Well, we can get 90 billion from the smokers." That will get smokers to stop and it will get people to demand some kind of sliding scale I was talking about. Same with obesity. Three hundred thousand people die every year because they are obese. They cost money. Just think what problem you'd have right now if the government said, "Anyone who is more than 20 percent overweight is going to have to pay X dollars additional on their Medicare or Medicaid bill." The pressures of economics are going to make clear to the public you can't have something for nothing.

LK: When we say this, it will be economic-driven rather than because it's the right thing to do.

KOOP: That's right. Almost everything I look at in medicine is being driven by economics. It isn't ethics and it certainly isn't quality of care.

LK: Will everyone have health care in the twenty-first century?

KOOP: I think the big sleeping giant is the group of uninsured. These are the working poor, not the real poor, because they get

Medicare and Medicaid. When Mr. Clinton came into office he started talking about the uninsured, who numbered then 34 million and now number 43 million and will number 63 million in the year 2000. That's going to be a critical mass that they and society will say we can't tolerate. This will trigger one of two things: Either we readjust the present system of managed care so it becomes more palatable, or the government will say, "You always told us you wanted market forces to drive the economy of medical care delivery and we let you do that since 1994 and you have failed. Now we will institute a national health service which will cover everybody and here's how much each of us will be taxed to cover the cost." That's a definite option for the early years of the next century.

LK: What will be the ramifications in the next century of Jack Kevorkian's work in this century?

KOOP: I think you are going to see economics driving the move toward assisted suicide and euthanasia under the guise of giving people autonomy to make decisions at the end of their lives. The push will be to make the decision. In Michigan Kevorkian is viewed as a hero. The *British Medical Journal* calls him a hero. My opinion is the guy is a serial killer. If you say that somebody who is dying and is in agony should have the right to commit suicide, everybody will say yes because it's considered the compassionate thing to do. But almost none of the patients Kevorkian killed was in pain, they just didn't want to die of their diagnosis. I don't think you can trust a medical profession that is a healer and a killer.

LK: But do you see it increasing in the medical profession?

KOOP: Yes. It's going to end up before the Supreme Court, and I don't know what they're going to say. Sooner or later, it will start at a state level and it will spread.

LK: What ethical decisions will doctors in the next century have to make?

KOOP: The ethics will center around decisions at the end of life, and that doesn't necessarily mean old life. It could be posttrauma life or the life of a newborn baby born in less than pristine condition. History can teach us here. Look at what happened in Germany at the hands of Bavarian medicine and psychiatry. You can plot a slippery slope from the first decision that there exists life not worth living, the insane and later amputees from the First World War and eventually Gypsies. I can't believe people who say there is no such thing as a slippery slope. I've seen slippery slopes, and they happen. This discussion about a burgeoning elderly population and the economic problems produced by it will force ethical issues to be subverted.

LK: And those issues being subverted would be—

KOOP: How long should people live? Should frail people that cost us more than robust people be given the same kind of medical care?

LK: It's been suggested every business tell its employees each has a half-hour to get out of the building and go for a walk. Do you—

KOOP: Yes I do. Johnson and Johnson started it and turned it into a profitable business. They lost a lot of money in the first year, and in the second year they broke even, and now they market it to other companies. If you keep patients healthy and if they lose weight and stop smoking, the bottom line on the health care bill always goes down. More and more places have exercise areas and facilities. It's expensive to initiate but it works.

Media

"Media" is a word I think has been used too much and certainly has been blamed, rightly or wrongly (put your money on the latter), for most of the trouble in the world. "Media" is a word with what seems to be an ever-changing definition, so it doesn't surprise me one bit that we are confused by what the media are and what they can or can't do. Certainly, they sell us products, give us information, and divide us into groups based on what we want to know and what we want to buy. And certainly there are ramifications, as you are about to learn from these three individuals.

Much has been made of the fact that new technology and the resulting changes it forces in the media will eliminate a staple of every twentieth-century morning: the newspaper. On Wednesday morning, September 15, 1982, technology did change the newspaper. But it didn't eliminate it. The newspaper got better. *USA Today* was introduced to America, and today it can be found in airports and hotels around the world. The man responsible for this new medium says we are going to have to continue to tip the newspaper boy or girl every Christmas in the twenty-first century. Al Neuharth has always enjoyed change but hopes those working in newsrooms everywhere will pay attention to the problems and new decisions created by change.

The marketing of ideas and products is the bailiwick of Joe Turow, professor of communication at the Annenberg School for Communication at the University of Pennsylvania. You may have never heard of Joe, but you'll certainly know his subject if you've ever been called by a telemarketer. Here's a preview of the coming century: Those calls asking how you are today are not going to go away.

Frank Lowe is the guy responsible for those wonderful "Pardon me, do you have any Grey Poupon?" television commercials. His company has also produced the popular "Lucky," the sweating construction worker who takes a Diet Coke break at the same time every morning, much to the delight of nearby women office workers. Both are among the most successful ads ever put on television, and as a result, I thought it would be worthwhile to explore the future of advertising with a man who is quiet and reserved and has no opinions.

AL NEUHARTH

FOUNDER, *USA TODAY*; CHAIRMAN, FREEDOM FORUM

Media people should take a little harder look at whether the instantaneous dissemination of information gives us any degree of study or appraisal or whether we're just throwing it all out there. And consumers of this information should say to themselves, "Well, it's interesting," or "It's exciting," or "It makes me mad as hell, but maybe I'd better withhold judgment until I get the full story." Now, I doubt any one of those pieces of advice will be followed by any group.

LK: Will there be newspapers in the next century?

NEUHARTH: Sure.

LK: Newspapers that we can hold?

NEUHARTH: There will be newspapers printed on newsprint with ink, mostly colored ink. Despite all the new means of gaining or retrieving news and information, many of which are or will be mind-boggling, there will still be newspapers that people will want to hold in their hands as they hold in their hands magazines and books and read them.

LK: Reports of the deaths of newspapers are premature?

NEUHARTH: Ted Turner said at a newspaper publishers' convention in Chicago in 1981 that newspapers would be dead by 1990. Didn't happen. The demise was predicted when radio came into being and again when television appeared. Now it's predicted with the Internet. I think it will dramatically affect newspapers but it will not mean their demise.

LK: Newspapers like *USA Today* have on-line access. That going to be standard in the next century?

NEUHARTH: I think most daily newspapers in anything but the smallest cities will supplement their printed product with on-line delivery of news and information. It will be specific information that people don't want to wait ten or twelve or twenty-four hours to get, and that includes sports scores, stock market information, and probably breaking news stories. For example, the *Dallas Morning News* broke the story about an admission of guilt by the accused in the Oklahoma City bombing case. It broke on a cycle when they weren't publishing, so they put it on the Web and got a lot of attention and then printed more details the next morning. You're going to see more and more of that. The reason it's not going to be dramatic is because most consumers don't have the time to sit down in front of a computer and punch in to get what they want. So until, or unless, computers and on-line information become more affordable and more portable, I don't think they'll be competitive for mass delivery.

LK: Will we subscribe to a newspaper on the Internet instead of having it delivered to our doorsteps?

NEUHARTH: I think we will do both. I don't think reading a paper on the Internet will be a substitute for reading a paper that you hold.

LK: That going to happen in the next four or five years?

NEUHARTH: I don't think they'll be as affordable as newspapers or magazines or television or radio, and I don't think they're going to be as portable. You can't take them to the bathroom.

LK: That's important?

NEUHARTH: Very important. It's possible we'll end up with small computers where you can retrieve information and hold them in your hand, but it's not likely to happen so systematically that it's going to wipe out newspapers.

LK: Will we see more national newspapers?

NEUHARTH: I think there will be specialized national newspapers in areas like sports, for example. It's possible someone would attempt a general interest national daily, but my hunch is with *USA Today* having a sixteen-year franchise, it's probably unlikely. Had I been asked that question sixteen years ago I'd have answered yes.

LK: No afternoon large-city newspapers?

NEUHARTH: I doubt metros will be published in the major metropolitan areas because the time and distance and competition for people's interest in the afternoon and evening is just too great. I think afternoon papers will continue in smaller communities.

LK: What societal shifts could kill a newspaper?

NEUHARTH: I don't think there's anything in the next century that's likely to kill off newspapers as we now know them, in terms of being printed on newsprint with colored ink and delivered to homes.

LK: But doesn't the fact more people work in their homes mean fewer will read while commuting?

NEUHARTH: Newspapers being read on the way to work only occurs in major cities where you have mass transit, so the majority of newspapers are read in the home or office traditionally, and that will continue. With more people working in the home there's going to be more time for reading.

LK: What will a newspaper twenty years from now look like?

NEUHARTH: It won't look dramatically different than it looks now. You will continue to see more color because even the good gray lady, the *New York Times*, is starting to print in color and has invested huge dollars in order to do that. And that's a belated recognition on the part of the print media that this is the television generation. Even the *Wall Street Journal* is starting to use occasional illustrations and small pictures on page one. It may be easier to find what you're looking for; there may be even more departmentalization, with a place for everything so different members of the family won't have to fight over the newspaper. More self-help and family involvement columns and features will appear. The content will continue to shift toward a more broadly defined "news." Newspapers are beginning to realize they are in the business of providing news-information-entertainment in the broadest sense rather than what the purists among editors a decade ago thought their job was. Editors are coming around to the fact readers want to be entertained as well as informed. And it won't be done by blurring entertainment with news because print and broadcast media can make a clear distinction through placement of the stories. For example, *USA Today* has a life section which is devoted to entertainment.+

LK: But if color is a way to get attention, isn't that saying you have to dumb down to get readers?

NEUHARTH: It's not dumbing down. It's the result of an audience that doesn't want to be bored. It's primarily because of the fast-moving and colorful television they've become accustomed to for a number of years now. We stole it from TV and put it on newsprint.

LK: A story in *USA Today* is shorter than in other newspapers. Is that a trend?

NEUHARTH: Sure. And short stories are going to get better as journalists understand that they are writing for the benefit of the reader and not to satisfy their own egos. It's a hell of a lot more difficult for a reporter who writes an eight-inch story that contains a lot of information than an eighteen-inch story.

LK: How about the use of bullets in a story?

NEUHARTH: Sure, bullets and plain talk. There have to be sentences and paragraphs that you're not going to have to fight your way through; that people can grasp and understand without studying. That means you can pack a hell of a lot of information in your short story. The mistaken criticism of *USA Today* and other publications is "You're too short, therefore you don't have a lot of news and information." Critics call that "shits and bits" but there's a lot of information in shits and bits. People are going to want more news and information than ever and they'll have less time in which to digest it.

LK: Will it be harder for people to understand a complex issue if the stories are shorter?

NEUHARTH: No. A high percentage of readers are interested in headlines and a synopsis but papers will offer in-depth as well. I think one standard is where the paper is published. If it's inside the Washington Beltway that's one standard, and if it's in Omaha there's another standard.

LK: Speaking of inside the Beltway, will we continue to read newspapers with an obvious editorial bent such as the conservative *Washington Times* or the liberal *New York Post*?

NEUHARTH: I think not. If anything, we are less likely to see politically biased newspapers funded by people with a political or international interest because the public is getting too smart for that. The *Washington Times* will be around as long as its sponsor continues to lose money but chooses to fund it. In the case of the *New York Post*, its head is interested in a printed voice inside New York City, and it will be around as long as he (Rupert Murdoch) is around. Some think having a voice is more important than making a profit, and I guess that falls under the First Amendment. Readers want to be informed rather than dictated to.

LK: Will newspapers ever pay for information the way television news shows do?

NEUHARTH: I doubt it. The public is dubious of stories where they know the source has been paid a fee. They're also dubious of anonymous sources, and there's been a real decrease in the use of that. You'll see newspapers with a policy that doesn't permit using anonymous sources. Papers will have their reporters work harder at getting the source to permit identification.

LK: What will be more important to the reader in the future: more international news or more domestic news?

NEUHARTH: Without a doubt there will be greater growth and interest in international news than in domestic news. The more people see and hear and read about what's going on elsewhere in the world, the more they want to know. It started with CNN. As for areas getting more attention in the next ten or twenty years, I would have to say China and the Pacific Rim and maybe Latin America.

LK: Why is there a need to know, and why is it growing?

NEUHARTH: It feeds on itself. The barriers are coming down around the world. And the more that people read or see or hear, the more they want to know and the more they want to go. The two most rapidly growing businesses in the next century will be the news and information business and the travel business. So those of us who gather information have a great opportunity to figure out ways to deliver to huge audiences in China, for example. Leaders there and in some other countries are doing their damnedest to keep barriers up but they can't.

LK: Anyone who is or, since we're talking about the future, will be the owner of a newsstand doesn't have to worry about being out of a job in the next century, right?

NEUHARTH: I think so. We'll still deliver to homes and to street corners but I don't think that form of delivery is going to show any dramatic growth. Still, I don't think it will disappear. It is possible the total daily circulation of newspapers will be flat or down a little from what it is today.

LK: Tell me about niche media. Are you concerned about its growth or is that healthy?

NEUHARTH: Not concerned at all. I think that's another way of reaching larger total audiences. While not many direct satellite TV channels may have a huge audience, they have a devoted audience, and in the aggregate they add up to more than we had when we were just three major conventional networks. I think there is potential danger but it's what those nervous critics point to. That basic hunger for more knowledge ultimately will dominate with most people. And while some segments of the audience may say, "All I care about is my kind of music and sports," eventually as they change in age and lifestyles, that will expand. What the critics overlook is it's a hell of a lot better to have any audience read or watch TV or listen to the radio than not read or watch TV or listen to the radio. Remember, most of us learned to read through the comics in newspapers.

LK: So people will buy newspapers twenty years from now for the same reasons they bought them twenty years ago?

NEUHARTH: I think the basics of a broad-based general interest newspaper will not be changed. What's offered up may change. But, for basically the same reasons, they'll buy a newspaper.

LK: Do you worry that eventually someone is going to chip away at the First Amendment?

NEUHARTH: I have some concerns that the more reporters, editors, and publishers that we have and the less professional judgment that they have in what they put on the Internet, the more the critics are going to say the First Amendment is too damn broad. We've already seen it where we start out with a V-chip to protect kids and pretty soon someone is deciding on everything that goes out. That's a real danger.

LK: You're concerned about the V-chip?

NEUHARTH: The V-chip for the present concerns me a little bit but the fact everybody from the president on down is saying we've got to edit what our kids have a chance to see, now that concerns me because you go back to Lenin or any opponent of free speech and free press in this century, that's how they started. They took away a little bit of what people were allowed to see and hear and say and pretty soon they've taken it all away.

LK: Who will do it?

NEUHARTH: What we need to be concerned about is politicians for momentary political gain will see some of those pressures and say, "Let's play with that for my benefit in the next election." And that is where the challenge to the First Amendment will come. In this country I hope and expect that the Supreme Court will still understand and uphold that there is a First Amendment. But we in the media must understand that to preserve a free press we must deserve it. Only a fair press can remain a free press.

LK: What do you say to the editor who, fifty years from now, has to deal with a First Amendment issue? What direction can you offer?

NEUHARTH: It's not a matter of fifty years from now. I think most editors have failed in the last fifty years, or since I've been in the business. Most journalists and media people wave the First Amendment flag as a protection for them. Very few of us have been able to show the general public that the First Amendment is for the general public. It's not just for publishers or editors, it's the people's right to know. It'll be individuals or groups with their own agenda and their own perspective challenging First Amendment purists, and then some politicians at a lot of levels, whether it's in city hall, the statehouse, the courthouse, or the White House, and they're going to make some political hay with that. Politicians will fan it, respond to it, and fan it again.

LK: We see news happening live now. Is that difficult to react to when you consider we used to have a day or two to think about what we've just heard or seen before drawing a conclusion?

NEUHARTH: I think there is a danger and there's evidence that initial reactions to major breaking stories are wrong. There was a major knee-jerk reaction to who planted the Oklahoma City bomb. People were convinced that was probably some group of Arabs who decided to get even for New York City. The mere mention of that possibility by one or two people on the air gives people that first impression and takes a hell of a lot of time to overcome it. So there's an inherent danger. There isn't any question those who look at one headline or hear one sound bite sometimes get the wrong impression because of the quickness of it. Again, it is more important to be fair than to be first.

LK: How will people in the next century describe journalism in the late twentieth century?

NEUHARTH: Historians will say the public standards for news increased in the last years of the twentieth century over what they had been before, and not everyone in journalism was fully aware of it. Conversely, historians will also say the mainstream media's performance was much better during this time than ever before, and the public isn't fully aware of this. Good journalism and financial success go hand in hand.

LK: What scares you about the twenty-first century?

NEUHARTH: Nothing. I wasn't scared in this one so there's no reason to be scared in the next one.

JOE TUROW

PROFESSOR OF COMMUNICATIONS,
ANNENBERG SCHOOL FOR COMMUNICATIONS,
UNIVERSITY OF PENNSYLVANIA

Make sure your children are conversant with the world around them. People who don't know how to use information are not going to do well in the twenty-first century.

LK: What are the media going to look like in the next century, and will the definition of the media change?

TUROW: The basic form of entertainment and news won't be drastically different. We're still going to have news and movies and television shows and sports. But the issue is going to turn on two things: how we get the stuff and how much we're going to share it with other people in the United States. More and more the media are going through fractionalization, globalization, and conglomerization. These are the three tendencies that have been going on for maybe ten or fifteen years now—

LK: Wait a second. Is "conglomerization" a word?

TUROW: You figure it out. Make up another word.

LK: I'll go with it.

TUROW: The merger of smaller telephone companies, like Bell Atlantic and NYNEX, into a single company is an example of conglomeriation. But to explain these three driving forces: Fractionalization means the media is being chopped up. Until the 1980s Americans watched three networks and a public television station. Videotape recorders were hardly known, cable was a very small part of America, and computers, for all intents and purposes, did not exist in the home. Now, think what people have today. The networks' share of the audience has been drastically reduced because of cable and the rise of independent stations, and because of the VCR and the growth (though still tiny) of things like the Internet and the use of the computer for games. All of these are taking people away from the typical television set on many points. So we're having an erosion of network ratings and a growth of segmented markets. Same thing with magazines. They've grown tremendously in their number and diversity of audiences they try to reach. And that's because advertisers are interested in chopping up audiences so they can be efficient. So television and radio have gotten into the act of reaching smaller and smaller audiences that advertisers are interested in. Now, that's just begun, but it's going to continue way past the year 2000. The idea will be to target with commercials and shows as specifically as possible, even to the point of talking to the individuals. You know how you get direct mail addressed to you saying you have won whatever it is, well, that's part of the electronic universe. Advertisers have learned how to address you electronically, so it's going to be quite possible to not only talk to you by knowing your name but advertisers will find out a heck of a lot about you. And they will give you discounts and rewards for answering questions about yourself. The more you answer, the more discounts you get.

LK: This happens over cable TV?

TUROW: Cable, phone lines, and it will be on-line with computers. It's already being done in a number of places.

In the future advertisers are going to be able to direct a commercial to you specifically by knowing what your interests are and by knowing what you've told them and given what they already know about other people who match your basic characteristics.

LK: More people will know about us than those who know about us now?

TUROW: There are a lot of people who know a lot about you now. But marketers are going to have records of what you've bought from them. It's called "relationship marketing," because as you build relationships with customers, you learn more about them and then you can start talking specifically to them. So we're moving to the point where marketers will say, "If you want to watch this movie, normally it costs $1.50 but if you will watch our commercial, we'll give you two movies for a dollar." This will be true on the Internet and cable. It's called "digital insertion," and companies will be able to insert commercials for you or people like you. The larger point I'm trying to make is that, increasingly, media programming will become categorized by types of people and tailored to individuals.

LK: And that brings us to globalization.

TUROW: Globalization is happening as the reader reads this. Companies are no longer seeing individual territories as their major area of business. Instead, they are looking toward the whole world as their business area. Companies from not only the United States but Europe and Asia are getting into it. It's happening in the record industry, the television industry, and the movie industry. Past the year 2000 you will see ten, maybe twelve companies that control distribution and exhibition and maybe production in most of the media materials most people see. This has the potential for conflicts of interest between a news division and an entertainment or corporate division owned by the same company. ABC and Disney is an example. *Time Magazine* and Time Warner is another example. Rupert Murdoch owns this publisher, HarperCollins! In the main lanes of popular culture we will have a relatively small number of companies controlling media outlets. Maybe even more important, there's going to be a tie-in with product manufacturers and distributors, like toy companies and fast-food companies, so there will be a blizzard of activity when a movie comes out because of all the joint ventures in the pipeline. We'll have $200 million worth of promotion because of these joint ventures sending out this incredible wave of publicity.

LK: Why does this sound scary?

TUROW: I think it sounds scary because, in the case of conglomerization, there's a potential danger of privacy violations. We will be working with marketers, whether we know it or not, who can make our lives an open book. But we'll be giving this information willingly. Go to the supermarket today with your supermarket card and every time it's used, your purchases are tracked. Then there's the question of community: the issue of what American society is. I'm really concerned that when we have a media world that is so segmented, people can be encouraged to go into their own world. You're tired of the garbage outside and walking down the streets of a big city and everybody's annoying you so when you come home, you want to be with a narrow community, from a media standpoint. So surrounding you with images that fit with your perception of the world, you may be further distancing yourself from other people in our society. That weakens the sense of the larger society, and that can have severe problems.

LK: Such as?

TUROW: Such as caring. Such as thinking of people who don't belong to our community but do belong to others. Such as not thinking the kind of money we spend and vote on should relate to people who may live just two miles from us but in this virtual reality of our experiences have no relationship to us. People across the way could go down the tube and we sit in our own media universes and gated communities and don't care.

LK: So then it can be suggested the burden is on these various media playing to these segmented audiences to say, "By the way, say hello to the folks across the street," or something like that.

TUROW: We're going to need some kind of cross talk between different communities. When you had three networks reaching 90 percent of people watching TV, that was incredible. The ability to talk across communities is rapidly eroding.

LK: So where is this going? Do people remain in their worlds or is there some kind of media to bring them back?

TUROW: I say there will not be the kind of media that can pull people back.

LK: We are seeing a proliferation of big bookstores with coffee houses and cafes. Does this suggest a willingness of people to escape gated communities and have a face-to-face talk with each other?

TUROW: Yes, I think people will want to meet but the meetings will be with people like themselves. Bookstores in upscale areas that have the kind of safe environment will see the aging baby boom generation as customers. The sense of a bookstore is you will meet other people with a similar proclivity. You are going to see these meeting places extend on-line as well. That's the issue: Where is there a place where people can fight verbally across different demographics and lifestyle interests, and my contention is that's becoming slimmer and slimmer.

LK: Is this happening because of technology or is it occurring because of human nature?

TUROW: Both. People like to be among themselves. Advertisers have been under the impression Americans were united by World War II and that generation would accept global mass media—watch the three networks and nobody has a problem with it. They said that during the 1960s America began to sort of break up because of civil rights and Vietnam War demonstrations, and baby boomers were more self-indulgent than the previous generation had been, and as a result, the new technology started appearing at just the right time, and they started taking advantage of the fractionalization of the United States by targeting people in the places they wanted to be and with the communities they wanted to be in.

LK: There is discussion about our technical ability to watch *Good Morning Bangkok*, which suggests we will have the ability, as well, to be tolerant of others?

TUROW: Actually, *Good Morning Bangkok* will further fractionalize the American audience because people watching that aren't watching the news their neighbors two blocks away are watching. You can watch *Good Morning Peking* and I can watch *Good Morning France* and we're watching totally different things.

LK: Are we going to use the telephone as much as we do now?

TUROW: Yes, but it's going to be supplemented with the Internet and videophones and all of that. Now, that said, keep in mind one long distance company is already trying to charge long distance rates on the Internet. The Internet for long distance is a lot cheaper, but we will actually hear an Internet voice and that is going to become more and more sophisticated.

LK: Do you worry we are losing the art of conversation?

TUROW: We already are. People don't strike up a conversation with people they think not to be like them. We are taught not to talk to strangers, and it has become part of our culture.

LK: Will parents be able to block out television programs they don't want their children watching?

TUROW: You're talking about the V-chip. In a technological sense, the V-chip is in its infancy right now. But in the next century as computers and television become synonymous, it's going to be easy. In fact, once television becomes digitized, a program will carry a lot of information on it designed by different kinds of groups. For example, you're a liberal parent and you find out the PTA has a monitoring service that suggests what shows are good and bad for your kids. And down the block there's another family who are fundamentalist Christian and they find out Reverend Wildmon's group has its own monitoring service. Now, everybody's got one hundred channels. So with the V-chip both families will have to accept those guidelines from the television industry. With the process I'm suggesting, it will be possible to tune your TV to the guidelines of the particular organization you care about and that, digitally, will select for your children based on the kind of norms that you care about.

LK: So there will be a Falwell chip and a Church of Christ chip and the Mormons and so on?

TUROW: That's right. It will guide your children to the programs they (the organizations) care about. And I see the ability to have a computer use what's called an "intelligent agent," which can determine what kinds of scenes you don't want for your kids. It's a customized approach.

LK: Will people still write letters?

TUROW: I think longhand is obsolete. I think e-mail has actually increased letter writing although it's a different kind of letter writing. Before e-mail I never wrote to friends. Now I get twenty-five messages and I respond, but the fact is people are writing e-mail and letter writing is a growing phenomenon.

LK: It does appear, then, the only place where we will interact with people from different socioeconomic backgrounds is the office?

TUROW: In a relative sense, yes. You see it on television now. All the shows with people of different races has them in a work context. Work sitcoms and work dramas (like *NYPD Blue*) tend to be fairly integrated. But when you deal with family shows they are all-black or all-white.

LK: What makes you think in the future we will become aggressive in how we receive information rather than being the passive sponges we have always been?

TUROW: We will be much more aggressive about it because there's going to be more of a way to interact with the material. For one thing, we will still be tired when we come home from work and don't want to spend the amount of time looking for something that interests us. So you'll have an "intelligent navigator," a kind of electronic waiter that will know what you want to see and what your interests are, based on what you've done before. It will choose from among the choices available and maybe even give you a synopsis. It has the potential of getting us out of the V-chip mire because it will follow what your preferences are.

LK: We are watching live events. It seems there's no longer a filter of what we see which allows us to think about it and then come to a conclusion. Is that good or bad?

TUROW: It's called "instant history," though I'm not sure that's the right term for it, but certainly the desire for reaction is speeded up. It's forcing policymakers, in a sense, to make decisions more quickly than they otherwise would have made them because their sense is "Gee, all these people saw it and we have to react." We get impatient if we have to wait an extra three seconds for a computer to load. People are talking about faster and faster modems, and what happens is technology breeds this desire for speed. And from a policy standpoint, that will have implications in the year 2000 and beyond. I don't believe we see reality just because it's live TV though. It's only one slice of a particular world that may be only a photo opportunity.

LK: So is the burden on people in the future to get a little smarter about what they see?

TUROW: Yeah, we have to make people a little more sophisticated about video images. It's a problem though, because people either believe what they see or they become cynical, and both are improper reactions. News and entertainment are, essentially, a battle over the definition of the world. You've got various sources in public relations, and interest groups and political organizations are always maneuvering to have a reporter write this or that, and we don't know, for example, why this person is on this television show. One of the things I tell my students is interrogate the newspaper, interrogate the television show. Don't dismiss it as simply false because if you do it then you miss tying into a national conversation. Newspapers are part of a community or national conversation, and we have to understand that to be good citizens. I worry our conversations are becoming narrower and narrower.

LK: What scares you about the next century?

TUROW: We are going backward in many areas. Look at indicators of what's happening in America and then look at the late nineteenth century, and you see very similar things. You see people concerned about immigration, there's a general feeling that wealthy people don't have to deal with people who are less well off, and what that does is increase the tensions between the classes. And this is exactly what was going on in the nineteenth century. The other issue is we are between cold wars and now have an opportunity to work out a bunch of our internal problems about inequities within society, where the society wants to go, transportation, housing, all of which require talking across groups and perhaps coming to some sort of idea about where people are coming from. We have to get a sense of ourselves and look those problems in their collective eye. It's ironic we are so divided at a time when there are so many problems that we actually can deal with and do so without the worry of also having to deal with a Soviet Union.

LK: In another fifty years will the Annenberg School for Communications be teaching a class called "How Not to Be Bullshitted by the Media"?

TUROW: I'm teaching that class now.

FRANK LOWE

CHAIRMAN, THE LOWE GROUP

I can't even give advice to myself.

LK: How must advertising change in the next century?

LOWE: I think we're already seeing dramatic change and I think this will continue and accelerate. First of all, we are seeing the tremendous increase in the number of television channels. This will mean that the audience will become even more fragmented. Then, there's the fact that these channels are becoming more global through satellites. This means that clients can increasingly reach a global audience with the same commercial. Next comes the dramatic rise in the universal comprehension of the English language because of business, satellite television, and programming in general. This will mean that on the global channels it will become increasingly possible to run advertising in English. Already it is common and even chic to run ads in English in many European countries. Finally, there is the change in the content of programming, particularly in sports. This has led to a dramatic rise in advertising spending from products that can be associated with this programming, such as soft drinks, beer, sportswear and equipment, computer hardware and software, cars, and financial services. Twenty-five years ago packaged goods dominated advertising. But today the giant budgets are for the categories I've just mentioned. Strangely enough, in many cases, the things being advertised are more important in people's lives today than the washing detergents and toothpaste from before. I think what we're going to see is that consumers are going to be able to decide what they want to watch and what they want to listen to and what they want to be influenced by. In the past that wasn't easy to do. So, we've now got to do advertising that consumers want to watch as opposed to have to watch.

LK: Does that mean you have to be entertaining in your advertising?

LOWE: Unequivocally yes. For a long time, advertising in Britain, which is perhaps the most creatively sophisticated market, and other

European countries have seen entertainment as an important ingredient. Strangely enough, the trend started in America in the sixties but was abandoned in the seventies and the eighties but now it's coming back. Keep in mind: Television is an entertainment medium and people expect entertainment, whereas the printed word was more about news so press ads were more about information. I think you have to leave the consumer a little richer for your visit than poorer. So the best ads today have wit and drama because otherwise they can so easily get ignored. And the ability to ignore them has been enhanced by yet one more dramatic change—the remote control. More than 40 percent of people in the United States and the UK admit to zapping television commercials. You can be pretty sure they are quick to zap the ones that bore them.

LK: Why don't you just make ads people will watch?

LOWE: We try to. But such is the amount of money spent on advertising that clients are obsessed, particularly the CFO, with proving the ads will work before they run them. The problem is that no one has yet devised a satisfactory method of research. All too often I have seen advertisements rejected by research because consumers tend to reject the unfamiliar but which still run because of a courageous client who has been rewarded by the fact that later on, with familiarity, people have liked the work because it is fresh and innovative. In consequence, they have liked the advertiser and the products. But this needs courage. Yet all too often, again because of the amounts of money involved, the agency gives the client ads they like and ads that research well as opposed to advertisements that come from their own gut and that they feel the consumer will like. If you think of advertising as an art, albeit a commercial one, it is worth noting the fact that most new movements in art and music and architecture, for example, have been frequently rejected by the generation in power, only to be picked up by the generation of the future. The way research works now is I sit eight people down in a room and I ask them to push buttons to show how interested they are in the ad they are watching. But I am putting the consumer in an entirely false situation because consumers don't actually look at advertising that way. They see it as the thing intruding into their program and when it comes on maybe they turn to their wife or kids or husband or whatever or go and get a beer. But in a focus group that doesn't happen because they are told to watch the ad. In real life they don't think about it at all because they aren't interested.

LK: And this means what?

LOWE: First of all, it means advertising is getting duller and duller and duller. Secondly, there were about 6 million television commercials transmitted in 1995 and, of those, 82 percent were thirty seconds or less in length. That's because the client is saying "I need frequency." They confuse frequency with impact. But a commercial has no impact if it isn't seen. So while it may appear on a chart as having been seen, that doesn't mean it was seen. So, ads are getting shorter because research efficiency tells you to talk to the consumer more times. Many think that the more times you show an ad, the better the chance people will remember it, and that is absolute bullshit if it's boring. It's like meeting a person. If they're interesting you only have to meet them once to remember them. A boring person you can meet twenty times and still not remember who they are.

LK: Ads will continue to be thirty seconds long?

LOWE: I doubt it. There are many fine ads that fit well and are very memorable with only thirty-second messages, but there are frequently needs and opportunities to use a longer time length so a mood can be created or a story can be told, and to give people some time to absorb the message. So I believe we will see longer ads which will be helped by the diversity of channels making air time, in a sense, more affordable. Even in the most expensive time slot anywhere in the world, the Super Bowl, all too often it is the client who has the courage and the money to buy sixty seconds and the courage to show a bold advertisement which gets remembered and even, in a way, to be thanked by the consumer. All the research we have done recently tells us that the most important consumer measure on effectiveness is likeability. This will lead to dramatic change. Until now, there has almost been a conspiracy of mediocrity and a great suspicion of creativity. What ads do you remember?

LK: Can't remember any.

LOWE: Exactly! Thank you very much. Isn't that terrifying?

LK: But I remember ads from the Super Bowl.

LOWE: You've just made my point entirely, because aside from being expensive, the Super Bowl has become an advertising program within a program and clients and agencies have learned that here to be dull is to be invisible.

LK: We have technology to edit out or edit through ads.

LOWE: That's right, we do. And that is going to make ads become better. Not only do we have the zapper to zap but we have more channels to turn to. I am sure most people reading this book will agree that they switch away from advertisements all the time to have a quick look at the news on CNN or to get the weather or to catch up on how a ball game is going. If we are to restrain these people from going elsewhere, the ad's have got to be more and more brilliant and fun. Why else would they give us their attention? After all, most products and services we deal with are relatively trivial. The important things in life are health and education, employment, and whether we have any money in the bank. It is hardly vital to the human condition that we drink one kind of beer or eat one kind of candy. Or, if Nike will forgive me, what kind of sneakers we wear. What is important, of course, is whether Michael Jordan wears them.

LK: So ads in the future will become more entertaining?

LOWE: Well, I think at the end of the day it must change. But at the moment I think we're still on the downward slope and I don't know when it's going to change.

LK: The moving camera and the use of black and white or a tinge of color with a black-and-white background is popular. Will we see more of this?

LOWE: I suppose so. It has to do with the fact that a lot of the people doing those ads replace the lack of an idea with a technique. I remember many years ago Rupert Murdoch asked me to do four talks in Australia when his newspapers moved into color. And while I freely admitted that color would enhance good ideas, I also pointed out that bad ideas in color would simply be colorful bad ideas. Mind you, talking of bad ideas, the effectiveness of advertising will be to a great extent dependent on the effectiveness of programming.

LK: We're doing some interviews in this book about programming. What is your perspective on that as an advertising man?

LOWE: I have the perception that programming is getting worse. But that may be because with so many channels it is just impossible to feed them with quality material, and, in any event, at the moment I feel that all too often we aim for the lowest common denominator, which is a pity because television is the most powerful influence on people's lives. Certainly, we should not imagine that just because there are so many channels available people are going to watch what they are given, particularly as increasingly there are others things to do in life than watching television. I am quite convinced, for example, that my children's generation and the ones that follow will be much more into doing things in all forms of education and leisure activity and will in consequence watch less television, particularly if it's not very good. Perhaps this is where the Internet and interactivity will play a role.

LK: I'm going to ask you some questions about the Internet, but let's look at all these channels and the narrowing audiences. Will Frank Lowe have to do ten different ads to cover what once was a general audience but is now splintered?

LOWE: I don't think so. Because the message for each individual product is normally the same for all audiences. Coca-Cola used to do advertisements for Sprite specifically targeted to Hispanic audiences. Yet we have found with the campaign we have been running—Image is Nothing. Thirst is Everything—that this appeals to all Sprite drinkers. What we will find is that with the increased number of channels and the narrowing of audiences we will be able to target more clearly, which has already meant a rise in the number of products advertised because clients with smaller budgets can afford it.

LK: There's the issue of creative boundaries, which always comes up when we talk of advertising. Right now, nine P.M.. is the time when we put on ads which suggest things sexual. Will that be pushed more and more?

LOWE: Yes and no. People will always try to push boundaries. On the other hand there is the wide body of opinion which finds that the gratuitous use of sex in advertising, particularly when aimed at younger people, is offensive. And nobody has the right to sell at any cost. My own rules here are that I would never wish to approve an ad for transmission when children are watching which I would not feel comfortable watching with my own children. Incidentally, that is not necessarily before nine P.M., which is a ludicrous watershed, as any parent will tell you.

LK: But right now we have this nine P.M. time. Will it become eight P.M. or will it move to ten P.M.?

LOWE: I'm not sure this matters, since children seem to watch at all hours, particularly during holidays. The question is the content, not the time. By the way, I am not so hypocritical as to suggest that sex should not play a role in advertising, it's just a question of how it's handled. If it's funny and normal, then that's fine. But if it's smutty or crude then it's not. Just the same as at home between parents and children.

LK: Liquor ads were shown on a Corpus Christi television station in 1996. This has made many wonder if liquor ads will become common on television?

LOWE: Again, I have always been puzzled by the exclusion of liquor ads on television, whether enforced or by agreement, for I am quite sure that children came to drinking beer and then hard liquor through their parents or peer group and not through advertising. Certainly, I cannot conceivably accept that advertising plays any role whatsoever, for example, in the problem of alcoholism, for we all know that alcoholism is a social problem caused principally by unhappiness, frustration, too much money or too little money, or even genetics, as we are now being told. Certainly, it cannot be laid at the door of advertising. Even smart and sophisticated imagery associated with alcohol can hardly be as powerful as television or films where alcohol is constantly consumed. Yet I do believe it will be attacked, probably more strongly when cigarette advertising has died because there is always a body of people who knows what is best for everyone else. But when they do step forward I hope they remember prohibition.

LK: So there will be more liquor ads?

LOWE: Probably. But I also hope and believe there will be a strong enforcement of the drinking laws so that alcohol is not freely available to children outside the home. I say outside the home because I have brought my children up to have a glass of wine from time to time and to enjoy a glass of champagne on a special occasion, making it a "normal" part of life, as opposed to something that is forbidden until you are eighteen.

LK: This is a good place for the transition to your thoughts on the future of cigarette advertising.

LOWE: I think it is doomed because there is an influential body of opinion that is opposed to it and because it is generally accepted that cigarettes cause cancer. But I don't think it will make any difference to the sales of cigarettes, only to the proliferation of brands. I've never believed that cigarette advertising was an influence on children compared with the natural curiosity of the young to try things; to be influenced by their peer group. I can't think of an ad that had as much influence on teenagers when I was young as the picture of Humphrey Bogart smoking a cigarette with Ingrid Bergman. Of course, I know that banning it is against the First Amendment. And I know it is hypocritical of governments to license the sale and to take money from taxes while banning the promotion of cigarettes. But I think it will be banned.

LK: What does this do to athletic events and public gatherings that are sponsored by tobacco companies?

LOWE: Once the pressure groups ban cigarette advertising, they'll move on to sports sponsorship, and eventually they'll probably succeed. Organizations in the sporting world will see it coming and gradually move to find new sponsors.

LK: What kinds of restrictions do you expect to be placed on advertising in the next few years?

LOWE: I think there will be a considerable lobby, not that there isn't already, but a bigger one, to stop ads that talk to children directly and tell them what to buy and what not to buy. We live in a society where a verbal, cohesive minority can actually seriously influence the silent majority. I don't see children being damaged by telling them to have Cocoa-Pops instead of Rice Krispies. I mean, they go into the shop—there's the Englishman talking—they go into the store, as you say in America, and there's 500 boxes lined up on the shelf. Well, that's advertising, isn't it? And many have the offer of sending this or that in and getting baseball or basketball cards in return and it's all the same thing.

LK: Will advertising continue to have an American sensibility or will we see a foreign McDonalds?

LOWE: In a sense, "yes" is the answer. Fifty percent of the world's advertising expenditure is incurred in the United States. But more important, 80 percent of the world's multinational companies are based in the United States and many of them, quite naturally, tend to sell their products across the world in the way they have succeeded in the United States. But this will only work where the national heritage of something is totally unimportant. For example: Pampers. People don't care that they are American, they simply care if they are the best. Or alternatively, where companies are selling a bit of the United States. Coke, Wranglers, Southern Comfort. There is a long list of products that are essentially American and would sell for this reason from Venice, Italy, to Venice Beach. What I hope here, however, is that all those people who are selling this way reflect a little bit about the environment in which they are selling. For while it may not matter what you put up in that famous road in Tucson which is regarded as the worst main street in America, it does matter what you put up, whether advertising signs or stores or fast food joints, in places where they would upset or vandalize the historic environment. And just to say it's acceptable because it works is not acceptable. I don't know whether it was McDonald's concern for the environment or Milan's pride in their city which caused them to build an authentic McDonald's without disturbing the classical architectural front of the building, but I am grateful for it.

LK: We spoke earlier about the Internet. Will we see ads there?

LOWE: Well, of course, we already have them, though most of them are fairly crude and rather dull. So the first factor that will affect the increase of ads on the Internet will be the increase of speed in downloading. Next, however, and probably more important, is the fact that the Internet, unlike television, does not have a captive audience.

So unless you have a category where information is really important, it will not be much help. For example, I can't see people looking up advertising to promote instant coffee on the Internet. On the other hand, there are major categories where the Internet is valuable for information, but it will not take the place of normal image-building advertising. For example, we have built Web sites for Mercedes-Benz, but we still need traditional ads to create the Mercedes image which will then lead the consumer to the Web site for information. You want to go to Hawaii? Click it on and see what islands there are and what hotels are available on those islands and what they cost and there will be a little review of each. This will increase as the new generation which is computer literate grow up with the Internet as part of their normal life. But I can't see the Internet working for what brand of instant coffee we should buy, since they're all the same and it's not a serious purchase. The Internet will be used for serious purchases such as motorcars.

LK: We just call them cars here. Will the Internet ad be interactive?

LOWE: Absolutely. We don't know how far this thing is going to go. The amount of information you can get about people who consume your products and put into data banks is absolutely extraordinary. You will be able to target people and you'll be able to talk to them and they will talk to you. It will come down to shopping of course. We've built thirty or forty Web sites for clients here and in Europe and we can monitor exactly how many people access the Web site and then we can find out what they liked and didn't like. It's in its infancy, just like advertising was in the fifties, but it's going to change, and very dramatically.

LK: Will there be any way to avoid providing information if we feel uncomfortable about it?

LOWE: I hope so. A lot of people feel very worried about the proliferation of essentially private information. They don't like the idea that companies that have managed to put together mailing lists where consumers provided information to one company are then sold on to another. And I personally resent the fact that I get mailings from one company which I know are based on demographic information and which I know could only have been provided by someone else.

LK: Privacy will be lost?

LOWE: It will be much harder to maintain, there's no doubt about that.

LK: Are we going to be able to smell ads?

LOWE: Some of them smell already.

LK: I mean the other kind of smell.

LOWE: Well, we already have scratch-and-smell ads in magazines, but I can't conceive we can manage that through television or radio. And I am pretty sure you wouldn't want it!

LK: Will celebrities continue to be used to sell products?

LOWE: Yes. Aside from the fact that celebrities are admired and people aspire to be like them, they are a short cut to getting attention. But it doesn't always work because consumers are not so stupid as to fail to realize that celebrity endorsements are often done because large quantities of money changes hands and that use of a particular product is not the reason the celebrity got where he or she is.

For example, while I can fully understand that Nike would sign Michael Jordan because their products could help him play better, it will be interesting to see whether Tiger Woods can enhance the sale of American Express cards since the use of a credit card can hardly contribute to his skills at golf.

LK: Will the fifty-yard line at a Chicago Bears game have an ad in the next century?

LOWE: I'm sure it will. Absolutely. It's just a question of time and money and somebody getting around to doing it. Look at Wimbledon. The players are walking billboards. In cricket, which is the bastion of sporting integrity, they now cut into the grass the names of the sponsors. It is extraordinary how this new medium has developed in cricket and rugby where the playing field itself is continuously used. Hasn't happened yet in soccer, but its time will come.

LK: What scares you about the coming century?

LOWE: The fact I won't be around for much of it. I'm furious I've learned so much and want to accomplish so much now that I'm older. And I can't help but think, God almighty, I only have another twenty or thirty years and I would love to see all the things that my son will see.

From a broader perspective, I hope there will be a better balance between the rights of commercialism and the rights of society. As of now, commercialism is running a little unchecked.

LK: Will there be ads on postage stamps?

LOWE: I hope not. Is nothing sacred? But then I come from a country that still has its head of state on postage stamps.

LK: You are concerned about commercialism, aren't you?

LOWE: I think there has to be a balance between selling and the world around us. They have a force to make people's lives richer but they can also be a force to impoverish it. If you look at the United States, which has so many things to admire, there are also so many things not to admire. Urban and even rural environments are increasingly clogged with gas stations which are hardly beautiful. Used-car showrooms have more bunting and flags than anything you'd see on the 4th of July. And there are the never-ending facades of fast food chains and billboards. I know the reasons for this are all about making money and there is nowhere better at making money than in the United States. I would love to see some of the big corporations say to themselves, hang on a minute, this is a really nice street, and as a result they wouldn't put up forty-two umbrellas and eight canopies and a giant golden arch or pictures of the Colonel. It will only come about if there is a debate by the people. But if this attitude goes on forever unchecked we could hand to our great grandchildren an uglier world than when we found it, which I think would be very sad.

LK: It would be a great ad campaign if a company did it.

LOWE: I'm sure it would. More important, without wishing to sound pious, it would show a great change of heart. Of course, the question becomes, who takes down the umbrellas first?

LK: How would you do an ad for the twenty-first century?

LOWE: I don't know. Advertising has been a great force for good in the twentieth century. It has been the means by which more people have found out about and used more products than ever before. And their lives are richer, more rewarding, and more fulfilling for that. The changing of the millennium is a massive change and I think that is a moment where people can reflect on exactly where they are headed and perhaps think about changing direction on a number of things they know are going wrong and don't particularly like. The last hundred years have been a bloody nightmare, with world wars, famine, starvation, and drugs. It's an appropriate time to take stock and ensure that we are truly doing things for the best, in a social sense as well as a commercial sense, before we continue on our merry way.

Planes, Trains, Automobiles, and Spaceships

On a flight from London to New York aboard the Concorde, I was given the chance to visit the cockpit for a few minutes, which, of course, turned into a little more than a few minutes. The captain and first officer tried to explain how one computer was talking to another computer, and it was apparent an "argument" of sorts was at hand. Now, I have been voted, consistently, the Worst Passenger of the Year by the National Worst Passenger Association, and the idea of flying faster than the speed of sound with two computers in disagreement was quickly making me a contender for another year. The captain explained the aircraft is always seeking the most efficient path and reacting to winds while all the time trying to provide a smooth ride. Hence the flashing lights. After we landed I saw the captain on my way out and asked if the computers finally agreed on something. "Of course," he said, "they always find common ground." I walked down the jetway feeling silly that I was glad human beings weren't flying the thing, because otherwise we'd still be over Nova Scotia or whatever you fly over to get to JFK while they continued to argue.

Getting from point A to point B is going to involve irony in the next century: A myriad of sophisticated I-don't-know-what will be inside our jets and cars and trains, but making the trip will be simpler to do. I'd like to introduce you to four people whose jobs are based on the next century.

John Hayhurst is a Boeing Company vice president in charge of building future aircraft. He says we'll continue to be fogged in, snowed in, severe thunderstormed-out, and all the other things that make me such a reliable award winner. Today he is focused on making variations of the popular Boeing 747. He says my chances of getting decaf coffee with skim milk in seat 2B are very good for the twenty-first century, which, in effect, leaves nothing else to be asked.

Thomas Downs's office is in room 2002 of Union Station in Washington, D.C., but it's on the fourth floor. You're about to learn the reason and, even more, you'll find yourself agreeing it makes sense. Amid the shelves of train sets the Amtrak president has a postcard view of Capitol Hill, though Mr. Downs is quick to say he and Congress don't always see eye to eye. But the relationship is getting better and better, and one reason is his ability to explain the train business to committee members and to the rest of us. He has big plans for Amtrak in the next century, and the way he tells it, we're in for a hell of a ride, especially after the year 2002.

The next century is going to see the end of the sexist joke about men refusing to stop for directions because, if I'm reading Neil Ressler right, men aren't going to get lost. The Ford Motor Company vice president in charge of building cars for the future says satellites will guide us out of tight spaces, like having no clue what city you're in, much less what street you're on, while somebody in the next seat is asking, "Are you sure this is the way?"

A face-to-face sit-down was held at NASA headquarters in Washington, D.C., with administrator Dan Goldin. He has been a frequent guest on both my radio show and my CNN program, and in every interview I've been amazed at the enthusiasm he exudes about the job. Goldin is part boss, part cheerleader, and part visionary, and I think those qualities are essential for anyone sitting in the big office. The shelves around his desk are filled with models of rockets and shuttles and, as I was soon to learn, launch vehicles. And he is quick to pull one down to explain how it did-does-will work.

And now sit back, relax, and make sure your tray table and seat are in their full, upright, and locked position because I'm going to take you for a quick tour of future travel.

JOHN HAYHURST

VICE PRESIDENT, 747–600X AND 747–500X PROGRAMS,
BOEING CORPORATION

Tomorrow's leaders will be characterized by a boundless curiosity, the natural propensity to evolve with the environment, the ability to work effectively with and through others, and the relentless pursuit of excellence.

LK: What is flying in another fifty or sixty years going to be like?

HAYHURST: Very difficult to predict that far out. I think in fifty to sixty years we are going to see at least long distance travel will be at faster speeds than we have today.

LK: Is that supersonic?

HAYHURST: Faster.

LK: What's faster than supersonic?

HAYHURST: The word "supersonic" means greater than the speed of sound. The Concorde today flies at twice that speed, or Mach 2. That far out, there's a high probability there will be airplanes flying at two and one-half, maybe three times the speed of sound.

LK: If we're flying that fast, will the plane be as large as a 747?

HAYHURST: In fifty or sixty years they could well be. I think the biggest thing we'll see before the size is that supersonic planes will fly farther. Today's Concorde has the range capability to just about make it across the Atlantic and can't fly across the Pacific at all because of the distances. So one of the issues for supersonic is not only speed but one that will have a greater distance capability.

LK: Where do you want to fly?

HAYHURST: Well, how about California to Asia? The distance from New York to London is about 3,600 statute miles. The distance from Los Angeles to Tokyo is one and one-half times that distance.

LK: Are you thinking this way because that's where a lot of business will be occurring?

HAYHURST: There will be a lot of business there but air travel in general is likely to grow at a much faster rate in Asia than it is in the U.S. and Europe.

LK: Why?

HAYHURST: Because of their rapidly growing economies, the disposable income that's available for leisure air travel is going to grow at a faster rate in Asia than elsewhere in the world. As the economies expand there will be some, but not as great an, increase in business travel as well.

LK: Do you expect business travel to maintain the same proportion of air travel in the future that it does now?

HAYHURST: Leisure travel is growing at a faster rate than business travel, and we see that trend continuing for quite a while to come. I don't think business travel will disappear because of enhanced telecommunications. While that equipment is useful for routine communication, it will never replace the need for some face-to-face transactions. It's hard to build relationships between people solely over the telephone or by satellite or by some form of picture phone or whatever.

LK: Aircraft are going to get bigger?

HAYHURST: We'll certainly see subsonic aircraft get bigger. I suspect within the next ten years we'll see airplanes with at least another 100 to 200 seats more than a 747. And perhaps in fifty years we'll see 800- to 1,000-seat airplanes. Now that's subsonic travel. The technical challenges are much greater to make supersonic airplanes that big. The next generation of supersonic aircraft might have only 250 to 300 seats and probably it will take longer for them to grow in size than the subsonics.

LK: If business travel is declining and leisure travel is increasing, why do we care how fast we get there?

HAYHURST: There have been a fair number of consumer surveys taken among the leisure travelers which indicate they place some value on travel time and might even be willing to pay a bit more for it, but not a first class fare, simply not to endure a ten- or twelve- or fourteen-hour flight.

LK: If passenger aircraft are getting bigger, what's the percentage of class seating going to be?

HAYHURST: It varies from airline to airline but typical 747–400s today have 5–6 percent of total seats for first class, 20 percent for business class, and the balance tourist, but some airlines have 747s on some routes with 50–60 percent business class.

LK: Your newest aircraft is the 777. Does this mean the next one will be the 787?

HAYHURST: I don't think so. Our focus is to build upon the existing airplane models that we have by developing what are called "derivatives," like stretching the body or increasing the takeoff weight so it can fly further or maybe even put new wings on the same body. The impact to airlines is that we can help them control costs for pilots and mechanics by reducing the amount of time they spend in training when moving from one model to another.

LK: What will a cockpit look like?

HAYHURST: There's a joke in the aviation industry that the next generation of cockpits will have a crew consisting of a person and a dog. The role of the dog is to make sure the person doesn't fall asleep. Every airplane for a long time to come will be designed around two pilots, and I think we'll see increased automation where it makes economic sense and provides some safety benefits. The appearance won't change all that much; however, the instrumentation will likely become lighter weight and less costly.

LK: Can you overautomate an airplane?

HAYHURST: The real goal is to use automation wisely. We use the concept called "human-centered automation," which means employing automation to assist the pilot in functions for which humans are not particularly well-suited, such as long-term monitoring tasks.

LK: But will we have the technology to make this plane do what we want it to do and the pilot will have nothing to do if we put it in place?

HAYHURST: We are not smart enough to predict all of the events an airplane may experience during its service life. We know, however, that human pilots are remarkably adaptable and have the unique ability to analyze and solve problems in real time.

LK: I understand, but will we have the technology where we could actually do that?

HAYHURST: It's probable, not highly probable but probable. Much of the technology exists and is being used today. Our autopilots, systems monitoring, and crew alerting systems make it possible now for an airplane to be programmed on the ground at the departure airport and, except for taxi and takeoff, fly automatically to another airport thousands of miles away and land safely in almost any weather without pilot intervention.

LK: Is weather going to be a factor in the future?

HAYHURST: I think we'll see improvement in detection equipment on board as well as on the ground and a better prediction capability. Nobody's going to be able to eliminate wind shear, which has contributed to several accidents in the past on landing. But we will have equipment which enables us to better pinpoint where these wind shears occur and when they are going to occur so the crews can either fly around them or be better prepared to deal with them rather than be surprised. And the effects of low ceilings and low visibility may be reduced by new technologies like synthetic vision, which enables the pilot to "see" a real world image through the weather.

LK: Airlines and airports will still take weather delays. In other words, La Guardia will not be a fun place to be in December?

HAYHURST: It's never a fun place to be in December. Some say in July, as well. But I think there will be navigational equipment which may enable tighter spacing of takeoffs and landings and by doing so could reduce the amount of the delay between consecutive takeoffs and consecutive landings.

LK: Will aircraft still have to be de-iced?

HAYHURST: We don't have an efficient way to prevent ice buildup today to the degree anybody would be comfortable with it. There is anti-icing equipment on the wing and around each engine but it's difficult to justify designing equipment to accommodate the overnight buildup of snow when an airplane is parked at night and sits until a seven A.M. departure the next day. But we will see more in the future of stationary devices under which the airplane taxis while being sprayed with de-icing fluid. And new technologies are being studied that may make de-icing a less expensive and less disruptive task in the future.

LK: Here's the big question about the future. We still going to have overhead luggage racks?

HAYHURST: (Laughs.) Yep.

LK: What's it going to be like loading passengers on a plane that seats eight hundred people when everyone stops in front of an overhead luggage rack?

HAYHURST: The ideal way is to have a way to guarantee the return of a passenger's luggage at the destination at no risk of loss. A lot of that is driven by what is outside the airplane rather than what is inside the airplane, the infrastructure at airports.

LK: It sounds like you're saying you want no carry-on luggage at all.

HAYHURST: You are never going to eliminate carry-on luggage, simply because it will be a long time before every passenger can reasonably expect to experience being able to receive his or her bags within fifteen minutes after landing where nothing ever gets lost or damaged. I also think that business people in particular are going to want to carry something on the airplane because a lot of businessmen want to work and they're not going to go on with nothing in their hand. We've seen some designs in Russia already where they enter the airplane through the lower deck, leave a bag in a fixed rack, and then pick it up as they walk off the airplane. It's not an efficient use of space and there's always the risk of someone walking off with the wrong bag.

LK: So overhead luggage racks remain. Space for bags under the seat remains?

HAYHURST: Overhead luggage remains. Space under the seat will remain. It's interesting though, there's a much higher propensity among U.S. passengers to carry on luggage than there is elsewhere. And there's also a much higher propensity among U.S. passengers to use the space under the seat in front of them rather than rely solely on the overhead bin space.

LK: Tell me about food service. Will gourmet meals be served, or are we moving away from that?

HAYHURST: It's a function, somewhat, of flight length. Certainly there is a possibility of handing you the food in the box as you walk onto the airplane. It's not served on the airplane, only liquids are served. That's an economic decision. We've already seen a reduction in the amount of food on airplanes in the U.S. today. Long-haul flights will still serve hot meals with a selection and not too much different from today for a long time to come. There's another cultural issue: If you fly from Chicago to Detroit, which is a forty-five-minute flight, at most, somebody will serve you a drink. And if you happen to fly at seven-thirty in the morning you might get a muffin. Now, if you fly from London to Paris, which is the same flight time, you will get a full meal. The flight length is the same but the passenger expectation in different parts of the world varies. It's possible a restaurant chain will cater food on board. It's all a matter of what airlines think will enable them to capture profitably a larger share of the air travel market.

LK: Will each seat on an aircraft have its own entertainment system?

HAYHURST: Video on demand is coming soon. Under five years. The people who design the interiors of our airplanes sometimes refer to seats as upholstered electronics boxes. We're going to see more functionality in terms of entertainment, in communications, in business services. It could be video on demand and a choice of twenty or thirty or forty or fifty of them rather than just one or two. Certainly integrated telephones, maybe games, in some parts of the world maybe gambling, maybe built-in PC capability so you don't have to lug a laptop on board, you just carry a disk and all of that is going to be coupled with less weight and less cost.

LK: What other kind of bells and whistles will we see when we sit in the seat of the future?

HAYHURST: We're going to see much lower-cost communication particularly in first and business class seats than we have today, like satellite telephones, faxes from airplanes, and so on. But it's a two-edged sword. Some businessmen like the idea they're going to get on an airplane knowing they are not going to be disturbed for ten hours. Others want to work every waking moment.

THOMAS DOWNS

PRESIDENT, GENERAL MANAGER,

AND CHIEF EXECUTIVE OFFICER, AMTRAK

I think the opening of high-speed rail service in the Northeast has as much potential to stir the imagination of the American public as the Diorama did in the 1939 World's Fair, which celebrated the automobile.

LK: What will riding on a train be like in the next century?

DOWNS: It's probably going to look a lot like the service already looks in Germany and France and Italy and Spain and Japan. It looks like a primary source of intermediate-distance transportation. Those countries have already made the investment we've been trying to struggle with for two generations. For instance, in France nobody thinks about flying intermediate distances of two hundred to three hundred miles. Instead they get on the TGV. And you also don't think about driving that kind of distance because you can be on a two-hundred-mile-an-hour train. You can be there a lot faster and be there in the heart of the downtown. I think significant highway capacity additions have ended in the United States. We went through a period in the sixties and seventies where the Interstate program was opening hundreds of miles a month. We're not opening hundreds of miles a year now. Highway capacity additions are so expensive that even places like California with huge financial resources can't afford them. A two-lane expansion (that's one lane each direction) of I–5 and the cost was going to be $130 million for every mile. Congestion is locked into our future for another decade on the highways because we're not building any right now and we keep adding more to the fleet and more miles of traffic. In the air, we just opened the last airport you and I will see in our lifetime in Denver. It was twenty-five years between the opening of Dallas–Fort Worth and the opening of Denver, and I think with Denver's experience of cost overruns and technology and what it's doing to flight cost in and out of Denver, that's probably the last major airport you're going to see built in the United States. Congestion isn't caused by running out of space in the skies, it's caused by running out of space on the ground for airports and runways and terminal capacity that is going to limit aviation.

LK: Do you think, though, that Americans are going to be willing to give up the independence of a car and be willing to get on a train?

DOWNS: We are spending $700 million to electrify and rebuild the line from Boston to New York to get the speeds from South Station in Boston to Penn Station in New York under three hours. The analysis is showing me, after we do this and put high-speed train sets on board there and after the debt service and every other expense, we can probably make $150 million a year in net profit. Can I make an argument there's a marketplace for this between Detroit and Chicago, or Milwaukee and Chicago, or St. Louis and Chicago? You bet I can. Can I make an argument there's only one viable way to have transportation growth happen in southern California between San Diego and Los Angeles, and that is high-speed rail? You bet I can. If you drive on I–5 right now, it's a parking lot either direction at rush hour. Everything is at a complete halt. It's too short to fly, and if you're flying from San Diego, well, you're still at LAX, and that's not where you want to go. If that is the case, then we can put a 125-mile-an-hour train service in place there and that trip becomes downtown to downtown, and that's a viable alternative for a business commute or weekend recreation. Portland to Seattle? Same thing. Expansions at Sea-Tac and Portland airports are enormously expensive.

LK: Are you saying we'll get on the train because flying and driving are so bad and not because trains are that wonderful?

DOWNS: Every time I'm in Europe on a train I'm struck by this: Look at Spain's Ave system, which runs eighteen high-speed train sets, which is the amount we've ordered for the United States. The service is incredible! You are on board and there's hardly a sound, it has great suspension, and you can set a glass of Coke on the table and it never moves. People remember old-style rickety cars that go *clackity-clack* and moan and groan. That's not new rail service. It's going to be like a cross between a luxury jet and a cruise ship in terms of a travel experience. You are on the ground. You're doing 150 miles an hour, you're stopping at major downtown areas such as Thirtieth Street in Philadelphia, midtown Manhattan, downtown Baltimore, and downtown Washington. You can't do that with an airplane, and you can't do that with a car. The car and the airplane have run their respective courses in terms of capacity and even their ability to treat people as human beings. Europe and Asia have made a different set of decisions for economic and mobility reasons than we did and it seems to work for them. It can work here.

LK: Tell me what these trains will be like.

DOWNS: The stuff we're ordering now are sets of equipment with six cars and locomotives on either end, 16,000 horsepower, electric, and they'll run at 150 miles per hour. We have the technology to run in either diesel or electric drive mode, and when you think about corridors like Chicago-St. Louis-Kansas City, it's possible to run passenger service at 125 miles per hour with traditional powered service that isn't electrified.

LK: You say there will be no more federal subsidy of Amtrak by the year 2002. In fact, you have that date on your office door. That going to happen?

DOWNS: Well, that's based on having a dedicated funding source to get us caught up on our capital. For a number of years, Congress decided not to kill us off but to starve us off the great road of capital. In 1986 our capital appropriation was $2 million, and that's about enough to fix broken windows around the system. One idea is to dedicate a half-percent of the existing federal gas tax to an Amtrak capital trust fund. That would rebuild stations and the repair yards and the equipment we need. But we also need an authorization bill which sets limits on our liability with other railroads and allows us other operating efficiencies which we don't have yet.

LK: Has Congress been a friend to Amtrak?

DOWNS: Congress has a tough affection for Amtrak. They've been hard on us by accident and by design. But they know a lot of people throughout the country are friends of rail passenger service. Unfortunately, once you have some initial successes, when they see we've reduced operating expenses by $130 million they say, "Well, we'll act like you reduced it by $200 million and give you a new target to shoot for." It's like the Olympic high jump: You jump until you fail.

LK: What do you say to future members of Congress about the passenger railroad?

DOWNS: It's important, that's what I say to them. I can't imagine another generation of Americans coming along and understanding why our generation threw it away. No other industrialized country has done that. They keep their railroads capitalized for hard economic reasons and not for nostalgia. We have an aviation trust fund and a maritime trust fund. We think rail passenger system has the potential to be the only mode for growth right now.

LK: To have government out of the railroad business, you need what?

DOWNS: I need government out of the highway business and the aviation business and the transit business, and get the playing field level. Or give me a railroad capital trust fund.

LK: Will a fare from Washington to Miami on the train be the same as flying?

DOWNS: Depends on the class of service. Between Minot and Devil's Lake, North Dakota, or Devil's Lake and Minneapolis, where there's not a lot of air service and the only other thing you could do is drive and the highways close up in the wintertime, well, that's an essential service for those folks and we provide that at a fare that's lower than the airlines on a coach side because we get great volumes.

LK: Almost all passenger rail lines in America and in every other country don't make money.

DOWNS: There's not a passenger railroad in any country in the world and in the history of the world that has made money.

LK: Then how can you say to me we're going to exist without government help?

DOWNS: In the past, two things have carried passenger rail service. Luxury accommodations like you used to see on the Broadway Limited was very upscale and very expensive. Trends show Americans are staying home more and not going overseas and have a willingness to pay for first class service on trains. The other is mail. We do $65 million a year in mail. We're going to double that in the next two years. Those two growth elements are what's going to help us defray a subsidy of the coach end of the run between Minot and Minneapolis for the elderly or the young or the handicapped or those who can't fly, or for folks who can't use the highway year-round.

LK: Will Amtrak retire its old stock? Your engines average twenty years old and the cars are something like fifteen years old.

DOWNS: Well, some of those cars will become baggage cars and mail cars. We have ordered $700 million worth of high-speed train sets and facilities, and we borrowed the money to do it. That's not a federal investment, that's the private sector marketplace, which by 1999 will yield high-speed rail service between Boston and Washington, D.C. That will retire almost all of the Metroliner equipment in the northeast corridor. We're still taking delivery on two hundred of the Superliner IIs, the bilevel cars we use out West. And we have just ordered one hundred new AMD–103 locomotives from General Electric with 4,200 horsepower that gets us 15 percent less fuel consumption. So we'll have new equipment but we won't have the stations or repair facilities and major overhaul facilities rebuilt. We borrowed about $2 billion to do this and have working capital to invest in the railroad. Now we have to make it because we have a lot of debt service to make in the next fifteen to twenty years.

LK: Tell me about the future cars.

DOWNS: There will be on-line live wire service, you'll get the New York Stock Exchange, you'll have terminals for your computer where you can plug in and not use batteries, there will be onboard fax-modem capability for computer workstations, and there will be video. It'll be beyond anything the French have in place.

LK: What will the train station of the future look like?

DOWNS: Hopefully, like Union Station in Washington, D.C.

LK: Does that mean train stations will be old train stations?

DOWNS: Train riders expect not just a grand station but retail space as well. They want to shop and eat and see a movie. That's what you'll see all over the country. Grand Central in New York will become a giant retail and passenger concourse. We want to rebuild the Farleigh

Building in New York and make it look like this. Los Angeles is finally struggling the right way with a gorgeous old train station to turn that into both retail and office and train station complex. Cities like Meridian, Mississippi, are spending $6 million to rebuild their station and have inner-mobile facilities for bus service and taxicab and an airport jitney. They get a revitalization of the downtown when this is done. There are three important things in real estate: location, location, and location. There are three things that create location: transportation, transportation, and transportation. If you have the best site in the world but people can't get to it, well, it's not the best site in the world. Amtrak goes straight downtown. Memphis, which was once one of the worst train stations in the country, is now, between the city and the state, investing $19 million for complete reconstruction of the station, office complex, retail, and parking. I think train stations will be the visible flagships of the renaissance of rail passenger service in America. Maybe it's nostalgia in the minds of the riders but they're writing real checks and they're riding real trains. A downtown gets a real activity center. Union Station is the most visited facility in Washington.

LK: What cities should pay attention to what you've just said?

DOWNS: I want to encourage Chicago, St. Louis—which has one of those gorgeous HH Richardson monuments and right now Amtrak is in a trailer two blocks away from the train station—and Kansas City too. Every city that has rail passenger service could do what Meridian, Mississippi, and Anniston, Alabama, are doing with their train stations. I'm not talking about a hokey thing like closing the downtown streets and bringing in new street furniture. Let's bring people downtown. My real challenge is Albuquerque, New Mexico. We stop the Southwest Chief there twice a day, thousands of people get on and off and see the town. Four years ago the station burned to the ground, and all that's left is a slab of concrete. You get off and there's broken glass and vendors with card tables selling crafts to passengers. All the customer sees is a parking lot. I'd love to see the mayor and the governor make an investment there. I can't imagine being responsible for a city and spending hundreds of millions of dollars on an airport with an inability to spend $3 million or $4 million right in the downtown.

LK: Is it your sense Albuquerque will do anything?

DOWNS: Well, it's always the times are hard and they don't have enough money and they'll think about it and things are getting along. Olympia, Washington, held bake sales and car washes and raffles until they raised money for a new station. Volunteers now do the landscaping and carry the bags because they care about the future of their town. California has spent huge amounts of money to rebuild every single railway passenger station. That's twenty-six railway stations. There's no single regret. California ran out of road capacity and air capacity faster than anywhere else. California usually gets there first. They're already there in rail passenger service, and this is the land of the Lotus and the automobile and they're spending a billion and a half dollars because they know rail service is their future.

LK: You from California?

DOWNS: No, Kansas.

LK: What scares you about the coming century?

DOWNS: That we never deal with anything in America until it turns into an overwhelming crisis. Having spent a number of years as the guy in charge of policy and planning at the Federal Highway Administration, I could easily see how road capacity could never keep up with the insatiable demand for driving. Once we built the infrastructure and the urban sprawl and the suburbs into the system, the growth of the automobile was inevitable. People think nothing of driving thirty miles one way to go to work each day. That's a formula for national gridlock. Everything has its limits, and this century we haven't acknowledged the limits on the automobile. We always think there's another road just over the horizon. There can't be.

LK: Are children in the next century going to be playing with a model train set?

DOWNS: The Amtrak American Flyer. That's one of the things that went with this new design. The licensing went to Lionel to make these trains.

LK: Will it go faster around the track?

DOWNS: Yeah, and it'll tilt around the curves.

NEIL RESSLER

VICE PRESIDENT, ADVANCED VEHICLE TECHNOLOGY,
FORD MOTOR COMPANY

*I tell my little kid, you will be living a life of continuous learning
and you can't ever get to the point where you think you know
everything you need to know.*

LK: As we speak, there are luxury cars, mid-size cars, economy
cars, sport utility vehicles, small trucks, and vans. Can we expect those
categories to change?

RESSLER: There will be fewer "platforms," as we say, but more
variations on the platforms. We will have vehicles that look different
but share a great many common parts (Ford's Fiesta, KA, and Puma all
share the same "platform," for example). We will have generic group-
ings and certainly luxury cars will be one, mid-size family transportation will be another, economy cars will be there. The area of sport utility vehicles and trucks is not as clear to me. It's hard to predict. They
may in the long run be replaced by some other "something" that
nobody's thought of yet.

LK: You haven't thought of yet?

RESSLER: No. The future is a pretty risky business.

LK: What will dashboards of the future look like?

RESSLER: There'll be a tendency toward more of the visual driver
interfaces: screens and electronic message centers and stuff like that.
We'll see more integrated controls where you don't have a box for the
heater and a box for the air-conditioning and another box for the radio.
It'll tend to be more of a flowing functional look.

LK: Visual driver interface?

RESSLER: Yeah, like route guidance. Turn left. Go a mile. Turn
right. And instead of having screens for the radio and the clock and
the temperature you'll have one screen which tells you whichever
function you're interrogating. Potentially, you'll see different ways to
describe matters that might concern you, like the proximity of a car
in front of you. If you have an obstacle detection device, maybe

something audible also, that tells you you're about to back into somebody.

LK: So when Ressler backs out of a parking place, he doesn't smack something behind him.

RESSLER: Right. The most obvious one is route guidance.

LK: Nobody's going to get lost, then?

RESSLER: Nobody should. The city street networks aren't digitized yet, meaning there isn't a computer map of the city, but that's going to change in the future.

LK: We'll no longer have a paper road map?

RESSLER: We'll have that too. But the computer in the vehicle will have a road map of the streets in the city. Route guidance depends on two things: knowing where you are and knowing the road system you're trying to move around on. Knowing where you are utilizes the global positioning satellites, which are in stationary orbit over the Earth. If you want to go someplace you need to understand what the network of roads is. You have a digitized map of the city, and in the computer memory is where all the roads are: which are one-way, which are two-way, and so on. It sounds like space age stuff but it actually works.

LK: Until the city changes the one-way street the other way.

RESSLER: You have to have a mechanism for updating it. As soon as you turn and the computer senses you have not followed its instructions it immediately calculates an alternative route.

LK: Does this suggest we won't have blind spots?

RESSLER: The same kind of technology will be used. You will be able to sense presence where you don't have direct vision. We work very hard to reduce the way the roof structure blocks your view, but there are strength requirements too. The roof has to withstand certain loads.

LK: What else will we find on the dashboard?

RESSLER: More room. There will be more leg room, more knee room in the future. Instrument panels will be more of a flowing theme that comes up one side of the car across the front and back down the other side. It'll be more smoothly integrated with the rest of the vehicle.

LK: Will we still have seat belts?

RESSLER: We will. We'll learn more about how to do air bags so they provide protection without the unfortunate side effects that rarely but sometimes occur. The population will be more safety conscious than it is today. In Michigan we've doubled the percentage of seat belt use over a ten-year period. You can also start to imagine things like smart cruise control, where you go down the road and upon approaching a car ahead of you the control will slow the car down and, if necessary, apply the brakes. It will provide automatic traffic pacing and will be available within the next few years. That will lessen rear-end collisions.

LK: Will cars be larger or smaller?

RESSLER: There are two things happening: There's pressure for reduced external size, these large wide vehicles with overhang—you know, parts of the car that are ahead of the front wheels or behind the rear wheels—are becoming slowly less and less acceptable. So they won't be as big on the outside. But people are expecting more room on the inside. So we're in a conundrum here. I think part of that could move us in a direction of having higher cars because people like to have proper headroom and good visibility, particularly older folks.

LK: Are we still going to have four-cylinder engine cars?

RESSLER: Yes, I think so. The internal combustion engine in increasingly sophisticated forms will be with us for a long time. It's a very efficient power plant. There have been a large number of alternative power solutions that have come up: the rotary engine, turbine engine, the Scotch yoke engine. Those have all kind of fallen by the wayside, and you're left with this reciprocating four-cycle internal combustion engine, which is lighter, less friction, and cleaner. That kind of engine utilizing some kind of liquid fuel, natural gas, methanol, ethanol, liquefied petroleum gas, but the bulk of the engines in the beginning of the next century certainly will be internal combustion. The smaller cylinder will occupy a growing fraction of the total.

LK: And this is because the cars will be smaller?

RESSLER: And lighter too. It'll be driven by environmental concerns and concerns about fuel economy.

LK: Let's talk about the electric car. Do you foresee a time when we'll walk into a Ford showroom and say, "Give me a Lincoln that's electric"?

RESSLER: I doubt it for a Lincoln. But there will be a time when there'll be a market-driven offering of electric vehicles in Ford showrooms. Its time isn't now but its time is coming. You won't see tens of millions of them, but I think you'll see a lot of them. Congested urban areas are where they'll make their real gain.

LK: When?

RESSLER: We're ten years away. But the thing you're trying to predict is the rate of development of next-generation battery technology. I can imagine a time when we'll have batteries that are available in reasonable quantity at acceptable prices, such that you could have an urban commuter vehicle with a range of 100 to 125 miles.

LK: This sounds like the electric car will always be in the city and won't be found on the Interstate?

RESSLER: I think that's correct. In order to have a battery that would store that much energy to drive an electric vehicle four hundred to five hundred miles, you'd have to have a truck with a trailer full of batteries behind it.

LK: For just a moment, forget the problems you have designing cars right now and tell me what a car fifty years from now might look like.

RESSLER: In a world like we live in, five years is a long reach. I'd say we will continue to use personal transportation because the country is too big and too spread out to rely entirely on mass transit. Cars will be smaller than they are today and will have some different form of motivation. I'd be surprised if fifty years from now we were running on gasoline or, for that matter, any type of carbon-based fuel. By that time we'll have fuel cells or super batteries or, if we learn how to store it, hydrogen.

LK: Let's talk about roads. Will the speed limit increase?

RESSLER: If it does it won't be by much. We're slowly recovering back to the pre–Jimmy Carter fifty-five upper limit. Montana has no speed limit, and that will continue to be the exception. I suppose it could go to seventy-five but you'll never see these unlimited speeds as have been used in Europe. As a matter of fact they're imposing speed limits now.

LK: Will roads ever become automatic, as I read about in science fiction?

RESSLER: The technology is challenging but the infrastructure makes it a daunting task. You're starting with a country that's letting its roads deteriorate and then imagine you're going to install a new or significantly modified highway system that has internal guidance and tracking control capability. The infrastructure is necessary to make those things work. We won't see any widespread use anytime soon.

LK: Will we become serious about rebuilding the highway system?

RESSLER: We have to. Our roads are worse than those in many places you go in the world. There will be a gradual awakening because it's becoming intolerable. I even question whether our road repair procedures are as good as they used to be. In years past, road crews would clean out a hole, put the patching material in it, and then roll it. Today they throw shovels of blacktop in a hole that has water in it, make sure the blacktop makes a mound, and then let the cars smash it down.

LK: How much longer can this be ignored?

RESSLER: We're beginning to see politicians make the speeches about the deteriorating conditions. We'll go through a brief period trying to figure out who's at fault, and we'll never figure it out. We are starting to talk about increased taxes allocated specifically for road repair, and that's the beginning. In this country the first step to correcting a problem is for there to be a widespread awareness of it, and I see it growing. I think we'll start to see action in less than ten years. Bridges are going to be built with carbon-reinforced deposits as is used in race cars and it has a longer life than steel.

LK: Will we have flat tires in the future?

RESSLER: Less so. The spare tire is almost redundant. Tire companies are producing "run flat" tires, which means you can drive fifty miles on a tire with no air. It's held up by the stiff sidewalls. Any vehicle with a "run flat" tire has a sensor in the tire which alerts the driver if the pressure falls below some threshold level like ten psi or something like that.

LK: How do you see the auto-buying public changing?

RESSLER: That is the $64 question! If you knew what people being born today are going to want to buy in twenty years, you'd have the ticket to the future. Having said that, I think affordability is a matter of growing concern. Shoppers are growing increasingly sophisticated, and it isn't only in the developed countries where I'd say that. Modern communication has brought the lifestyle in the developed countries to the people in the emerging markets, and they're going to be more and more insistent on having everything they see elsewhere in the world.

LK: So do you expect the steering wheel to be moved to the left side in England and Japan and the Asian markets?

RESSLER: No. We as a producer need to make it efficient to do a vehicle that can be adapted to left- or right-hand driving and we're doing that. At the Tokyo Motor Show we had five different products you could buy in Europe and America, with right-hand versions for the Tokyo show. Our job is not to change the world; our job is to adapt our products.

LK: Tell me about security in vehicles.

RESSLER: It's technically possible to have a locator on every vehicle going into some central station so that if your car were stolen you could activate something on your key fob and have a signal broadcast. That requires a lot of infrastructure, but if thievery continues to be as critical a problem as it currently is and if our electronic antitheft systems don't bring it to a much-reduced level, it could come. The wild card is these electronic antitheft devices are extremely effective, and we see a precipitous drop in the theft of all of our products. Those things really do work, and as more and more of our fleet of vehicles have these antitheft devices, it's going to be tougher and tougher to steal cars. In fact, that's why this business of hijacking cars with people in them has grown, because it's too hard to steal one after the person has locked up and left.

LK: Do you foresee cars having a chip or something in them so they can't be started if the car senses alcohol on the driver?

RESSLER: It's technically feasible to do. Same electronics as before. I don't know how much demand there is for it but you could do it.

LK: I was just wondering if it could become a standard part of the car.

RESSLER: They start out as an option. This is the pattern started with antilock brakes, air bags, and so on. Some features start out like that and then wither away. Other features start out the same way and grow rapidly to the point where it's a necessity to have them either widely available or standard on the car just to sell the car. Where this would fall between those two bookends I don't know.

LK: Will we have keyless cars?

RESSLER: We've designed systems that use something like a credit card but there doesn't seem to be a big demand for it. People seem willing to use keys. We already have remote keyless entry where you push a button and the car unlocks. We are also building systems which will keep a car from being hot-wired and stolen because the car won't start without the ignition key, and that's a functional addition of having a key. We could get rid of the key today if that's what people wanted.

LK: Do you expect the trend that began with Saturn, where this is the price, we're not going to dicker around with you on it, you pay it or you don't buy the car—do you see that continuing?

RESSLER: Our feedback is more people dislike this bartering than like it. Maybe it's our country. There are other cultures in the world where that is an accepted way of doing business. Doesn't seem to be here, so my personal guess is we'll evolve in a direction of this is the price and here's what you get and we'll move away from the dickering and bartering that typified purchases in the past.

LK: What do you say to the young people whose parents run the service station in town and they're interested in taking over the business? Will there still be a market for the local repair shop with new cars?

RESSLER: There's a role, but the appearance and migration of sophisticated microelectronics has made that task a lot tougher than it used to be. We have lots of microprocessor-controlled functions within a car. We have multiplexing, which is a very different way of communicating signals around the vehicle rather than the old way of connecting a wire between every device, and those are all tough to diagnose. You have to have the right equipment, and you need people who are very knowledgeable. It truly is a technician as opposed to a mechanic.

LK: Is what you're saying is that in another ten years nobody can change the oil in his Ford that's sitting out in the driveway?

RESSLER: That's the part you will be able to do. What's tougher to do is diagnose an electronic problem. But there are two answers to that: One is the neighborhood garage goes out of business, and the other one is the neighborhood garage figures out how to do it.

LK: Which one will happen?

RESSLER: The latter. People are pretty resourceful when it comes to staying in business, and I think over time what we'll find is the neighborhood repair shop will become increasingly able to carry out work that today is a pretty tough job for them.

DAN GOLDIN

ADMINISTRATOR,

NATIONAL AERONAUTICS AND SPACE ADMINISTRATION

This is a time of change, and during change come dislocation and disruption, but there's unbelievable opportunity, and I hope people look forward with optimism and say, "We're going to make it through this tough time of transition to the twenty-first century." Don't hold on to the past with an iron grasp and not allow us to go forward.

LK: Where are we going in the next century?

GOLDIN: We are going to extend human presence into space beyond earth orbit on a sustained basis. The flight of Shannon Lucid onto the Mir space station in 1996 signals a permanent presence by the United States in outer space. As we get into the twenty-first century it's going to be back to the moon, to Mars, maybe Europa (a moon of Jupiter), and I foresee in the twenty-first century our having a research station on an asteroid which could be like the research station we now have on the South Pole in Antarctica. These would be the initial penetrations by humans out of Earth orbit. This is the final frontier, as they say on *Star Trek*.

LK: What are we going to research? Are we looking at the Earth or are we looking the other direction past Pluto?

GOLDIN: A number of things. There are two types of benefits. One is a scientific one with fundamental knowledge necessary to improve the life of people here on Earth, and potentially the life of people off planet Earth, out of the solar system, or is life unique to planet Earth? The other is commercial. Are there resources which will allow the sustained presence of human beings on another planetary body? Are there resources on those bodies which could sustain an economy? And we have to make sure the cost of doing it is less than the benefit.

LK: Do you see people in the next century booking a weekend to go to the moon?

GOLDIN: How soon in the next century? Planes were invented at the turn of the last century and were used for a variety of oddball things for a while, and then we started using them for war and then people started using them on a commercial basis, but they had to be very affluent to do it. It wasn't until the sixties that everyone could use it. We take air transportation for granted. In the next five to ten years I see flights of humans into space that are not run by government entities. So as we go into the twenty-first century there's going to be a transition from government operations into space to private operations. But yeah, it'll start for the very affluent, but as time marches on and we get better and better vehicles, maybe some time later in the twenty-first century is a possibility.

LK: So there could be United Airlines going to the moon and American Airlines going to the moon?

GOLDIN: Yeah. It will not be the government doing it. As I speak, we're handing over the shuttle to the United Space Alliance, a new company, and we're doing that intentionally because if you get up in the space frontier you can't get the government in it. We're building the X–33 and the X–34 working in cooperation with companies, hoping they will make it commercial. Indeed, at some point in the twenty-first century somebody may go up to an orbiting station that is a hotel.

LK: NASA will be the umbrella organization over all of this?

GOLDIN: NASA will be very different. I foresee a few decades from now, instead of our budget being 60–70 percent dedicated to Earth orbit, the NASA budget being weighted to being further away from Earth. There will be the Federal Aviation Administration and there will be the Federal Space Administration.

LK: There won't be a NASA?

GOLDIN: There will be a NASA but NASA will not be focused on Earth orbit. NASA will be focused on deeper space activities.

LK: Let's talk about deeper space activities. When do we go to Mars?

GOLDIN: I believe first of all we'll go back to the moon. We need to know if there's water there, and we think in some of the craters on the south pole of the moon there might be water, so we're going to see if there are resources on the moon. If there are, then we'll be back. If there aren't, then we won't. It's open. We have to have four things before we can have sustained presence in space: (1) We have to figure out how people can live and work efficiently and safely in space. (2) We have to get the cost of transportation to space down by a factor of ten to one hundred and we're doing that now. (3) We have to figure out how to cut the cost of operations in space by a factor of thirty. And (4), we have to establish if there are ways of living off the land. Go back to the explorers of four hundred years ago. The ones that tried to take everything with them died. But those explorations that took tools to live off the land survived. So we have to use robot spacecraft to find out where there are possibilities for sustained presence, because then you can do it for low cost. For instance, we think there is subsurface water on Mars. If you can find the water you can break it down into hydrogen and oxygen. We can breathe the oxygen and we can burn the hydrogen. This is the problem: We don't want a feel-good mission. We want a sustained presence. I think we can solve these problems in the next ten to fifteen years and after that, we can be off to anyplace we want to go.

LK: Explain this to me. If we go to Mars, what are we going to do? Put more people there?

GOLDIN: Everyone has questions. "I want to know for certain, Mr. Goldin, what's out there?" It is human nature to explore. I don't know what we are going to find, but if we can find a potential for scientific payoff and economic payoff and if the potential of that payoff is greater than the cost, we go.

LK: We will go to Mars but we won't go to Venus, correct?

GOLDIN: I'd say the probability of going to Venus is very low. We might go to Europa, a moon of Jupiter. The Voyager spacecraft passed by and found it was almost a perfect sphere. It looked like the highest spot on Europa was about one hundred meters. Not high. There appear to be some cracks in the surface, and some think they contain liquid water or frozen water, ice. So what I'm saying is everyone focuses on Mars, but we need to focus on places that might be in the life zone. Now it is a fundamental aspect of life to answer this question: You go to the beach, you look up and ask, "Where did I come from?" This is an aspect of life that is very important. I don't know. Maybe life is unique to Earth and there's no other life anywhere else in the solar system. Or the universe. So scientific intellectual knowledge is one reason as long as it doesn't cost too much, but also the possibility of new resources.

LK: What do you think?

GOLDIN: I learned in life that I don't know what I don't know, and I know when you go to the frontier, you learn. I will not speculate.

LK: Would you like there to be something outside of what we have here?

GOLDIN: I'd like to believe that life is not unique to Earth. There hasn't been any evidence yet that says life is unique to Earth.

LK: Let's talk about the international space station. That's going to be completed in 2002. There will always be people on board?

GOLDIN: Yes.

LK: There have been troubles on board Mir, the Russian space station. Are you worried this could cause a delay or a rethinking of the plans?

GOLDIN: It is going to be a point of concern but we have worked our way through the latest issues, and right now the Russian factories are full of equipment and every indication is they are going to be there on time.

LK: The international space station will be composed of whom?

GOLDIN: Including the United States, fourteen countries to start: ten from Europe, Canada, Japan, and Russia.

LK: Does the success of space exploration in the future depend on international cooperation and participation?

GOLDIN: No, it is enhanced by international cooperation but it doesn't depend on it. America is a bold country and we're going to open the space frontier. We'd love to do it with other countries but we're going to do it.

LK: It is not contingent on other countries?

GOLDIN: No, but it is desirable to have other countries. The United States will provide worldwide leadership. We will be the catalyst to bring countries together to open the space frontier.

LK: Do you see the space station being a kind of UN in the air, a means by which disputes can be solved between countries because they are together on a mission in space?

GOLDIN: We're not there yet. The Berlin Wall, when it came down, was symbolic of the end of the Cold War. When Winston Churchill described the Iron Curtain, well, that was the signal of the start of the Cold War. So we have these bookends. We're going into a period of rapid change, and it's making people's heads spin. We're going from a bipolar world to a multipolar world. We used to have the East and the West blocs and now it's kind of fuzzy. We're going from a manufacturing age to an information age. We're going from domestic economies to a global marketplace. We're going from a time when companies and countries could have products which lasted decades, and now within six months, you can lose a product.

While all this turmoil is going on, the population will double in just two generations, and I'm hoping if we can stay on a track where we are dominated by economics and opportunities and growth instead of war, and if we successfully build this international space station, that's going to signal the start of the new era. It is very symbolic. Think about this: Russia and the United States spent fifty years aiming nuclear missiles across the oceans at each other. When I was in industry, I was responsible for the system engineering on the land-based ballistic missiles and had a couple thousand people in my organization. All of a sudden, in a period of months, we went from that condition to the United States and Russia building the international space station along with other countries. We showed that for fifty years we knew how to use science and technology to build weapons of mass destruction that threatened humanity, and the symbolism here is unbelievable. Now we're working together in space to do work on bio-med, understanding combustion, working on robots, advanced materials. What a productive life! I would say if we go down this path this will be a real litmus test that the world is taking a new direction.

LK: Will there be more than one space station in the future?

GOLDIN: The space stations beyond the first one will be commercial. To open the space frontier you want to start bringing in industry.

LK: Will there be different kinds of shuttles in the future?

GOLDIN: Let me correct you. There is the shuttle and then there are different kinds of launch vehicles now under development. The shuttle has the solid rocket boosters, which take it 100,000 feet high and then they separate and have to come back. Then there's the external tank which uses up all the fuel and then burns up. So the shuttle is a two-stage vehicle. It's costly to maintain. Now the launch vehicles we're looking at take off and land without dropping anything. It's totally contained. Hopefully, these can cut the cost over the shuttle by a factor of ten.

LK: So the launch vehicles could take off from Washington National Airport and land there?

GOLDIN: Initially they'll take off from and land at remote areas, but ultimately we're going to try and figure out how they can take off over populated areas. You bet. The first launch vehicles have rocket engines, which means the engine takes all its fuel and oxidizes it. The next step is to scoop up air in the atmosphere with a launch vehicle so you get even more performance. The first launch vehicle will be flown in 1999 from the Mojave Desert and we'll land it in Montana. The adventure has begun. This is no longer science fiction. The second one will be launched in 2003, and around 2005 we'll go commercial with these things.

LK: Right now you need the tanks on the side of the rocket to get off the ground. By 2003 you're still going to need tanks?

GOLDIN: Oh yeah, but we'll carry fuel. We won't have to carry as much oxygen, and that makes the weight of the vehicle lower, and that means we can take more into space.

LK: And they will actually be on a runway and take off the way a 757 does?

GOLDIN: No, they'll take off vertically. But it is conceivable, as we get the reliability up, it could land at La Guardia. We're going to have to work with the Federal Aviation Administration and, as I said, we're now pushing the boundaries; we're actually talking to the FAA because they're going to have to license how rockets land. They may have to change their name. Here's another example: We went to the Russian Mir space station to pick up two Russian cosmonauts. The shuttle landed in the United States. We brought aliens back from space. Just handling passports, we had to work with the U.S. Immigration Service because it wasn't a standard port of entry. Now, we don't intend to pay for the production of these vehicles. We want private industry to do it. If they're successful, we hope they go to Wall Street, get investors, build it, and we'll just be a customer.

LK: Kennedy Space Center still going to be as prominent as it is now?

GOLDIN: Oh yes.

LK: Will there be more of them?

GOLDIN: The heavy lift cargo, the things going directly to space, will come out of Kennedy. But maybe at the end of the first decade of the twenty-first century, Federal Express or UPS will want to have a really fast package delivery service. You know, let's say I have to get a package from Washington, D.C., to Tokyo and it's very important, high-value stuff, well, there might be more.

LK: Will there be ads on the sides of rockets?

GOLDIN: You won't see ads on any NASA spacecraft, but when the vehicles become commercial, I think there is a probability you'll see ads then.

LK: Are we going to still have to worry about space junk?

GOLDIN: Yes. We haven't found a way of taking it out. We are working through the UN to put in design standards for spacecraft so we don't generate space junk.

LK: Do you see a time when there might be a galactic garbage truck of some kind?

GOLDIN: Before you get to that, we need to do some recycling here. Once we get the reusable launch vehicles, I see a day when they go up and bring back spacecraft that are no longer operating instead of leaving them up there. Now, we might just slow down the orbit of the space junk and let it burn up in the atmosphere. That could be done with an Earth-based laser that would slow down the orbit, but I don't know if it's going to work yet. If it does, we're ten years away from doing it that way.

LK: The United States has signed a document saying if we ever get to another planet, no one country can own it. Do you worry we could be challenged on that?

GOLDIN: There are some very serious issues that we have never been willing to think about. On one hand, we don't want to start intergalactic wars, and I think we want to utilize the space resources appropriately. On the other hand, there are going to be a number of commercial interests that are going to develop, and I think we need to understand the ramifications of that. A private company might do prospecting on Mars. Let's say they hit the mother lode. Well, who owns it? That is a potentially serious problem, although I think "opportunity" is a better word. So you can see in this example there will be some very serious aspects of space law. Each country has to do things in its own national interest first but then we have to consider we're in a world where we're going to have to work together. It can't be America only. I just think as the reality of operating on other planetary bodies becomes closer to reality, it's not just a question of national sovereignty. It's a question of public/private rights. Life is a balance of adjusting things.

LK: But it's private industry you're talking about.

GOLDIN: Yeah, and private industry is going to have some opportunity, but we have to understand the implications of what we're saying.

LK: What scares you about the twenty-first century?

GOLDIN: You're never going to get me to be scared. I see unbelievable opportunity if we deal with all these changes properly. I see an opportunity to begin to understand how life formed and evolved and to answer the basic questions of humankind. I see an opportunity for unbelievable productivity. I'm not worried. My only concern would be that we go back to our ways of the twentieth century where we didn't get to understand other cultures and we solved those problems with weapons. But the problem is those weapons are so deadly now that we could have an extinction of humankind. That's my only worry: that we go backward and not forward.

LK: When's the last time the shuttle flies?

GOLDIN: 2008. And the next generation will not say "NASA" on the side. It'll say "United Space Alliance" or "American Space Alliance." NASA wants to go to the next level of the frontier. We want to put a telescope into orbit and take it out half a billion miles from the sun and point it into space within one hundred light-years of Earth and search those stars for an Earth-like planet. And then we want to remotely sense that planet and see what gases are in its atmosphere, and then we want to take a picture of that planet with a resolution to see if there are oceans, continents, clouds, and mountain ranges. That's what NASA wants to do.

LK: That all?

GOLDIN: We want to develop spacecraft that travel at Mach 25 (25,000 miles an hour), which is escape velocity and required to get into orbit. We want to be able to predict weather within hours, weeks, and months, and be able to tell farmers five years in advance what crops they ought to be planting and if there's going to be drought or torrential downpours. We want to predict natural disasters. We want to look down on Earth and manage our natural resources. We want robots getting signals from space to plow the fields. We're going to look down from space in 384 colors to see what stresses are on the crops: too much water, too little water, so we can tell farmers how much water to put in their fields, if there's too much or too little fertilizer. We're developing a cyberglove so if an astronaut gets sick on the space station, we can put the cyberglove on and a physician on the ground can feel the texture and the moisture of the skin of the one who's sick. We're working on cyberspace simulation in three-dimension so the astronaut who's not sick on board could run a simulation on how to do an operation and with a command from the ground they could fix, say an appendix, in space.

LK: This is starting to sound like the job of the Divine.

GOLDIN: It's the human mind.

Expect to see within the next ten years:

1. If they exist we will find Earth-size planets around stars within one hundred light-years of Earth.

2. We will have a much better understanding of the possibilities for life on Mars and the capability for sustaining life.

3. We will know if there is a liquid ocean on Europa and if it contains life.

4. We will peer out to the very beginning of the universe.

5. The international space station will have been completed and we will have figured out how people can safely live and work in space, and the great adventure will begin of people leaving Earth orbit to go on to other planets.

Education

I decided this section should include the words of people who are on the front lines of teaching. So you are going to meet three individuals: one at the elementary school level, one at the university level, and one who believes privatization is the only answer for education.

You will note a majority of the advice being offered throughout these pages uses the word "learn," so it makes sense to look at how we teach today and how we might do it differently and with better results tomorrow. To this end I knew right away John Golle was going to be on my list of people to talk with. He has been making a lot of noise about public schools in the past ten years and is considered the foremost advocate in America for privatization of public schools. He is a person who, when challenged to step up to bat if he thought he could do better, did just that. Today he runs Education Alternatives, Inc., which is one of the largest privatized school groups in the country.

Because every educator will tell you the critical time for learning occurs in the early grade school years (the current view is if you don't have a child's attention by the third grade, that child is lost), I decided to sit down with someone who teaches elementary school teachers. After all, if a teacher can't teach, a student can't learn. I found this person in Dr. Larry Smith, chairman of the Department of Elementary Education at Ball State Teachers College in Muncie, Indiana.

Dr. Richard Levin, president of Yale University, works the opposite end from Dr. Smith and, consequently, the work of one eventually affects the work of the other. His predecessor, Benno Schmidt, left the university to work with Chris Whittle, another proponent of private-based education, in the Edison Project. And so it becomes all too obvious that we are interconnected and one's action someplace will show up later in another place. The most fiery debates I've ever moderated have not been NAFTA or abortion or the DH rule, but education. That's good. It shows we care, and I'm confident this will be the case in the years to come with these three lightning rods at work.

John Golle

CHAIRMAN AND CHIEF EXECUTIVE OFFICER,

EDUCATION ALTERNATIVES, INC.

You need the proper skills to make it over the bridge from the have-nots to the haves. You have to be able to read, compute, communicate verbally and in written form, and if that can be done, it will manifest itself in both the workplace and your personal life.

LK: How many school systems will be privatized in the future?

GOLLE: Looking into the twenty-first century we perceive the percentage will increase. What has happened in public schools is there's no competition to speak of, and as a result, legislators, policymakers, and school board members will be forced to turn to competition in order to improve the vast majority of the schools.

LK: And that competition will come from privatization?

GOLLE: Yes, I think so. However, the mix of public and privatized schools will never be a fifty–fifty mix. If just 10 percent of the 43 million students in K–12 attended a privatized alternative, that would probably be enough to change the rest of the system.

LK: So government is still going to be in the school business?

GOLLE: I don't believe the educational system will be totally privatized, but without privatization I don't believe government will be able to reform itself. We need a market-driven public education system with different offerings so the consumer has the ability to choose among different providers, all of whom will meet the minimum standards.

LK: This sounds like the wealthy children go to the privatized schools and the poor children go to the public schools.

GOLLE: That was the initial criticism of privatization, and the facts prove just the reverse to be true. If your son and daughter are going to a school and they are getting straight A's are you going to move them out of that school?

LK: No.

GOLLE: What if your child is failing? Dropping behind and hanging out with bad kids, and you have a free choice as to where the child could attend? Would you move him out?

LK: Absolutely.

GOLLE: And who do you think is showing up at all the charter schools? Parents can vote with their feet.

LK: So you see yourself as a lever to make the other guys better?

GOLLE: That's exactly what we are.

LK: How's education going to be paid for in the next century?

GOLLE: That's the most perplexing problem facing policymakers. The question is: "How are we going to get the economic buying power into the hands of the parents?" We might achieve this goal by means of vouchers, school choice, or some other alternatives, but legislators are going to have to give this power to the parents.

LK: Some would say if there's a privatized school in Town A and there's another privatized school in Town B and the same company runs both, then it's the same lessons. Valid?

GOLLE: It's a concern right now but it will go away. One of the issues this country has to deal with is that of academic standards. Right now there's little logic. Each state sets its own standard. This is completely inadequate. I'm talking to you from Minnesota. Fifty miles away from me is Wisconsin. Minnesota and Wisconsin have very different criteria for someone who graduates from high school.

LK: So you want a national goal?

GOLLE: I think we must have national standards in the next century.

LK: So every fourth grader knows the same thing?

GOLLE: Exactly. And our standards must be competitive with those in Germany and France. We're woefully beneath their standards, and the world in which to compete is getting smaller, and in the next century it's going to be even smaller. But it's important to understand too, we have a different society and a more diverse population than France or Germany. But because the French baccalaureate program is one of the highest academic achievements that you can receive, we're putting it into our Boston charter school. They'll go to high school thirty-six hours a week rather than the current twenty-four hours and they will be fluent in a second language and they will have mastered advanced mathematics and science programs. That's a good standard, but we would not be able to put it into use all over the United States.

LK: Are we going to have a national board meeting every few months to decide what is essential for every fifth grader to know before becoming a sixth grader?

GOLLE: There will be a percent of curriculum offering that will be the "national hurdle" and then there will be another percent based on the norms and ethnic makeup of the local level. Might be a fifty–fifty mix, I'm not sure.

LK: So the other percentage, the local one, differs from community to community.

GOLLE: Yes, as it should. We have a significantly diverse population, and the diversity is growing. We shouldn't try to create a cookie cutter and stamp out clones. We need to respect the differences. Our respect for those differences is one of our strengths as a country.

LK: Are there going to be a number of companies doing what you do so there will be competition for the contract with a school system?

GOLLE: Competition exists now. Disney is in this business, and I expect you'll see more of that. It will be healthy competition, and the reason is that this is about a $280 *billion* industry.

LK: Schools going to be year-round?

GOLLE: The idea we have to assemble everybody every day from eight-thirty to two-thirty is ridiculous, and giving summers off is outdated by at least thirty years. Students will be in school longer hours and year-round. In addition, we are failing to prepare high schoolers adequately for trade positions. Insisting that everyone go to college and be a nuclear physicist is already proven to be an inept and undoable goal. Every year Europe sends a percentage of students into trade areas depending on their likes and dislikes and aptitudes. We need to start doing that.

LK: Will privatized schools look different from public schools?

GOLLE: Two things are going to happen. First, municipalities will sell their schools to private enterprises in order to get them back on the tax rolls and to recoup tens of billions of dollars of money, which isn't too different from what is already happening with prisons and hospitals and airports. Private enterprises will operate schools and be under contract to meet certain performance and cost standards. Secondly, the physical plants themselves will change dramatically, especially in the secondary level. You'll see far more types of education in the workplace as opposed to what we now call high schools. You'll see on-the-job training in high-tech areas, manufacturing and engineering. High schools can't afford to purchase the equipment, so it makes sense to take the student to the workplace where the equipment is in use.

LK: There will be more independent study in the workplace?

GOLLE: Sure. The equipment is there. The know-how is there. Your attendance and skills will go up. Now this kind of education isn't going to be easy because many state laws don't allow this or make it difficult to do because unions want to protect jobs.

LK: Are there going to be teachers' unions in private schools?

GOLLE: Unions which have been successful will see a significant rollback of their power in schools. As a result we fully expect that AFT and NEA will allow their unions to represent non–public school teachers, which is something they rarely do now.

LK: Will teachers continue to be state-certified, or will your company have its own standard the teachers must meet in order to work?

GOLLE: It's likely there will be both, though I'll tell you now the certification program run by states is inadequate. There need to be more internship and proven capability before we turn our children over to someone with little more than blind faith.

LK: But if there are four privatized school companies doing business around the country, does that mean there will be four certification standards?

GOLLE: It's possible. The post office and United Parcel and Federal Express have different standards for employees, but the consumers don't care. All they seek is that their packages arrive on time at the least possible cost. We as a nation should be less concerned with what technical preparation a teacher receives and more concerned with holding teachers responsible for what students learn and the manner in which they treat students. Right now we place great importance on the certification process and degrees of teachers and virtually hold them unaccountable for what children learn.

LK: How about security in schools?

GOLLE: It's a large problem. But think how people reacted when the airlines brought metal detectors into airports. What an inconvenience! The lines! How long is this going to last? Is it really forever? Now, we just take it as commonplace because nobody wants to ride a plane with someone carrying a firearm or a bomb. We would hate to see similar security in schools but, quite frankly, I expect it—particularly in our inner city schools where guns are commonplace. Schools have to be sanctuaries where students and staff can enter free of any concern they will be harmed.

LK: Metal detectors then in both elementary and high schools?

GOLLE: Yes. The age of those carrying weapons is getting younger and younger.

LK: Cops in the hallways?

GOLLE: Not in the traditional sense. We have people there now but they don't carry firearms and they are supplemented through video cameras. The purpose of this isn't to keep the good guys in but rather to keep the bad guys out. Our company uses electronic surveillance and training of the staff and we've done a good job with this, which results in higher attendance by both students and staff.

LK: What about discipline in the classroom?

GOLLE: Discipline is a misunderstood item. The need for discipline is the result of two things. First, a teacher's ability to control an unruly child has been significantly lessened because of rights groups. This is wrong. Some children have emotional and/or behavioral needs that can't be met in a normal classroom, and these children should be moved. Second, children are disruptive because educational offerings are so bad. Teachers are boring. These children come out of a video arcade with 486-computer graphics, only to sit in a wooden chair and have someone lecture to them. That's the way we taught fifty years ago! When they become engaged in active learning they won't be bored. When they aren't bored, their behavior will improve.

LK: Is there going to be a computer on every desk?

GOLLE: I'm not sure you need a computer on every desk but we're using one computer for every four children. A computer is a learning tool because it can bring the Internet into the student's lap. It's a good administrative tool because we can measure a student's ability rather than waiting until the end of the year. We will do it every week and we will have the ability to take corrective action if there's a problem. And it will help a teacher keep track of who's there, special diets, and so on.

LK: Will privatized schools subscribe to a specific Internet program to teach, say, the third grade?

GOLLE: All schools will do it. We'll subscribe to a variety of services because we're smart enough to know one size doesn't fit all. People develop intellectually at different rates, just as they develop physically at different rates. In the next century students will be able to learn individually by means of a textbook or their teacher or a computer program and technology depending on their individual needs.

LK: Textbooks in the next century?

GOLLE: They'll look different than they do now. A student every year will have an individualized textbook printed on demand by course, by teacher, and by classroom. One chapter might come from one publisher and another from another publisher, and some software from a different vendor. We might discard it at the end of the course.

LK: Sports?

GOLLE: Absolutely. There will be more extracurricular activities in schools for both boys and girls.

LK: Do you see the role of businesses changing in relation to schools?

GOLLE: Corporations through their taxes are already the largest provider of dollars for educational services. The government says businesses spent $40 billion in 1995 on remedial training to teach employees what they should have known when they were hired. So businesses are paying for the education of employees twice. If we can deliver individuals who have higher skills and are ready to work, corporate donations will increase.

LK: Would first grade start at the same time it starts now?

GOLLE: First grade is a misnomer. It means the children are six years old because we group them by age. Preschool is very important and we have less preschool than Kenya right now. The period from age three to age six has been proven to be the most important time to stimulate children intellectually and get them ready for a more organized educational offering. For every dollar spent in preschool we save $6 in remediation costs later on.

LK: So when someone is four years old in the twenty-first century will he be in preschool or first grade?

GOLLE: We won't have grades anymore. Instead of asking what grade a child is in we will be asking whether the child can read and write. We should start to say the children are in different academic studies. For example, we might inquire, "Is your child in English yet?" or "Is your child doing algebra yet?" rather than "Is your child in third grade?"

LK: So there won't be grades one to twelve?

GOLLE: In our Tesseract schools (model used by EAI, which emphasizes society's responsibility to find and nurture a child's talent), we don't have grades per se, and we don't give out report cards. We have personal education plans (PEPs) that set forth the students' agreed-upon goals and accomplishments by subject areas versus letter grades. It's more helpful than just saying a student is an eighth grader who received an A or a B. Grades mean nothing. Albert Einstein was learning disabled. If you throw that label on a child today, watch what happens to that child's self-esteem. Eighty-eight percent of prisoners were told at one time they were "learning disabled." If you feel badly about yourself you won't care much for others.

LK: Well, how long are we going to stay in school?

GOLLE: School is looked at as a job by students. But it's a job for which you don't get paid, and too many times you're told you're stupid or ignorant and put in special classes where fellow students make fun of you. How long you going to stay in that job? We need to tailor education to suit each person.

LK: So someone could "graduate" from secondary school at age twelve?

GOLLE: I suppose it's possible. Some very gifted children do that now. We have a very simple belief: Every person has gifts and talents, and it's our responsibility to find and nurture those gifts and talents. Students will be tested continuously because of technology. No more single global test at the end of the year. We'll test weekly. Instead of saying, "This has got to be learned within one semester," we're going to say, "You must learn this material. We don't care if it takes you one week, one month, or one year." Then the students will "graduate" when they master the necessary knowledge and skills expected that will allow them to be employable in today's society. In addition, college credits will be integrated into high school so students will be able to work toward both high school graduation and college or career courses.

LK: This is based on knowledge and not age.

GOLLE: Age is a falsehood.

LK: What about competition? Students won't be in the same class under your plan.

GOLLE: Competition is with yourself as opposed to other kids. This is different from the way we do it now with a bell curve. You get a job in the workplace and you're told to go work with John on a project. But you've spent all this time in school trying to beat the brains out of John. So there has to be a change in how we look at competition.

LK: How about special education? Will that be handled by a privatized company, or will there be another group handling this?

GOLLE: We have to stop labeling children. We have given students negative labels like "learning disabled," and we pull them out of classes for "special treatment." These actions stigmatize children and make them feel bad about themselves. They see themselves in a negative light, and before long they start dropping out. Certainly some children's needs can best be met outside of the regular classroom, and I think more and more of that will be provided by an independent contractor.

LK: If there's a privatized school in the community does that principal answer to you or to the school board?

GOLLE: There won't be a school board. The principal is hired by the parents and held accountable to achieve agreed-upon results. Local school boards have become politicized and mostly controlled by the unions. They've become redundant.

LK: What do you say to those fifty years from now who will be in the education business?

GOLLE: Don't repeat the past. We have gone through fifty years of a transition from moving public schools in an agrarian society to an industrial society to a high-tech society, and we didn't transform our schools along the way to accommodate that movement. I know fifty years from now will be a very different world but we just can't forget the lessons from the past.

LK: What scares you about the twenty-first century?

GOLLE: I have never in my life been exposed to as much racism and elitism as I have in the last ten years, and I see it getting far worse before it gets better. The strength of this country is its diversification, and as is typical in anything, the strength is also the weakness. There is increasing polarization between races and classes, and it scares the dickens out of me. Education is the leveler in this. It is the bridge between having and not having.

John Golle's list of future issues that schools must face:

1. Financing. Urban environments are punished because they have more needs but less tax base to meet those needs. How we finance public education will change dramatically from local property taxes to state/federally driven formulas.

2. Standards. Educators will need to think in terms of helping students to compete internationally and prepare students for that goal. For example, Spanish is going to have to be a required class.

3. Home schooling. It's gaining popularity. Educators need to be aware it's driven by parents who believe their children are in the hands of people who are less than competent. And with the Internet this is only going to become more common. While the sample size is small, students in home schooling score higher than students in public schools.

4. Unionization. It's going to become less powerful. I predict people will be less willing to put up with their demands when the results aren't positive.

Dr. Larry Smith

Chair, Department of Elementary Education,
Ball State Teachers College, Muncie, Indiana

Don't look for simple answers to complex problems.

LK: What is going to change after the year 2000 in how we teach elementary students?

Smith: We are going to see the greatest change in our schools that we've ever seen in the history of education.

LK: Aside from that, not much then, right?

Smith: Yes. We have got to integrate technology into our curriculum much more than we are doing now.

LK: What does that mean?

Smith: We're still in the stone age in schools when it comes to technology. Our teachers don't have the knowledge base yet and are in great need of staff development. Now by that I mean teachers spend an inordinate amount of time on their own just to learn how to use the technology, so there will have to be someone available to spend an afternoon a month for a year or two years to teach the teachers how to use technology effectively.

LK: When you say "technology," you mean books? Television? Computers? What?

Smith: Television, computers, video. I think books will be used less and computers used much more.

LK: Fewer books?

Smith: We'll still use books to teach reading and for the enjoyment of literature and so forth but for science and social studies, we're moving more toward the use of multimedia.

LK: How will a student learn history in the twenty-first century?

Smith: If we study the *Titanic* and assign the class to research the story, everyone in the classroom will wear a headset and we'll use a CD-ROM and we'll find out the structure, what happened to it, we'll watch the newsreels, you'll click on the *New York Times* and read what they said about it, and even if you can't read, it'll be read to you. So this is going to help the students with reading problems because the information will be read to those children. They will get a multisensory approach to that information because it's coming in auditorily but they can actually follow along with the print too. They are hearing it and they are seeing it. Everyone in the classroom will be doing different things at different times depending on their particular level. This is exciting because we'll get personal information from people who were on the *Titanic* who have already been interviewed and so we'll use multimedia in history rather than have the student research it in the library.

LK: And will this be done with a single monitor in front of each student, or will there be a large one in the room?

SMITH: There will be large monitors in the classrooms because the teacher will need them to present instruction. But every student is going to have his own computer that can be taken home for homework. It will have cordless transfer capability to a larger computer that stays with the teacher. It's likely these will be purchased and given to the children if they can't afford it themselves. The teacher will make the assignment electronically, they'll be graded and sent back electronically. You'll have a paperless classroom. And the business of staying home because you didn't get your assignment done is no longer going to be an excuse.

LK: Will the quality of students be different?

SMITH: Their expectation of learning is going to be different. We are moving from an auditory world to a visual world in education. Young people are no exception. They learn visually. In the future we will have to figure out different ways of instructing the child. I think we're at least ten years away from being up to speed on this because that's what our students at the university are being taught, so there's going to be a lag time. We used to have an overhead projector and maybe a videotape but now we use computers to do our presentation and an integration of multimedia which includes videos and CD-ROMs.

LK: Will teacher/student ratio change?

SMITH: It might come down a little bit. Right now it's around one teacher to every twenty-two students. But keep in mind, if the ratio is lowered, you're going to need more classrooms, and that means more buildings. We have enough teachers now to lower the ratio but we don't have the facilities.

LK: Will students begin with first grade in the next century?

SMITH: What we now call first grade will be occurring in kindergarten. This is going to happen because we have inadequate child care for preschool children. I think in the next century we'll see four-year-olds and maybe three-year-olds attending preschool at the public school. The result will be a move to push the curriculum down and have the child begin sooner. There are very few parents who stay home with their children, and we will see schools take over the need for quality child care. Look, schools already open at six-thirty in the morning to accommodate the working parent and stay open until six-thirty to seven at night. This is just a continuation. Teachers won't be doing the child care, though. That will be handled by others.

LK: Do you think parents will be minimally involved in schools?

SMITH: I will tell you we are pushing in education to get parents more involved and I will say you'll see parents more involved in the future because educators will insist upon it and parents are going to want to. Parents haven't been involved because of their jobs, but I also believe it's the fault of the schools as well. Today we invite the parents into the classroom and ask for their assistance much more than before. And that will continue. Being a parent in the future will mean being more participatory in your school. It is going to take parents and teachers to effectively educate the child.

LK: What do you have to say to parents in the next century?

SMITH: Become involved with your children's school, which is the same thing we're saying this century. Be aware of what's going on in the schools. Since both parents work, or if there's one parent in the home, one parent works, you still have to spend some time with the child, and that means checking his homework.

LK: There's the key word, "homework." Elementary students will have it in the twenty-first century?

SMITH: Yes. But it won't be a computer disk or a CD-ROM. It's all going to be on the Internet.

LK: This is starting to sound like companies will put out a number of programs and you subscribe to one and you get the software and it will work with you through the homework as it works with you through the lesson in class.

SMITH: There will be companies setting up communication packages in schools and we'll buy systems, and that's where we'll get a lot of educational material. Teachers' organizations, consortiums of university and public school educators, and maybe even corporations will review the programs. It won't be a government agency doing it, but maybe something like a standards board in each state will monitor the programs. I see it coming into the classroom via the Internet for one to three years and updated daily.

LK: Does this mean the teacher will do less since there's television and a computer doing the teaching?

SMITH: The teacher will be doing different things than before. The planning will be different. It's common for the classroom teacher to present the information by talking. The teacher still is doing 80–90 percent of the talking in class. But I really think, as we prepare for the twenty-first century, the teacher will begin doing less talking and more guiding in preparing lessons using technology which presents the information much more effectively than the teacher talking.

LK: Are you saying the teacher will be a facilitator while the computer teaches?

SMITH: No. Absolutely not. I think some things have to be learned through direct instruction, such as arithmetic. But as the math becomes more complex, students won't learn the step-by-step procedures to find the answer.

LK: Is that something you're comfortable with? Less face-to-face in a way, and the medium, to take from Marshall McLuhan, is the message.

SMITH: It's more effective for learning, though, than having the teacher talk at you. It makes our lessons more powerful and keeps the student's attention longer.

LK: Some would say this will make a child less imaginative and creative because the computer or whatever is doing the work for him.

SMITH: To the contrary, the child will become more imaginative because he'll want to try more things to figure out how to use the machine in a variety of ways. I really think it will help us become more understanding of diversity. They will have pen pals in various countries and learn how to interact with each other and learn about cultures. The child in Bombay will talk to a child here in Muncie, Indiana.

LK: Will they know how to write in longhand?

SMITH: I think penmanship is going to become less and less important as we use the keyboard more and more. And I think that's good because a lot of children have trouble writing as a result of motor skill difficulty, but with a keyboard their work will look as good as the next person's.

LK: Do you anticipate students staying at home?

SMITH: I don't know. As they get older they could learn at home as they learn responsibility. For a while home schooling will increase but I don't know how effective it's going to be. It will happen more in the middle grades and high school. Then we come to the other way a child could stay at home with a virtual school, which is already being tried out in California. I think there are things children still need to learn with a teacher and in a classroom setting. My big concern with the virtual school is that we'll start having a lot of people without social skills. They can communicate electronically but there is something to be said for the socialization which occurs in a school.

LK: Will elementary school teachers have to take classes in discipline?

SMITH: We do it now. But every case is different and you need some sense of how to manage young people. More classes won't help. We need to know how to deal with other human beings more than another class on discipline.

LK: Are there still going to be the Three R's?

SMITH: Four R's. Reading, writing, arithmetic, and research. We are going to have to teach our students how to use the Internet to do research. And that can only make our students smarter than we are today.

LK: If everyone has a computer, what happens to the elementary school library?

SMITH: Everyone enjoys reading for pleasure. Reference books, though, will be on CD-ROM.

LK: Is this the end of blackboards and chalk?

SMITH: Going to be used less and less. I really think today what we do with a computer in the classroom is what before they did with an overhead projector and transparencies. Presentation programs in use today and in the future will be in color, in motion. And that's much more effective.

LK: How about privatization?

SMITH: Well, I think there's going to be more and more of an attempt at it in the next century.

LK: You like that idea?

SMITH: Not particularly. We should focus on the public school, but there's a push to examine private schools, and there is going to be an increase in the number of schools that privatize.

LK: How's that going to work?

SMITH: Well, I don't think they are aware how difficult it is to educate students. And I think in terms of a child with special needs or a child who comes from a family with some sort of problem—it could be abuse, it could be drugs, but something's on that child's mind other than learning—it's virtually impossible to educate him until you get whatever's on their mind off of it. If the movement to privatization is such that it's going to take all students, I think they're going to find some students are not very easily taught.

LK: Tell me about teachers' unions.

SMITH: They'll exist in states like New York and Pennsylvania where they are entrenched. States aren't very prone to them and I bet in other areas they die out. Teachers tell me they don't find the union to be effective or helpful.

LK: Will teachers ever be paid enough?

SMITH: They'll probably never be paid what they think they're worth, but we are moving closer to what we all agree is a livable wage.

LK: What improvements will we see in elementary education?

SMITH: We are going to have to learn how to work more effectively with the dysfunctional child, and that includes both teachers and counselors. In addition, because we will bring younger students into school, you will see more education through play. Teachers involved in that are going to need a good bit of preparation that isn't being offered now although this university is doing just that right now.

LK: Some say that public education and its teachers have failed our youth. How would you respond?

SMITH: I don't agree. Elementary schools do a particularly effective job with children. There are those out there who say, "Teach the basics no matter what," but I don't agree with that because I think you first have to get the child's attention, and if the child is hungry or disturbed, the child isn't going to learn. Now, I will also say we need to systematically remove the people who aren't interested in children and teaching. Already we are doing more interviewing of prospective teachers. One of these days we will see a review of senior faculty about every four or five or six years by peers, parents, school board members, and maybe even community leaders. In the future, you may not have tenure as we know it today.

LK: How will funding for schools change in the next century?

SMITH: I'm seeing some really interesting things starting to happen. Corporations are very interested in education now, and I see them wanting a partnership with schools. I think you'll see corporations help us move into the communication and information age. The movement of technology into schools is slow. You will see a corporate contribution to a local district becoming mandatory if that corporation intends to do business in a community. This could be money or it could be equipment or it could be expertise or it could be some kind of adopt-a-school program. You will see different kinds of assessments in the states so there is more equality among districts. I see federal dollars to schools increasing in the next century. You will see more states offer tax cuts and give that money to the schools rather than the taxpayers.

LK: Is the trend to build more elementary schools or fix up the ones you have?

SMITH: I mentioned earlier how we are moving curriculums from the first grade to kindergarten and as this continues, we're going to have to do something about child care, and that may mean building more schools. If we go to year-round school we're going to have to put air-conditioning in them.

LK: Do you see year-round schools?

SMITH: I think it will happen. Yes. Remember, the academic year as we know it today was based on farming. We're no longer expecting the children to be available in the summer to harvest the crops, and I really think it's a more effective use of school buildings, and students with learning difficulties will not regress over the summer, which happens a lot now.

LK: We still going to have grades one to six?

SMITH: We're moving toward multi-grades. Teachers get to know the needs of each child, and that means the students can be with the same teacher for three or four years. We'll still have grade levels but the same teacher is going to remain with the student for a longer period of time. There's some real benefit to that but if you end up with a teacher who doesn't care much for you or you don't care for that teacher, there are going to be some problems too.

LK: Who's going to be an elementary school teacher next century?

SMITH: I noticed about a year ago that we're getting more men. In 1986, 6 percent of our students were men. Ten years later that number was 17 percent. Two colleagues and I have done a study of this and it appears most of these men come from single-parent homes and feel almost a calling to be good role models for our young people. It's not that the men who went into elementary school in the past weren't caring, but these young men see this as a career. Elementary school teachers will continue to have to be knowledgeable about children and effective teaching strategies. The new quality needed by a teacher of the future will entail being a risk taker. They are going to have to be willing to change things somewhat rapidly because technology will be driving it. School boards and administrators are going to have to rely on a teacher's reputation and let the teacher make those changes and support the teacher.

LK: What worries you the most about the next century?

SMITH: I'm really worried about drug use, particularly by pregnant women, and the effect it's going to have on our children. This is a very serious concern for all of us.

LK: Will schools in the future face angry parents telling them not to teach about drugs or sex, or is this just something we're going through for a while?

SMITH: We're teaching wellness. Don't drink, don't take this drug. Don't hit others. It's a perennial thing. There will always be liberals and conservatives, so there will always be this debate.

LK: But the burden will always be on the schools to do this, right?

SMITH: We have to teach good and bad. It's not okay to kill somebody. People say, "My kid has the right to do this or that," and I respond saying, "Yeah, there are some rights as to what you can do, but there are some things that aren't helpful, and we as adults have to help people." We have to be concerned about the welfare of mankind. That's elementary education. We get more and more people who believe it's okay to do their own thing, but at the same time, it isn't right to steal and it isn't right to threaten somebody with a knife, so we have to teach values. The teachers in the future are going to play a bigger part of the parents than they did this century.

Dr. Smith's list of books that should be read by every elementary student in the next century:

1. *Love You Forever*, Robert Munch

2. *Uncle Jed's Barbershop*, Margaret King Mitchell

3. *The Polar Express*, Chris Van Alburg

4. *Where the Wild Things Are*, Maurice Sendak

RICHARD LEVIN

PRESIDENT, YALE UNIVERSITY

To young people: Study hard, develop skills, and unleash your imagination. To everyone else: There is enormous potential in this society, so think big and think ambitiously about ways you can do things to make this world a better place.

LK: What should a student know by the time he enters college in the coming century?

LEVIN: Students have to be prepared in the basic skills of reading and writing and mathematical competence. They should have had some basic exposure to the sciences, a foreign language, and history. That's the short form of entry requirements for most colleges and universities. I don't think it's going to change very much. I have seen in recent years the degree of the preparedness of the students has moved more quickly than our requirements. For example, we found for a period of years that more freshmen were arriving at Yale requesting computer network hookups than sophomores using the networks. Students were getting increasingly computer literate in their high schools and as a result, putting demands on us. We don't have a computer literacy requirement now because we don't need one. One hundred percent of the students who come here are already there.

LK: Do you think colleges will become more vocationally oriented, and will broad-based departments like English become less relevant?

LEVIN: There's a constituency out there in the business world that has been quite vocal about how we need better technical education and better vocational preparation in this country. Frankly, while I think there will be advances in vocational education for some segment of the student population, I believe most of the four-year colleges and universities will, in the near term, continue to offer a liberal arts curriculum. It's the generalized ability to think critically and to read carefully and to weigh arguments and to solve problems that is the most important in having a successful career. Liberal arts provide that. You learn mental flexibility and acquire the ability to adapt to new environments.

LK: What do you say to those reading this who are about to go to college and are entertaining the idea of becoming English majors?

LEVIN: I think an English major is a perfectly adequate and, indeed, an excellent preparation for life. A good training in how to read critically is important in business schools and law schools. Most of our professional schools are looking for people with a broad intellectual range, so I would not discourage anyone from being an English major.

LK: A typical college curriculum will still be based on four years?

LEVIN: Probably. Some of my colleagues have felt the high cost of education suggests we should look at allowing students to finish in three years. I don't strongly oppose it but I don't see any dramatic impetus to change. If we made a three-year option here at Yale, I don't think you'd see any dramatic shift in that direction. One of the problems with looking forward into the future of education is it's so easy to project that what has happened over the last few years will be the same over the next twenty-five or thirty years. Yale has its three hundredth birthday in 2001, and I've gone back over the speeches and writing that were prepared at the time of Yale's two hundredth birthday about what would happen in the twentieth century, and let me tell you: They missed it entirely. They had no idea of the growing importance of science. In fact, the forecast from 1951 as to the look of the year 2000 wasn't very good either. I remember back in my undergraduate days when everyone talked about how technology would take over the university. Now, thirty years later, we still have stand-up teachers in classrooms and we may have that fifty years from now.

LK: Will we be able to receive degrees via the Internet?

LEVIN: Yes. Yale will continue to focus on the intimate day-to-day contact between students and faculty in real space, but in cyberspace there will be all kinds of activities both in on-line situations and during the students' own time. Britain has had Open University for years where you can get a degree while watching television or through correspondence. It serves a function but it's a small fraction of the entire population.

LK: Do you think students will go to libraries to read, or will they double click on their computers and read the research off the screen?

LEVIN: I believe students will make use of increasingly available information from over the network to do research and to study, and I see nothing wrong with it or dangerous to the quality of education. Our libraries are rapidly becoming the resource centers for helping students to learn how to access information over the Internet. The modern librarian is going to be a computer specialist, and the field will be redefined as "information services" for students and faculty doing research. That's a very positive development. Students and faculty will still need access to libraries for physical books, such as primary research materials used by scholars and old manuscripts and so on. It's going to be a long, long time before all of that is computerized. We have 10 million books in our library, for example.

LK: In the next century how will students pay for college?

LEVIN: That's a problem that needs to be confronted. Universities like Yale have long-standing policies of meeting, from their own internal resources, the needs of students who are going to be admitted. We provide the difference between what families can pay and what Yale costs. We're going to stick to that policy as long as we possibly can, because we think providing access to an institution like this is important not only for the economic diversity it brings to Yale, but for society as a whole. The big concern is the burden on the middle class, who can afford to pay but literally face a huge financial sacrifice doing it. I think that's the problem we're going to have to address. There may be some public relief on that front. The last three or four years have seen a slowdown in the rise of college costs, and I think you'll see that continue. I do believe we'll do better to control the rising costs, but you can't eliminate those increases altogether without changing the basic nature of the service you are offering. In other industries you can get increases in labor productivity by more output per worker, but in our context that means more students per faculty. To do that you change the interaction between student and professor and you can no longer offer the small seminar classes of twelve or fifteen students that at places like Yale are an important part of the experience.

LK: Yale will have as many employees in the future or fewer?

LEVIN: Hard to predict. A lot of the growth of supporting staff has been the consequence of growth in federal research grants or government mandates. We have many people here to satisfy regulatory requirements, assure compliance in a variety of areas, and handle paperwork. The tendency in Washington, on both sides of the aisle, is to rationalize some of these regulations.

LK: Is there going to be a Department of Education in the next century?

LEVIN: I think that's likely. There's an important federal role in a number of contexts. One of the things the federal government has done is have the freedom to be innovative and fund pilot programs and new educational techniques mainly in the kindergarten through twelfth grade area. I think that's useful and important because the states and local school boards tend to operate more formally and tend to have less opportunity to support innovation.

LK: How will the role of government in handing research projects to universities change?

LEVIN: It's imperative that federal research grants continue. I believe there's insufficient recognition of the critical importance of university-based research, especially fundamental curiosity-driven research, in the economic well-being of this country. The system we put in place at the end of World War II is historically unique and totally innovative. It is the idea that the federal government will take primary responsibility for funding basic research. It also will locate basic research activity in universities where students are taught as well as where research is conducted. And third, the award of grants is left in the hands of peer review boards; scientific experts rather than political hands. This has worked unbelievably well. So much of America's economic advantage today derives from being first out with major innovations, new industries, and new concepts. The Internet is the result of government-funded basic research. All the modern advances in gene therapy and pharmaceuticals and the use of genetics and molecular biology are the result of basic research funded in universities by the federal government. The things that led to these advances were not directed at a commercial application. But in recent years we've become more interested in short-term results. Congress and the government have lost focus, and they have shifted away from fundamental curiosity-driven research toward things with potential commercial application, and that's disastrous for the future of the American economy, because government can't pick commercial successes. We've been spectacularly successful at letting curiosity-driven research flourish in this country and then relying on the unique ingenuity of American entrepreneurs and the extremely well-developed venture capital market to bring to the market new products based on science. It's a great system and should be one of the highest priorities of the federal government.

LK: So between curiosity-driven research and short-term research in the next century, how do you see it playing out?

LEVIN: We have an uphill fight politically to convince the public and the government of the argument I just made. I believe I'm right but it's going to take a lot of education for people to be persuaded. There's a story of a physics professor at Yale doing curiosity-driven research back in the 1960s on the development of the laser. He was funded to develop an argon gas laser; his work was motivated by a general interest in the physical phenomenon of coherent light. Last spring I heard he was recuperating from an operation for a detached retina. That operation had been performed using the same laser he developed thirty years earlier. Nobody had the slightest idea that might be an application one might use that technology for.

LK: Will a bachelor's degree mean as much in the next century as it does today?

LEVIN: That's hard to predict. I think for an awful lot of careers today a post-bachelor's degree is required. Eighty-five percent of Yale graduates go on to some other degree. I think specialization and the demand for skills in the economy will probably force us to see continued emphasis on education beyond four years of college.

LK: And that brings me to the next question: Will people re-enroll in college for a month or two in order to maintain a handle on the changing technologies with which they work?

LEVIN: Absolutely. The role for continuing education in the professions and in all kinds of walks of life will flourish in the coming years. We've already begun to see this, and computer technology makes this all the more feasible. In the next few years you're going to see continuing education and refresher courses being offered over the Internet. A busy lawyer may not have the time to take three months away from his office and go to a law school. Instead it will be done over a computer. Engineering and business schools will be doing this too.

LK: What scares you about this new century?

LEVIN: I'm an optimist, and I see tremendous opportunity and potential. For all the criticism that someone in a job like I have faces, the fundamentals are really quite strong. Despite all the concerns nationally about declining test scores, students are much stronger on average than students were thirty years ago.

LK: Is there anything that elementary schools or high schools can do that they aren't doing now to make your job easier?

LEVIN: You asked what scares me. Well, I think there are things that need to be done better and in a more sustained way going all the way to the cradle for the preparation of those in the disadvantaged parts of our society. This is a source of great weakness in our urban public schools, where high percentages of people are growing up in difficult circumstances. The work being done here at Yale strongly suggests the earlier the better; the sooner you get access to kids you begin to develop not only the specifics of reading and writing and language recognition, but the general predisposition for learning and interest and having a longer attention span. Head Start and programs dealing with even younger kids are terribly important.

LK: Elsewhere on the pages of this section it's been predicted schools will become year-round, and elementary schools will begin earlier, around the age of four. You agree?

LEVIN: I'm not an authority but I do think with the change in the workplace and both parents working, it makes sense.

LK: How about learning a foreign language?

LEVIN: Do it.

LK: What language?

LEVIN: In a way, I don't think it matters greatly. From an educational point of view, any number of foreign languages are equally valuable. We are seeing shifts in the patterns of enrollment in foreign language as a consequence of the changing realities of the world's political and economic situation. For instance, more study Spanish and Asian languages than study French now. We have a growing Korean language program here at Yale now, in addition to Chinese and Japanese.

LK: Do you see the time when college athletes are paid?

LEVIN: I suspect many are already. We are holding to the amateur ideal, and we don't even give athletic scholarships. The increasing professionalization of college athletics is disturbing, and I do worry about it. The commercial value of athletics to many institutions is going to continue to lead to stronger and stronger pressures to compensate the athletes. I don't know if it will literally be salaries or the schools will be more liberal about what constitutes appropriate financial aid.

LK: But it's not going to happen at Yale, right?

LEVIN: I'd be very unhappy if that happened.

LK: Will high schools become privatized?

LEVIN: They're starting in elementary schools now, and I think the results are mixed. My predecessor, Benno Schmidt, is heading up the Edison Project. They've had a good first year. I don't see this taking over the marketplace, but I see the trend of private schools growing and perhaps providing a model by which public schools can be run. That would be the greatest contribution this movement could make. If the ways in which they succeed can be imitated by the school boards and the school superintendents to produce constructive change within the current system, that's a good thing.

LK: What kind of research would you like to see being done in the twenty-first century that isn't being done now?

LEVIN: One of the great lessons of the history of science, and I guess this would extend to all scholarship, is that the future of knowledge is unpredictable. If we knew which way knowledge were going we'd know it already.

LK: Yeah, but nobody would buy this book.

LEVIN: We've operated in what's been a very decentralized system where people pursue their own research interests, and the community of scholars in a field judge whether it's worthy or unworthy, good or bad research. It's a system which can lead you to some dead ends and we can be taken up with fads sometimes. On the whole, however, it has served us well, so I'd hesitate to venture a view. We'd all like to see ideas that help solve the social problems in our society, but it's very hard through research alone to find solutions to those problems. I'd like to see attention given to cities and to people with economic hardship and broken families and so forth, but I'm not sure if it's a matter where more research is needed or more social commitment is needed or more involvement by the entire community is needed.

Making a Living

While most of us, if asked, would prefer not to work in the next century, most of us are probably going to spend a large portion of our lives doing just that, whether we're asked or not. So I decided to talk with seven people who spend their waking hours thinking about how we will earn a living in the future or how we will use our paychecks. They go to work to figure out how we'll go to work.

I can remember doing my late-night radio show when Richard Trumka won the presidency of the United Mine Workers in a hard-fought campaign throughout the West Virginia coal fields. The producers were able to track him down that evening, and he was kind enough to spend a few minutes on the phone talking about "the needs of working people," as he liked to say again and again. I could hear the devotion to that goal in his voice, and based on later interviews, I can report it hasn't gone away. Today Richard Trumka is secretary-treasurer of the AFL-CIO and still talks about the needs of working people, many of whom wear white collars.

Lester Thurow is an MIT scholar who has consistently urged venture capitalists and governments and corporations and unions to think globally. Today it's a cliché, but I recall an interview with him years ago, again late at night on radio, when he started talking about the need to see the big picture and not just the events down the street. He is a straight talker and always open to an opposing view, which makes for some pretty terrific debates. A caveat: You may not like his words if you're over sixty-five. And, for that matter, you may not like them if you're under sixty-five.

Ed Gramlich was the chairman of a presidential commission on Social Security, which delivered its final report in 1997. There was news on two fronts from the commission. The first was that the members didn't agree on any single plan to fix Social Security, so they delivered three variations on a theme. Second, they do agree there will be more studies of Social Security as well as Medicare and Medicaid before we even get to the next century. He offers some tough words as all of us seek solutions. I'll lay odds the words you are about to read will be heard over and over as America tries to be fiscally responsible as well as socially responsible.

The interview with John Seely Brown was a flat-out riot, and I hope to actually meet this guy someday. He runs "virtual office" research for Xerox Corporation and finds the tools that can make meetings more effective, which is code for "less boring." I can think of a lot of people who ought to take a class from JSB.

One of the biggest stories about the twenty-first century is contained in this section. Magdalena Yesil predicts the penny will go out of business after the year 2000. This means no more prices like $11.99, and it's worth the extra penny to no longer need a penny. Yesil is a founder of Market Pay, president of CyberCash, and as such is on the front lines of putting our dollars and coins into suspended animation somewhere. A black-stripped card will be swiped (not stolen, the other kind of swiped) through a machine, and that's how payments will be made rather than by actually handing over money. Magdalena spends a lot of her time talking about the future.

Alfred Berkeley is the president of NASDAQ, which is an acronym I still don't understand, though I like their TV commercials. He envisions a lot of change in how we measure daily conditions of the stock market and predicts we will be able to make transactions from our homes. I'm not going to be one of these forward-thinking investors—unless I can do stocks on my IBM Selectric, that is—but it's nice to have the option.

RICHARD TRUMKA

SECRETARY-TREASURER, AFL-CIO;

FORMER PRESIDENT, UNITED MINE WORKERS

Understand that change will come at an ever-increasing rate, and you can't stop change. However, if you're willing to join together, then change can be managed.

LK: In 1996, the AFL-CIO collected what it called "one-time only" dues from members for political activity. How certain are you this was only a one-time occurrence?

TRUMKA: It's not. I think unions are going to be more actively involved in political campaigns out into the future. Our members have told us they don't want to be told who to vote for, but they say, "Give us information about the issues that are of concern to us and we'll make up our own conclusions." Now, look at the twenty-first century out there in another forty or fifty years, well, people are going to be a lot more decentralized. We may have a different form of democracy, one that is more participatory. Everyone is going to be hooked up to a computer, so instead of asking your representative to vote for you, there may be referendum votes on issues. And if that's the case, getting the proper information is going to be more and more important for working people. So for a trade union, it's going to be more important to give them analysis and information rather than conclusions.

LK: So union members will type in their password on a computer and get Richard Trumka's take on both union as well as national issues?

TRUMKA: Absolutely. They'll be able to communicate with their leadership. I think they're also going to be able to vote on legislation that way. Instead of having one hundred senators block a vote on minimum wage, we may be able to send it out on a referendum vote and say, "Okay, next Tuesday we decide if the minimum wage should be increased," and, bink, we vote.

LK: The use of dues for political activity sounds like a union litmus test in which members are given a list saying, "These candidates we can live with and these candidates over here we can't live with." Is that accurate?

TRUMKA: Currently, we're just saying, "These are the issues, and this is how X voted on the issues, and this is how Y voted on the issues, and this is where X and Y stand on issues that are important to you. You decide." Now, that's important today and it's going to be important fifty years from now. There's going to be more forms of communication and it's going to develop a whole bunch of interesting issues. Remember, information is strength and information is power. Who gets to edit that information you get? If you can't digest all the information that's available, well, who's going to digest it for you? And those are issues created just on the political front. The borders are going to get blurred. Multinational corporations will be everywhere at all times. And one question that's going to come up is how do you raise revenue for the local citizenship from a corporation that only exists electronically in your jurisdiction? We're all going to have to deal with this. Multinational corporations aren't going to look after the citizens that are here. It's going to be the trade union movement or workers' organizations.

LK: Are you saying there might be, for example, the United Mine Workers union in Brazil?

TRUMKA: Hopefully, out into the future, mine workers in every country will belong to the same organization. They can move us around at the switch of a dial or the punch of a key; the only way we can protect ourselves is if we are linked through international solidarity. I think you'll see more international organizations. We're loosely linked right now.

LK: In 1996 there was an election at the AFL-CIO which was unique in that for the first time in forty years there was more than one candidate running for office. Can we expect contested elections in the future?

TRUMKA: The trade union movement has, historically, always been the most democratic movement out there. Yes, I think we'll see more of this and as the pace of change becomes more rapid, you need to change directions because it's more important. I don't think you'll see us lag by five, ten, fifteen years behind the event that necessitates change because we didn't see the change happen.

LK: Who will be union members?

TRUMKA: I think a lot of upper-level management positions will become unionized because they're going to be discarded and become the same as production workers right now. They'll try to use managers to do several different jobs. You may not have managers working for a corporation, and the number of full-time employees will probably decrease. That's going to mean managers need somebody to pull them together and to speak on their behalf and to negotiate for them so they get fair treatment and compensation. That's where we come in. Workers are going to be decentralized in the future. They won't be at a common work site so the need for an organization that gives them collective strength and voice will be far more important than it is today. And today, believe me, it's plenty important.

LK: This will be white-collar workers?

TRUMKA: White-collar, pink-collar, blue-collar workers. Middle management and upper management as well.

LK: We hear of the growing disparity between incomes of a CEO and employees. Will this begin to reverse as a result of unions, or will it continue in the present direction?

TRUMKA: In our heyday we were 35 percent of the workforce and we built the middle class. When unions started to decline, and that was a conscious decision by a number of White House administrations to compete internationally with a low-wage and low-skill type of strategy, they had to eliminate unions. Wages started to stagnate. Now anybody out there who believes that, without some type of worker organization, you'll get a fair deal and can share the wealth that you've created and the employers will do it on their own volition, I have this bridge in New York I'd love to sell you. Nobody is going to allow 1 percent of the people to have 99 percent of the wealth they produce.

LK: Are you saying there will be a maximum ratio between CEO salary and worker salaries?

TRUMKA: I'm not going to say there's going to be any kind of percentage or ratio. Here's what will happen: If we have the collective strength we'll bargain a good deal. If 100 percent of us in an industry belong to an organization, we'll get a fair share. If 50 percent of us belong to that organization, we'll get half as good a share.

LK: The trend in business is to outsource, or pay an outside group to perform a job that once was done in house in an effort to avoid paying health care and benefits for full-time workers. Will future contracts with corporations require a percentage of that work go to union employees?

TRUMKA: I think workers are going to insist on that. We might represent all the people doing X type of work.

LK: So you see that really happening?

TRUMKA: In fifty years a corporation will probably fit in this office right here. There will be two or three people. All the links to production will be decentralized. There won't be common work sites. Now, that raises social issues right there. How do we communicate and associate with each other? Tax issues. Workers' organizations won't be at the work site because there won't be a work site. The work site will be everywhere. So we're going to have to organize workers rather than a work site. But we're doing some of it now. We do it with bricklayers. Someone wants bricklayers, they call us and we send them fifty bricklayers who are trained, skilled, and have health and safety training, and are the most efficient bricklayers in the world.

LK: People will join unions in the next century for job security? Wages? Health care? What will be the driving force?

TRUMKA: All of the above.

LK: Somehow I knew you were going to say that.

TRUMKA: If you look at the fact that we're in a decentralized workplace, where people don't communicate with one another, where is their real bargaining power? When a company can get what you give them anywhere in the world and if you aren't organized, what is your bargaining power? You're sitting here doing this interview right now? Well, I could be talking to Joe and Jane Guachagaloop in Italy right now and they could be doing the interview just as easily, right? It can be electronically transmitted today. Well, in the future it'll get even more so and there's going to be a need for a workers' organization to prevent them from getting trampled on in the process. And the more decentralized it gets, and the fewer workplaces there are and the fewer commonalities among workers, the more their need for an organization to represent them, to get them power, and to be their voice.

LK: But will this be driven by anger?

TRUMKA: Some of it will be but it's also being driven by outright pragmatism. I want better wages. My employer won't give me what I deserve so I'm going to have to join together with all the other people that do my type of craft.

LK: You think we'll see labels on clothing or on cars indicating the history of the product? It was in whatever country and made by this union?

TRUMKA: Yeah, I think you will see it. There's already a lot of mislabeling. China, for instance, can bring only so many pieces of clothing into this country. After they hit the limit, then they label it something else by sending it through another country that says, "Made in Sri Lanka" or whatever. And countries are going to start specializing in this kind of stuff. Sri Lanka, for example, could become the "T-shirt state" or something like that.

LK: But there will be labels?

TRUMKA: Oh sure. Employers want to be their own nation states. They want to eliminate borders and countries and governments and do it themselves. They think they can divide up more equitably the world's resources and become extremely efficient worldwide. That's their dream. God forbid if society ever allows that to happen.

LK: Watch the transition here. What scares you about the twenty-first century?

TRUMKA: Corporations having so much power that nobody, including all the governments in the world, can do anything to change it. I'm not saying this is going to happen, but that's my biggest fear. And if the trend continues right now? Sure it can happen.

LK: Why?

TRUMKA: *Why?* If the unions, the last line of defense for America's workers, are eliminated, then it will happen. When was the last time the U.S. government stood up to Exxon and said, "Guess what? You *aren't* going to do something"? Nobody knows, and that's the issue. The last line of defense is workers. You take the Social Security-Medicare-Medicaid fights, and we were the last line of defense for them. The minimum wage? Who else fought and used their own resources when most of our members don't get the minimum wage? It's not fair that a CEO who works for one of the top five hundred corporations earns $12,414 a day. And it takes a minimum-wage earner eighteen months to earn what that guy did in a day. He goes to the john, and it takes the worker a month to earn what he spent in the john. That's not fair. You ask me about anger? American workers are angry about that.

LK: Do you anticipate unions in the next century will directly contact immigrants to this country?

TRUMKA: We're doing that now. The United Mine Workers helped my grandfather get citizenship papers when he came through Ellis Island. But don't start worrying about, for example, Mexican workers coming north. Worry about corporations going south.

LK: Will there be more right-to-work states?

TRUMKA: Right-to-work will be a nonexistent concept. States are probably going to become next to irrelevant because countries are being made next to irrelevant. I'm not saying I agree with any of that but I'm saying that's what's likely to happen. Right-to-work states spend less on education, less on infrastructure, their average wages are $150 a week lower than a non–right-to-work state, so if you're looking at the twenty-first century and need a high-skill/high-wage society, right-to-work just doesn't cut it.

LK: You think fast-food restaurants will be unionized?

TRUMKA: Absolutely. We have to have changes in labor laws because what we have right now is antiquated.

LK: Like what?

TRUMKA: Like the membership on boards of directors. We'll use our pension money and go to a board of directors and say, "Hey, we own 72 percent of this company and you are being hostile to our interests and guess what? We are going to downsource you, we are going to outsource you, and we are going to unemploy you. We are going to put people in who represent our interests." So forty to fifty years down the road, you're going to see a whole lot more worker involvement on the boards of directors and on the political level. Workers will start to understand their own potential.

LK: So you're saying there will be a mandatory union member on every board of directors to keep a check and balance?

TRUMKA: No. I see several members on those boards of directors. Look, workers own 25.7 percent of all the equity out there in their pension plans. That suggests we ought to have at least 25.7 percent of the directors right there. We're at 0.07 percent right now.

LK: So how's that going to happen?

TRUMKA: We're going to see new capital strategies initiated by the labor movement and managed by the labor movement in the next ten or fifteen years. As that happens, we will exert more control over the creatures we now call corporations. There will be more collective bargaining to get control. There will be legislation. And there will be lawsuits. All are viable strategies.

LK: The AFL-CIO is composed of seventy-eight separate unions. How many will it have in the next century?

TRUMKA: Twenty or twenty-five.

LK: More?

TRUMKA: No, total.

LK: So you're losing unions?

TRUMKA: No. They're going to be combined. They'll join together. There's a merger being talked about between the United Steel Workers, the Machinists, and the Auto Workers. That will be a Metal Workers Union. That's scheduled for the year 2000. You ought to add the Mine Workers and the Chemical Workers and OCAW into an Energy Union. As you see corporations restructuring and changing, workers' organizations are going to have to look to mirror them in a lot of ways and precede them in other ways.

LESTER THUROW

SLOAN KETTERING SCHOOL OF BUSINESS,
MASSACHUSETTS INSTITUTE OF TECHNOLOGY

*We will succeed or fail depending on whether we build a society
with a vision, and that is something we are willing to commit to
and work toward. And if you can't do that, then we split up and
become another Montana Freeman group where everybody opts
out. If you want people to opt in, there has to be a vision to sell
them.*

LK: What does America need to do in order to be successful in the
twenty-first century?

THUROW: We need a builder mentality, and we don't have it now.
We need to build things that we know aren't going to pay off while
we're still alive. And one reason for doing this is we're going to have an
enormous elderly population. You take the average person age sixty-
five today, well, he has about seventeen years of life expectancy, and
the average elderly person has about eight years of life expectancy, and
if these people are the majority of the voters, how do you do things like
build a biotech industry or even build an Internet industry? Sometime
during the 1960s the American Institutes of Health started putting $2
million to $3 million a year into biotech, and six or seven years later
you have the double helix, and two years after that you have DNA, and
thirty years later you have a big profitable industry. Government, in
this case, had to invest money which took thirty years before it came to
fruition. Or look at the Internet. Twenty-five years ago the Defense
Department decided it needed a bombproof communication system so
it built and maintained the Internet for about fifteen years and the
National Science Foundation did it for another ten, and now it's the
most exciting economic opportunity on the face of the globe. But there
again, it needed this enormous social investment. If you look at what's
happening in our government budgets of late, basically it's the elderly
who are squeezing all of these kinds of social investments out of the
budget because from a politician's point of view it's much easier to cut

infrastructure, R&D, and education than it is to cut pensions and health care for the elderly. In part because the young don't vote but also because those things don't pay off in one year and you don't see the negative things until twenty-five years later when you don't have a biotech or an Internet which can generate jobs into the future.

LK: This sounds like you're putting one class against another class.

THUROW: That's right, but I'm not putting them against each other, they are against each other. If you look at the data, in 1970 the average seventy-year-old had 40 percent less income than the average thirty-year-old. Today the average seventy-year-old has 20 percent more income than the average thirty-year-old. Both are unfair, but do I want to make my parents rich at the cost of making my children poor? The answer is no. The system is putting the classes against each other and you've got to have a balance.

LK: In the twenty-first century the vision should be what?

THUROW: Well, I've argued we don't know what the country should be doing for the year 2010 but we do know our society has to have a set of values and a vision that says, "Building for the future is important and generates welfare for people who are alive today even if they won't be alive in that future." We have to be willing to do it. If you want to put it crudely, we're in a situation where people are saying, "I won't build it unless it pays off before I die." Since World War II our vision was containing the Russians. That's gone away. You can't have a negative vision anymore. It's got to be a positive one, and that uses the key word "building." The interstate highway system was a vision thing, in Europe high-speed rail was a vision thing. Singapore has electronic libraries, and that's a vision thing. So we have to build a better America and to do that we have to be willing to make three long-run investments: in education and skills, in knowledge like research and development, and in the infrastructure like the Internet. In our current budget, that's what we're cutting back on.

LK: Will we find this vision or does it come from a leader?

THUROW: Well, if you have leaders you are going to have to have people who want to be followers. It's difficult to be a leader at the moment because "followership" isn't the spirit of the times. Now one answer is, that can change if we have a crisis. We had the Revolutionary War and up pops George Washington, we have the Civil War and up pops Abraham Lincoln, we have World War II and up pops Franklin Roosevelt. Have a crisis and we'll have a leader. The problem is a crisis is a very painful way to generate a leader.

LK: What kind of crisis will we have in the twenty-first century?

THUROW: The answer to that is nobody can say. What a democracy does worst of all is deal with problems that are easy to forecast but not evident, or problems that are occurring at a very slow rate. Example: The real wages of the bottom 60 percent of the male workforce are declining at the rate of about two-thirds of a percentage point each year. That's been going on for twenty-five years, and nobody's doing anything about it because it isn't viewed as a crisis if you look at it from year to year.

LK: What has to change within government to put the country in a good position to face a crisis?

THUROW: Look at our balance of trade deficit right now. It's $200 billion. That can't go on. We can't borrow money forever to keep this trade deficit. That's economic arithmetic but we're waiting for some kind of crisis where the rest of the world runs away from the dollar. And we know what the right thing to do at the moment is. We import oil as if we were a producer of oil when we ought to price it the way the rest of the world prices it, and that means putting a $4 or $5 tax on it and pay $6 or $7 a gallon for gasoline. This could have been done at the start of the Persian Gulf War but George Bush didn't want to do it. It can't be done today, but there was a moment in time when a leader could have pushed it through because it could have been seen as part of the Persian Gulf War and we're not going to pay those bastards anymore. Eisenhower took a symbolic event which was the Russians launching Sputnik and made it into something where we improved American schools. Events come along which in themselves aren't crises but they could be used to do something to solve some of the problems we have. Our government has a basic design to not make decisions. We can't really do anything unless 70 percent or 80 percent of the House and Senate plus the president agree. Fifty-one percent can't get anything. Forty-nine percent can veto the other 51 percent. Look at it this way: We have nineteen states with a combined population less than California. One group of 38 million people has thirty-eight senators. The other group of 38 million people gets two senators. Somehow that's called democracy.

LK: What kind of qualities will a leader need to possess?

THUROW: The leader of the future is going to have to be able to mobilize public opinion using the electronic media. Lyndon Johnson was good at getting things through Congress but couldn't deal with the public over television.

LK: That has nothing to do with having a good idea, does it?

THUROW: It has nothing to do with having a good idea. It has everything to do with selling a good idea. That and the fact it is so expensive to run for office that I think in the future someone will try to buy the presidency. Sooner or later someone is going to succeed, and then the question becomes what do we think of the system at that point.

LK: You think that will happen?

THUROW: I absolutely think that will happen. Right now 90 percent of the people running for office who spend the most on TV ads win. We have a Supreme Court that says, "You can spend an infinite amount of money on yourself, but people can't give you an infinite amount of money." Look at Ross Perot: The second time around he lived under the same sword the other candidates did and he didn't get as many votes.

LK: And if we do this, then the classes are brought together?

THUROW: That's right, because then we are working on a common thing. In the sixties we were all going to the moon. Something like that is going to be vital.

LK: What you're implying is more people in the next century should vote.

THUROW: In 1970 the group with the highest poverty rate was the elderly. Today the group with the highest poverty rate is those people less than eighteen years of age. Now, those are precisely the people who don't get the right to vote. What we've done is have a system entirely for the elderly, and we don't even let the young vote. Look at school bond referendums: The elderly systematically vote against education. In the long run that's the way to kill human society, or a prosperous human society.

LK: What kinds of industry will drive the U.S. economy?

THUROW: Microelectronics, biotechnology, telecommunications, civilian aircraft manufacturing, machine tools, robotics, computer software and hardware. If you look at telecommunications, for example, within ten years we will have all the technology necessary to close every retail store in America. Now, shopping is partly a social experience, but if you want to see the shop, the shopping of the future will be the Mall of America in Minnesota, where you have wave machines and Ferris wheels and shopping is part of Disneyland. But if you simply want to get good things cheap, you will do it electronically. L.L. Bean is a store in rural Maine and does $350 million worth of business in Japan, and they don't have a single employee in that country.

LK: Will those industries keep the United States in front?

THUROW: It depends if the United States makes those three investments we talked about earlier.

LK: Is there an industry the United States should develop or strengthen?

THUROW: Machine tools and robotics is the weakest industry right now. That's what produces our equipment. I'm not saying government should invest in industry, but we may need some long-run government investment in the science of robotics.

LK: Do you think the wealth of the country will continue to be controlled by a small percentage of individuals?

THUROW: It's more true now than it was twenty years ago. I think the answer can be found in how much money are you willing to put in to educate the bottom half of the population.

LK: Will there continue to be a middle class?

THUROW: It's getting smaller and smaller. And again, I go back to the answer to the last question. Are we willing to invest in education and training? The jury is out. I'll tell you this, however, the upscale stores like Bloomingdale's and Neiman Marcus are doing very well and the downscale stores are doing very well, but the middle-class stores like Sears, Macy's, Gimbels have gotten in trouble, not because they are managed by dumb people but because their customers have less money to spend.

LK: Let's talk about the social contract between those who work and those who own the business.

THUROW: That's one of the very fundamental fault lines in the business community because they preach the doctrine of teamwork being very important, and at the same time in the downsizing movement they are basically telling everybody, "You ought to think of yourself, and no matter what good things you've done for the team yesterday, if I don't need you today I'll fire you, and if I need you tomorrow I might hire you or somebody else, and then fire you or that person all over again when I don't need you again." And you also have a system where the key person is the knowledge worker, yet instead of attaching those knowledge workers to the firm the business firm is saying, once again, "You shouldn't have any loyalty to me because I don't have any loyalty to you." There's a very fundamental problem building up here because I've spent thirty years of my life in business schools and thirty years ago, had you asked, "What does the average MBA say about how to succeed in America?" that person would have said, "Be a team player and find a good company and make the right investments in that company in terms of your career and you'll be rewarded." Today if you told that to an MBA he'd look at you as though you were a mad person. These people have no loyalty to anything and they shouldn't. But you can't run corporations where the management cadres have no loyalty.

LK: Loyalty is important?

THUROW: Corporations themselves say it, because why else would they spend all this time talking about teamwork? I think you've got real schizophrenia here in the business community. Half the time employees are being told to think of this place as a home, and the other half of the time employees are being told don't think of this place as a home. The two sides of their mouths don't compute.

LK: So is this going to continue?

THUROW: As far as we can now see, yes. But in the long run we need to develop a new social contract.

LK: And that is?

THUROW: The honest answer is nobody knows. It has to be something the companies will actually live up to and something the individuals will actually live up to, and at the moment all we know is that the old one's dead.

LK: Would it include a promise of benefits to an employee in return for something?

THUROW: Well, the current social contract is fear: "Work hard because otherwise I'm going to fire you tomorrow morning." Human societies don't work on fear for every long.

LK: You see a role for a labor union in this social contract between employee and employer?

THUROW: It had in the past. But look at the current issue of exploding CEO salaries. They've gone up from about thirty-five times that of the average worker to now more than two hundred times that. CEOs set their own salary. So the question becomes why didn't that happen in the 1950s? Well, if John Lewis and Walter Reuther had seen that a CEO gets a 30 percent pay increase in one year, then every worker's going to get 30 percent, and if not, we'll bring this economy to a halt! They would have made it stick. So you as a CEO didn't raise your salary like that because you knew if you did your company was going to do it for everybody. So in that sense, labor unions in the post–World War II era were instrumental in imposing the social contract.

LK: So then will management in the future tie its salary to some kind of ratio with the average worker?

THUROW: As long as a company is profitable and management is doing good things the board of directors isn't going to worry about it. The issue ultimately is going to be decided like smoking. If you say, "What stops CEO salaries from rising faster than the general public?" the answer is sociology. Does it become so completely unacceptable, like smoking, that you simply have to stop? And we may be getting there.

LK: So this is an issue which reflects how we feel about ourselves today?

THUROW: Yeah. This kind of stuff is explosive because my impression is Americans are almost unique in that we aren't terribly envious of somebody that has enough money to have a penthouse apartment on Park Avenue, but when it comes to health care, we're Communists. If somebody else's kid gets health care and my kids don't and we work for the same company, I'm going to go through the roof. We're building up an incredible social time bomb with things like dual-class health care systems.

LK: Will more or fewer people join labor unions?

THUROW: Because of the organization laws now on the books I don't think the labor union movement is going to recover. These laws make it difficult to get Americans to join unions. We know sooner or later that if you continue with exploding CEO salaries and downsizing, the American worker is going to find some way to fight back.

LK: And a union would be the way?

THUROW: Yes. Maybe there will be something else that we don't quite call unions, but I don't think they're going to sit there and take it forever.

LK: You're optimistic about the future of a labor union then?

THUROW: I'm optimistic about some kind of organization to which the workforce joins. Traditionally unions have been populated by blue-collar workers, but if you look at the downsizing movement, that mostly affects white-collar workers and managers. Take the 48,000 people voluntarily "laid off" at AT&T a few years ago; very few of them were blue-collar workers.

LK: Who will be an economic superpower?

THUROW: The same ones that are now: Europe, Japan, and the United States. China might be in the twenty-second century. Ask me then.

LK: Let's talk about trade agreements. In the next century the U.S. will have new trade agreements with whom?

THUROW: You've got all the trade agreements you're going to have for the next twenty or thirty years. You've got the European Common Market, NAFTA, and there's talk of doing something along the Pacific Rim, but the people who are talking aren't talking about doing anything until 2020. In the Pacific Rim it's hard to figure out how to even put a trade area together. One country, Japan, is an economic giant and a political pygmy. Another country, China, is an economic pygmy but a political and military giant. Then if you throw the United States into the whole thing, there's no way to hand out voting power. If you do it on population, China runs the system. If you do it on economics, Japan runs the system.

LK: So don't expect a trade agreement of any kind in the Pacific Rim for a while?

THUROW: You're going to have a lot of talk about it but not much action. In Europe you could get it going because there were four countries with equal wealth and size and population (Italy, France, Germany, and England). In the United States you could get NAFTA going because there's one huge country making the decisions for all three, because the other two (Canada and Mexico) are small in terms of economics and small in terms of population. But in Asia, there's no dominant power, no countries of the same size, and no countries with the same economic development. China is huge but poor. Japan is small but rich. The fundamentals aren't there for putting together a group.

LK: Do you see tying future trade agreements to human rights?

THUROW: Yes. Issues like child labor. We may have to put up a sign saying, "This Shirt Made by Child Labor," so if I don't want a product of child labor, I don't have to buy it. Now, if you start in using minimum wage as human rights, then you get into trouble. What's a minimum wage in China with a per capita income of $400 is different from a minimum wage in the United States with a per capita income of $25,000.

LK: You mention the European Common Market. How will we do business with them as there are more members, and will we see a single currency in Europe?

THUROW: There will be a single currency but it won't be done quite as fast as they promised, which was 1999, but they're on the road to it.

LK: Whose currency will it be?

THUROW: Well, either the deutsche mark or the Euro, and I think it'll be the Euro because the rest of Europe will want a neutral currency rather than just using the deutsche mark as the currency.

LK: Any chance the Euro will come to the United States?

THUROW: The Euro creates problems in America. If you have a flight from the dollar, a large falling and people say, "I don't want to hold dollars any longer," and the Euro exists, well, then there's a place to go. If the Euro doesn't exist and you don't like dollars there's no place to go because all the other currencies are so small or difficult to get, you can't get into them. So I think the minute the Euro exists, the dollar becomes a lot more fragile.

LK: But if we're using a Euro will we be seeing more European products in the United States?

THUROW: Today we're importing 12 percent of our gross domestic product, which is double what we did thirty years ago. I expect to see something like that occurring in the future.

LK: In the next thirty or forty years where will we travel on business?

THUROW: The one part of the world which doesn't play in the global economy is Africa. Unless something radical happens in that part of the world, I think that's going to continue because Africa is the one part of the world where the per capita income is actually declining. In terms of where business will be done I'd say Europe or Latin America.

LK: In the next century what are the best and worst professions to be in?

THUROW: I don't know if you can say "profession," but you can say if you want to have a chance of being economically successful you have to be well skilled and well educated. If you want to be a failure, drop out of high school. The reason I use "skilled" and "educated" is that there's a whole set of professions such as tool and die and machinists which you typically don't learn in a university but typically pay higher wages than what a university graduate makes. So the question is can you get the right skills, and I don't think "the right skills" is synonymous with going to a university. For more than one hundred years the most economically successful person was involved with oil—John D. Rockefeller in the nineteenth century, Sultan of Brunei in the late twentieth century—but today it's Bill Gates. Until Gates, the richest guy was associated in some way with natural resources. Now it's a knowledge worker.

LK: What do you mean by "well-educated"?

THUROW: I think that's a good high school education, which is equivalent to what a European would get, and then putting on top of that a four- or five-year postsecondary skill training education system, which could be a university education but could also be equivalent to the German apprenticeship program.

LK: And what are skills that one needs for the next century?

THUROW: Do you have the knowledge skills and understanding to play the world game? Are you comfortable working in another part of the world, can you understand where people in the other parts of the world are coming from, and can you make a deal and understand how to make a deal with them?

LK: Should people in high school in the twenty-first century give serious thought to learning Chinese?

THUROW: Wouldn't be a bad thing to do. But even more important than learning the language will be learning the culture so you know where these people are coming from. You can hire a translator but that's not going to be enough. Global skills mean a lot more than language. Being good at that is going to mean the highest-paying job.

LK: A career or job with little promise in the coming century would be what?

THUROW: The jobs will still exist but they'll be filled with different people. Automobile assembly line jobs paid $20 to $30 an hour, which are the equivalent of college wages. They used to hire people who were high school dropouts. Today the number of those jobs is smaller but look at whom they hire: Everyone has at least junior college education and people skills and mathematical skills, and this means they're going to hire a very different group. So it isn't that there are occupations or professions that will disappear, but those occupations and professions will demand very different entry requirements to get into them. High school dropouts will no longer work on the automobile assembly line.

LK: What do you think the next century will have that we in this century didn't?

THUROW: The biggest thing, and we see it already, is there will be an increasing opportunity for you to economically opt out of any political jurisdiction. The fifth-biggest banking center in the world right now is the Grand Cayman Islands. There are no regulations, and that's where 30,000 people do their banking so they can avoid the laws of their home countries. And it can be done electronically. We see it in these religious cults. Look at the Contract with America where it said we are going to quit being a country and become fifty different countries and share a military.

LK: What scares you?

THUROW: That there will be all these nagging and festering problems and we won't deal with them.

LK: Are you looking forward to the twenty-first century?

THUROW: Yes, I am going to enjoy buying my groceries on the Internet.

EDWARD GRAMLICH

FORMER CHAIRMAN, ADVISORY COUNCIL ON SOCIAL SECURITY;
MEMBER, FEDERAL RESERVE BOARD OF GOVERNORS

Start saving.

LK: You've completed two and one-half years chairing a commission on Social Security, and I'm wondering if there will be more commissions appointed to deal with the same issue in the next century, and if so, what words do you have for the future members?

GRAMLICH: Lord help the people who serve on those commissions. There is a very difficult fiscal problem, among other problems, going on. For instance, Arizona is getting very full because so many retirees are moving there. And in another ten years the baby boomers will begin to retire, and that is going to be a huge population, larger than any earlier or, for that matter, later group of retirees. We are facing the potential of the cost of medical care for senior citizens (Medicare and Social Security) cutting into defense and education and any other federal government program.

LK: But the potential still exists for Congress or the White House to say, "Things look bad and we need a commission to find answers"?

GRAMLICH: People can create commissions whenever they want.

LK: Well then, looking back, what advice do you have for those councils or commissions that will pick up the Social Security ball and run with it?

GRAMLICH: You could probably look at the situation now and conclude we shouldn't have followed such a zigzag path to reach conclusions, but a lot of us were learning about the system and changing our minds as we went. I'm not sure there was any way we could have been much more efficient. We've had disagreements and they take time to resolve, and in the end some weren't resolved.

LK: Well, many say Social Security won't exist in the twenty-first century. What do you say to those people?

GRAMLICH: Even if no changes are made, the system runs out of assets in 2030. But that doesn't mean the system disappears because there will still be cash revenues coming in and benefits can be paid out. Worst case where we wait until 2030 and nobody does anything, then a 20 to 30 percent cut in benefits can still keep it going. But I think there are much better cases, especially if we act early. So, to answer those who ask the question, I say there will be a system in the twenty-first century but I think it's going to be different, at least I hope it will be different.

LK: What will be different?

GRAMLICH: If we keep with the present defined benefit system only, then there's going to be some combination of cuts in benefits or higher taxes. Some on the council have argued we move toward a different approach which features more defined contribution and your retirement is prefunded. That is, people will save for their retirement, and I think that's a good idea and I hope we move in that direction.

LK: And that will be done how?

GRAMLICH: The benefits are scaled or calibrated to that level of 12.4 percent, which is the sum of the 6.2 percent paid every paycheck by the employee and the 6.2 percent paid every paycheck by the employer and then, in addition, I'd have a mandatory contribution on top of that which would.go into a defined account that would be owned by people and not part of the budget. People would choose their investment, stocks or bonds or whatever. This would be a complement to Social Security and would give everyone a stake in the system.

LK: Some would say that's dangerous because most people don't know about stocks or bonds, myself included.

GRAMLICH: Well, pension plans have these problems and face them routinely. I worry about it some but I'd have the government or some chartered private agency manage the account and create what are known as index files or mutual funds that hold all stocks in a market so the risk is diverse and people are choosing whether or not to go into stocks or bonds. They would not be picking out individual stocks.

LK: If one desires, can the mandatory contribution be increased?

GRAMLICH: We'd keep it a certain percentage and if one wanted to, more money could be added privately as is done with an IRA, for example. I see the number at 1.6 percent of an employee's total income.

LK: Would it make any sense to just say, "Anyone born after such and such a year is on his own"?

GRAMLICH: We need a public pension plan and we need mandatory savings, and I don't think people can foresee how much saving they're going to have to do, especially when life expectancy is getting so high and there are ways the government could manage it and open it up to some form of privatization.

LK: We are, then, coming to a time when the government will say, "Folks, we can't do it alone, and individuals are going to have to start funding a portion of their own retirement"?

GRAMLICH: I hope it doesn't have to come to that point and that people will do it voluntarily because they recognize what is going on. Looking at the numbers, though, that is not happening. People seem fully aware they may not get their full Social Security benefit and it would strike me if they know it, then they ought to start saving. It sure isn't a rational point of view.

LK: How far away are we from that day when there will be a mandatory kick-in?

GRAMLICH: I don't know the answer to that, but I'll tell you we aren't that far away from the day when the government will be forced to scale back Social Security benefits, so we aren't that far away from the day when people will find upon retiring that Social Security only covers 20 percent of their previous wage income. We're ten years away.

LK: What then do you say to financial managers who advise their clients not to count on Social Security?

GRAMLICH: Well, in a way I applaud it because I don't think we save enough on our own for retirement. The fact is, however, that Social Security will be there, and with some immediate changes it can be made into a system that replicates what we have now.

LK: Is that the ACLU I hear knocking on your door when you talk about mandatory saving?

GRAMLICH: I don't think this takes away a person's freedom any more than taxes take away a person's freedom. The ACLU wouldn't be knocking on the door if I proposed a rise in the payroll tax and, in a way, this is more freedom because people get the money back.

LK: If you look at the way the United States operates, we seem to wait for a crisis to happen, let it happen, and only then will we deal with it. Is that what has happened with Social Security?

GRAMLICH: It hasn't happened until now. Changes have been made over time and done well in advance of the crisis. I hope we can keep it going. If you're talking about crisis, let's talk about Medicare because that crisis is already here.

LK: Some suggest increasing the age to collect benefits. Good idea?

GRAMLICH: Something like that will happen. We've offered three plans at the advisory council, and increasing the age for benefits is implicit in two of the three. In the year 2000, the retirement age begins climbing two months a year for six years. Then it stays for twelve years and then begins climbing two months a year again. We might eliminate the twelve-year gap. Some want the age to be sixty-seven in the year 2000 and others want it to be sixty-eight.

LK: Isn't that unrealistic when you see so many older workers being tossed out and replaced with younger workers who will do the job at a lower pay scale? Will there be jobs for these people if the age of retirement is increased?

GRAMLICH: It's indeed a reality and there is an inconsistency. If people are going to live into their nineties, the government isn't going to be able to pay them those scheduled benefits for thirty years without a huge increase in taxes. So people could pay the taxes or they could change the date of their scheduled retirement benefit. As for not being able to work a particular job, that's too bad, but they can work other jobs. People have to recognize if they are unwilling to pay the higher taxes, which I think most people are, then they have to make some other accommodations, not in the age they leave their main job, but in the age they start drawing public assistance. We have to protect people when they are the most vulnerable, and that's when they are in their eighties and nineties, and one way to do that is have them take more responsibility for themselves when they are in their sixties.

LK: How should future generations deal with their aging populations?

GRAMLICH: The aging population is tough on a defined benefit pension plan because the present workers pay for the present retirees, and as the present population ages you have fewer workers and more retirees. Those workers have to pay higher payroll tax rates as a result. So by its nature, the system we have today is going to create problems. I'd like to see more prefunding where people are funding their own retirement. When that is done people save for themselves and the system gets more independence from demographics.

LK: Do you see more of a family role in the aging population than we've had over the past few decades? Older parents moving in with sons and daughters rather than going to a nursing home or something similar?

GRAMLICH: In comparison to many other societies, the American society has not developed in that way. We have Social Security to support Dad and Mom rather than have them live in their kid's home. So I think if that system hasn't evolved already, it's a little bit hard seeing it evolving now when there are a lot of dads and moms in relation to others.

LK: Will payroll taxes increase for Social Security in the next century?

GRAMLICH: If we go to defined contribution accounts, it doesn't have to happen. If we stick with the way we do it now, then that's a good prediction to make.

LK: Will this money go into stocks because of the higher rate of return?

GRAMLICH: All the plans proposed feature equity investment. But we agree if you define the contribution, then people making the investment ought to be free, at least, to put it in diversified portfolios.

LK: Would there be specific stocks that people wouldn't be allowed to put their money into because the retirement money could be lost?

GRAMLICH: No. I'd have the government buy the whole market with index funds. Once you get into choosing specific stocks there will be political interference. The fund manager, like my company or the government, would select where the money goes.

LK: So a bad day on Wall Street could mean a bad day for those with retirement money on Wall Street?

GRAMLICH: Yes. And it's a risk. But any slice of historical period shows stocks outperform bonds. There is always a risk the market will be down in the year you retire, but it won't be down enough to wipe out the gains over a working career. But, yes, it could wipe out a share of those. If the stock market fails to outperform bonds, then any of the three ideas we came up with in 1996 isn't going to look very attractive.

LK: And if the stock market went south, those with retirement money wouldn't be able to count on any guaranteed minimum or assistance, correct?

GRAMLICH: I wouldn't assist it, no. We don't do it with IRAs.

LK: Would the mandatory contribution be tax-exempt?

GRAMLICH: I expect it will be treated the same as we treat 401(k)s and IRAs, so the answer is yes.

LK: What do you say to the proponents of means testing in which a millionaire would not be entitled to Social Security?

GRAMLICH: I don't like that idea, because if people saved a lot then they don't get Social Security, and if that's the way we do it, then why save anything at all? That is an undesirable incentive. Means testing fails the incentive test. Nobody on the council supports means testing, which is one of the few things we agreed on.

LK: Jump ahead twenty years and tell me what Social Security will look like.

GRAMLICH: By that time it's close to inevitable that we'll have a scaled-back public system and we will have defined contributions to an individual account. It will be happening in most countries of the world by that time.

JOHN SEELY BROWN

CHIEF SCIENTIST, XEROX CORPORATION;

DIRECTOR, PALO ALTO RESEARCH CENTER

First, learn how to learn and learn how to love learning new things. Second, be open to new ideas no matter how bizarre they first seem because a lot of ideas are going to come at you and many will challenge certain background assumptions you hold. But if you give them the time of day you might find ways to use them.

LK: What are we going to find in an office in the twenty-first century?

BROWN: I question whether we'll have "offices" as we currently think of offices. We're moving into an era where, instead of thinking about the office, we think about the "workscape." Most of us probably spend a tiny fraction of our time in our offices. We spend as much time around coffeepots, conference rooms, hallways, airports, home, highways, and so forth, so we should break away from the frame of thinking most work gets done in offices; rather, work becomes distributed over the entire physical space that we traverse through or occupy during any eight- or twelve-hour period of our day.

LK: So we will still have an office building?

BROWN: We'll still have office buildings but I think you'll find offices will take more the shape of social gathering spaces where you can come together to have high-powered, high-performance conferences and informal meetings.

LK: No more conference rooms?

BROWN: There will be an increase in electronic-based conference rooms where you have powerful meeting capture tools that facilitate the streamlining of meetings and the ability to capture everything that is being decided at the meeting without the extra work of having to prepare minutes after that. There will be things like electronic white boards where anything that you write will be automatically captured and transformed into a document for you without any additional work.

Video and audio can be captured for later replay if you want, perhaps indexed by what you've been writing on the white boards and so on. So you'll see more emphasis on the social spaces of office buildings which facilitate coming together and having not just high-powered meetings but very productive, informal conversations.

LK: This sounds like we're going to be taped.

BROWN: I think you'll find meeting capture rooms have facilities for recording anything that's going on for later replay or transcription if you want. Think of a tape loop that records everything that's been said for one minute and then erases it after that one minute, so if somebody says a brilliant idea, others in the rooms won't have to say, "Oh, can you say it again?" You won't have to. You hit the replay button and the last thirty seconds will be replayed and the ingenious thought will be there. You can set it for thirty seconds or a minute or whatever you want.

LK: Let's go back to the office.

BROWN: The workscape.

LK: Sorry. There will be a desk and a fax machine and a computer screen?

BROWN: The type of equipment you think about today will be history. There won't be personal computers, there won't be telephones, there won't be fax machines. I doubt there will be pagers. Instead you'll see some kind of totally integrated communication appliances that will facilitate all your communication needs in one device. You will see a smart input-output basket that is a portal for taking any document in the physical world and immediately converting it into the digital world or taking anything in the digital space and converting it into the analog physical paper space. You'll see personal desks going away and see desks crafted for two or three people to sit around and be able to share information on the screen. The screen will also become part of the woodwork.

LK: It sounds like there will be many group projects and not a lot of individual working.

BROWN: There's a lot more collaborative work going on than the architects of office buildings today understand or the architects of informational systems understand. Most real work happens collaboratively. We need to find ways to honor how knowledge and ideas are actually created.

LK: Will secretaries be necessary in the workscape?

BROWN: There will definitely be a blurring of distinction between administrative assistants and executive assistants, and we may find ourselves going back to the original notion of secretaries. Those are the people who are really orchestrating the events that you find behind the scenes. So there will be secretaries but not in the way we currently view them or pay them. It will be an evolutionary change, a gradual change. Right now secretaries do a lot of this and aren't recognized for what they do, and there will come a point where we will recognize their skills and problem-solving abilities and they will become full-blooded participants in the workscape as opposed to these subservient roles.

LK: You were talking earlier of integrated appliances which will sit in an office —

BROWN: A workscape.

LK: Workscape. What will these be like?

BROWN: You'll carry them with you. I think you'll carry a wireless device that is your phone and is your fax machine and is also a small window onto the World Wide Web and so on. Every device you have will be "IP addressable" (Internet addressable), so every artifact that we have will actually sit on the Internet, and many will be highly integrated so they can carry on multiple functions all at the same time.

LK: What is it going to look like?

BROWN: Something like digital paper, which is the size of an eight-by-eleven pad of paper. It may be a quarter-inch to a half-inch thick. It will have high-resolution displays and wireless communication, a virtual keyboard (if you still use keyboards), and it would be something which connects into a set of almost-personal Web sites behind the scenes sitting on the Internet, which carry out the assistant tasks which you have created.

LK: This sounds like we're not going to need those yellow Post-it notes anymore.

BROWN: Each of us wants to be able to have the opportunity to craft the workspace as we want. We all work differently. We actually all think differently, and what you want to be able to do is have each person craft his or her digital workscape as he really wants. And the key property of the Post-it note is it allows you to put your persona on anything you want at a particular moment. Now, walk into ten people's offices and you'll see just how different each office really is. One person puts huge stacks of paper all over the place, another has a very pristine desk—

LK: And that always has been the case.

BROWN: Always been the case. So as we move more into the digital world that same ability to tailor the workscape as you want, to match your particular cognitive style of work, is going to become even more important.

LK: Do you expect employees will be in their homes for the most part and just show up at the office, excuse me, workscape, once a week?

BROWN: The key notion of a workscape is, it blurs the distinction between the office, the home, the road, and so on. The workscape is like a manifold which spreads over all of these places. I think you'll find that people are doing some work at home, some work at clients' workspaces, some work in the conference rooms, so work will happen all over the place. The key is going to be able to connect, or disconnect, or stay connected to your own workscape as you move around from these physical places without having to worry about "What did I leave over here?" or "If I update a file here is it also updated over there?" and so on.

LK: Will it matter where a headquarters is located and will cities like New York and Los Angeles still be big business centers?

BROWN: Yeah, I think they will. Out here in Silicon Valley you can't help but go to a restaurant, listen to a conversation at the next table, and wonder, "My God, is my company ready to do that?" You hear the buzz, and in the buzz you not only pick up ideas but you get a sense of what everyone else is doing and you start thinking about yourself relative to that. So I think the physical locale is actually going to be very important in terms of providing one kind of grounding in terms of your intuitions about what's going on in the world and how good you are relative to other people.

LK: Tell me about the office staff.

BROWN: There will be an increasing necessity to have someone around who understands multiculturalism, be it bilingual or bicultural, because translation is only part of the game, and there has to be understanding of what that utterance might have meant from that conversation. When you move to a global economy it becomes increasingly challenging to see the world from the other person's point of view.

LK: Will we still commute, and will there still be a rush hour in the twenty-first century?

BROWN: Commuting doesn't necessarily mean rush hours. If you are working wherever it makes sense at that particular moment there's no reason to believe it makes sense for everybody to jump on the road at eight A.M. to go to some centralized office buildings. You may go there anytime during the day and you may stay home. So I think you'll find a much more uniform distribution of travel. You won't find these burst modes of travel at eight A.M. and five P.M. I don't even think we'll have an eight-hour day anymore.

LK: Let's talk about travel. Are we still going to travel to meet a client and do business, or will we do it by teleconferencing?

BROWN: I think you'll find physical meetings where you get a chance to look the other person in the eye. Having some physical and social contact will always be important. Cyberspace will not replace physical space. But once you've established connections physically, you'll be able to extend that into cyberspace. At the same time, you will, no doubt, make connections in cyberspace that will lead to getting together in the physical space. So I see these as two complementary structures, each one aiding the other.

LK: A follow-up on the conference room where we're having a meeting. Will there be screens there so we can have John Seely Brown in his Palo Alto—

BROWN: Workscape.

LK: Yeah, and then someone in Bangor, Maine, on another screen, and everyone else at the table in a conference room someplace else?

BROWN: Every reasonably equipped conference room will have at least those capabilities. You want to blur the distinction between who's physically in the conference room and who's virtually in the conference room. This is what I've been talking about: blurring the boundaries between physical space and cyberspace.

LK: The move toward a workscape will begin with a small business or a large corporation?

BROWN: It could go a number of ways. A large corporation has the constant need to attract publicity, so they may be the first to change. On the other hand, if you look at the industry that does construction or the industry that makes movies, both are already well out in front in terms of being able to bring vast collections of tiny companies and teams together for brief moments to get the job done. That hints at a new kind of workscape. You will see, because of digital form and the Internet, the movie industry come together in virtual space as opposed to just physical space. So you may find an industry as opposed to just a firm doing it. The third possibility is a state. I've been thinking how California could actually experiment with building a new kind of fabric that brings commerce and learning together in this virtual space. There could be huge webs of mom-and-pop shops coming together to get products done but the same thing could be done for a university. Soon you will see these webs serving the dual purpose of work and learning, and you might see a state putting in the infrastructure that allows new ways to work and learn. We're twenty years away from the third possibility.

LK: Companies now are doing a lot of outsourcing such as hiring an independent contractor to do the payroll rather than have someone on staff doing it. Is security a concern?

BROWN: It already is a concern, and one of the challenges we face in the cyberspace age is how to really create a moderate sense of security. You'll be seeing some major progress within the next few years on this. It is a false hope to believe computer systems can be totally secure because it has as much to do with social-political practices as it does with technological practices.

LK: So there's going to be problems?

BROWN: There are always going to be problems, and especially if we don't address the social side of work and if we don't live in a civil society and if we don't have some moderate amount of trust. Work without trust is always going to be highly inefficient and without a technical solution.

LK: Will the workscape become more family-friendly?

BROWN: Absolutely. Remember, we are blurring the boundaries between living, working, and learning, so it stands to reason we will blur how families impinge on the workscape itself. A lot of times you may be working with a lot of your family members around you or in your periphery. You may find kids in the workscape. When you engage in knowledge-work you aren't going to have dangerous equipment around, so many of the reasons for barring families from being around the workscape or workplace are no longer quite so valid.

LK: Will there be opportunities for employees to get together in the workscape?

BROWN: I think as businesses go beyond the pure business process (engineering craze), they'll begin to realize knowledge-work gets done in a social fabric, and as much attention has to be paid to the social fabric as is paid to the business processes which structure the work. You will see increased attention to an understanding of trust and of each other, and a willingness to listen to highly diverse points of view We need to find ways to enrich the social fabric of work as opposed to just the syntactical business processes of work. We are going to blur the distinctions of what we think of as work, what we think of as learning, what we think of as entertainment, and what we think of as living. You are going to see yourself doing several things simultaneously where you can see a movie, have a conversation, and then have a flash about how to finish the painting. The distinction of when we had an idea and where it came from will blur.

LK: And one way to enrich the social fabric of work is how?

BROWN: Provide more opportunities to have informal conversations in meetings and to find ways to honor the multiple points of view that will be brought forth in trying to understand something. As we look at the chaos around us, we recognize that no one person is an expert all the time. You will find the value of cultural, intellectual, gender diversity is going to play out in very major ways as we move forward. Again, this is a way to triangulate on the best possible interpretation of something in that particular moment.

LK: If I call an off— Wait, if I call a workscape will a human being answer or will it be one of those voice mail systems where I punch "1" to talk to somebody?

BROWN: In calling other businesses you will encounter more intelligent but nevertheless automated voice dispatch systems. On the other hand, in the workscape of your colleagues (the community or practice that you happen to be a part of) there will be new technology to enhance your awareness of "the periphery." In other words, you'll know what's happening in everyone else's workspace that you are connected with. This, then, allows you to have a sense of whether that person is in or is busy, so you'll have the ability to pick the right time to place a call.

LK: And this is done by my calling them first and going through this with them?

BROWN: No. What you'll probably find is going through some kind of multicast technology on the Internet and you'll have an increased awareness of where others are at that moment and what others are doing. It may be, for example, a low-quality video stamp that says, "Yes, he's in the office," or "No, she's not in the office," so you know whether or not to place a call.

LK: You paint a picture of efficiency.

BROWN: Well, it's effective not just efficient. What we're looking at is how to decrease the deadtime when you're doing useless work, like trying to find a document you created a week ago. And how to increase the "live time" when you actually are creating value in the workplace, creating more time to think creatively, more time to actually collaborate with each other. Here at the Palo Alto Research Center, one of the goals is to design technology that is sufficiently powerful that it can get the hell out of the way and just basically disappear. We're looking at bringing calmness back to the office so that the things which really matter are the things you are focusing on, not the technology you are using. We need technology that fits the way an old shoe fits: so perfectly that you never rub up against it and it enables you to focus on the work rather than finding the right document, finding the right format, being able to scribble the right kinds of comments for the right kind of person, shipping them off, remembering addresses, and all of that. It will disappear.

LK: We are going through this now because the technology is still new, correct?

BROWN: In part yes, but also because the vendors of the technology add more features to the technology. The easiest thing in the world is to say, "I've added more memory, so I can add twenty-five new features." I'd like to say if you add twenty-five new ones, take fifty old ones away. Adding feature after feature requires no taste. It requires taste to step back and say, "What are the minimal features that are needed that can be crafted by the user on the fly?"

LK: What worries you?

BROWN: In the twenty-first century we're going to find change even more than it's happening now. This means the competitive edge of the individual, the competitive edge of an organization, actually turns on one's ability to learn. So what worries me is we're not putting enough attention on creating a learning culture. And that's the learning culture in the workscape, at home, and in the schools. So I think if you don't feel comfortable picking up fundamentally new skills every three to five years you're going to be in bad shape. That may cause an increase between the haves and the have-nots which will be determined primarily on whether you have a willingness or even an interest in learning. I think learning is quite different from being educated because if you look at most of us now many years out of college, what we've learned, we've learned from and with each other. Learning is fundamentally social. We learn in groups, from groups, in relationships, from relationships, and so on and so forth. I'll guess that twenty-five years from now we're not going to be talking about organizational architectures, but rather learning architectures. Corporations are going to have to think primarily in terms of how to redraft the physical spaces, the social spaces, and the informational spaces together in a way that enhances our employees and ourselves to engage in learning.

LK: Will fewer people be expected to do more work, or might we see more people in the workscape?

BROWN: My guess is you will see more people and they will be engaged in more creative activities that actually create content that gets consumed in leisure as well as in business. An example is Web sites. There are new ones coming on and there will be so many that a new kind of media will be formed that will employ huge numbers of people who are artistically inclined. There will be new jobs which blend the artistic component with the content component. Here at PARC (Palo Alto Research Center), I'm thinking about giving someone this job title: knowledge artist. I'm not sure what it means yet but it brings the artistic sensibilities to try to get to the essence of what some complex knowledge domain is about. We have a hard time getting something that is wonderfully simple but actually captures and honors the complexities of the idea. Picasso could take a pencil and sketch three lines and capture the full-blooded wonder of some person's personality. That's what I want in a knowledge artist. We're going to need more skills like that.

LK: What other job titles will we have in the next century?

BROWN: Knowledge architect. Organizational architect who can design structures that enable productive, effective work to happen. We have sacrificed creativity in the push for efficiency, and efficiency is what mattered most in the old economy. In the new economy we are walking into, creating new rules of the game is going to be very important. I see it in the shift from making products to making sense. We are going to find more work in the interpretive role: How do you make sense out of what is going on? You're doing this right now because you hear my words and try to figure out what needs to be explained further, which becomes the next question. You are engaged in sense-making.

LK: The next question is more of an observation than a sentence: You use the words "blend" and "blur" a lot.

BROWN: We have tended to see the world broken up into categories that actually aren't going to help us make sense out of where the world is going, so those categories are going to have to change or we're always going to be confused about what is going on.

We have to be freer to explore and to think out of the box. The value of thinking out of the box is going to be increasingly important as we try to gain competitive edges.

LK: In this century we were thinking within the box?

BROWN: We were thinking about constant improvement within the box, and now we have to worry about effectiveness out of the box.

LK: Because effectiveness out of the box will eventually come back and change what's in the box?

BROWN: Yes.

LK: I don't even know what I just said.

BROWN: It's a good metaphor.

LK: To be a good boss in the next century, what will someone have to bring to the table?

BROWN: There are two critical things a boss has to do: (1) be incredibly good at listening and listen to what is *not* being said as much as to what *is* being said, and (2) ensure that an open and honest communication is actually taking place. The boss has to communicate with clarity and simplicity without sacrificing the authenticity of the idea.

LK: Will future bosses have to be different than they are now?

BROWN: Yes. The boss has to be very skilled at both learning and unlearning. We have to be willing to challenge our own background assumptions and be capable of giving them up when they don't do the work they used to do. That requires the capability of learning and unlearning, and it's a terrifying thing for most of us. We tend to hear things over and over again in the same way and we get stuck in our own "box," if you will. We need to unlearn the assumptions in that box to see the world afresh.

LK: What's going to happen to paper?

BROWN: I don't believe the paperless office will happen anytime in our collective lifetimes. Clutter will still be around, but there are certain forms of paper that will go away. For example, I'm sure you won't find reference books any longer in paper form, you may find novels and you'll find new kinds of paper that are reusable. That is, the paper—we call it digital paper—can be first printed on with a special and very inexpensive new kind of printer or stylus and then, once you're done reading it and marking it up, you drop it into the input-output basket I was talking about earlier and—

LK: Let me guess, it comes out blank?

BROWN: It will suck all the annotations off of it and add those annotations to the original digital document as a new layer of information and then erase the paper for immediate reuse.

LK: So you can use the same sheet of paper for a year or something?

BROWN: Yes.

LK: One more question: Will we still lift pens from our office?

BROWN: Workscape. Yes.

Magdalena Yesil

Founder, MarketPay

Don't be afraid of or shun technology. It's here to serve you, so learn about it. Indulge in your curiosity. And it isn't going away.

LK: Are there going to be currency and coins in the twenty-first century?

YESIL: Absolutely, but they'll be mostly used in the electronic form.

LK: We won't have dollar bills in our pockets?

YESIL: We definitely will carry walk-around money. There's nothing I can do with an electronic coin when I'm thirsty and want a cold drink. I'll have to have a real dollar bill to pay to get myself a cold beer, unless, of course, I'm in front of a vending machine that accepts electronic payments. For most of my purchases, I will be paying with electronic representations of the dollar bill.

LK: What's that going to look like?

YESIL: It will look as it does today but there'll be no dirt and no paper. It's going to be on the screen at my office and on the screen at home, and that screen could be a TV screen or a PC. It could even be a screen on a computer game machine or a classroom desk.

LK: But if you're going to the 7–Eleven will you pay with electronic money?

YESIL: I'll pay, most likely, with physical currency. There is nothing more convenient than having legal tender on a piece of paper that I can exchange for a cold drink. Now, smart cards might be used in a case like this too.

LK: What's a smart card?

YESIL: It's a piece of plastic that has money in it. It's the next generation of the telephone cards we see today. You might even have a smart card issued by 7–Eleven. But there is always going to be a place for the paper and metal money that we use.

LK: Is the penny going to last?

YESIL: The copper penny as we know it will probably not be here in the year 2010. The lowest denomination will be a nickel.

LK: So tell me how we pay for things?

YESIL: I think people will continue to use their credit cards and probably even more so than they do now. They'll still write checks and they'll still pay with cash. Let me give you this example: My child comes home from school and he doesn't want to do his homework. Instead he wants to play a computer game against his cousin who lives in New York, which is on the other side of the country. I will give him an allowance in "Net money" which will enable him to play a computer game for a few hours on the Net and which will enable him to use a homework helper like an encyclopedia when he gets around to doing his homework. All of this will be paid with "electronic money." These aren't new sources of money. They are the same currencies that we know but now we're using another communications medium.

LK: Net money?

YESIL: That's an electronic wallet available from a number of companies, including mine, which is similar to a leather wallet. You put your credit cards in there as well as your cash.

LK: But this exists on a screen?

YESIL: Yes. You draw money from whatever payment instrument you're using, like a credit card or a debit card or your checking account or a stock brokerage account. Ideally, parents once a week can automatically deposit or download $10 or $15 (depending on their generosity) into a child's electronic wallet. That enables me to keep my child at home for computer games rather than letting him go to the arcade down the street, which most despise.

LK: A child will spend money to play computer games?

YESIL: Mostly. Also for a homework helper. But if I only have one child and his knowledge level is changing every year I might choose not to buy a specific program and instead just let him go in and rent software to do the research. He will be charged by a block of time like thirty minutes or he might be charged by the question. There will also be sources charging on a subscription basis.

LK: Where else will we need an electronic wallet?

YESIL: I think a common use of the Internet will be dating services for people who don't necessarily want to go to smoky bars. Chat forums have been a popular activity on-line. America Online says it's created a virtual community; people who are interested in Land Rovers or four-wheel driving or people with an obscure disease might want to talk to each other over America Online or the Internet. So in the year 2010, for example, we're going to see a lot of these communities sharing thoughts and experiences on-line. Some of these experiences will be paid for and others will be free.

LK: So we'll be cyberdating and take our electronic wallets along?

YESIL: Why not? Play trivia with your cyberdate! Or treat your date to a cybermovie where the two of you become the lead characters.

LK: Hey, whatever works. Tell me about cybercommerce.

YESIL: Commerce is the exchange of money, buying and selling. Anytime you have 40 or 50 million people connected to each other on a communication medium, they will conduct commerce sooner or later. You may have a 1958 Corvette I want to buy and I'll negotiate with you on the price and, ultimately, send you the payment so you can get it shipped to me. We've been conducting commerce using telephone lines. Now we've got the Internet or cyberworld.

LK: But if you buy the Corvette on-line, can I get paid while we're still on-line?

YESIL: Yes, if the payer has his checking account connected to his electronic wallet. There are going to be escrow agents on-line, certificate authorities that will authenticate a purchase will be on-line, and there will be third parties that we use today to build trust without even thinking.

LK: Are we still going to have mail-order catalogs sent to us that we can touch, or is that going to all be done on-line?

YESIL: No, I think we will still have mail-order catalogs. Mail-order catalogs are very entertaining. You can take them to bed and thumb through. You can take them on your car trip and look through. And you can pull out your cell phone and make an order. There's a lot of convenience to having forty pages with pictures. You can take a lot of information in within two or three minutes by flipping through that catalog. It would take several downloads into a computer before it would appear on the screen. Now, that said, there are lots of things I can do with my computer that I can't do with the printed catalog. I can scan my own photo in there and when I choose a yellow sweater, I can use my scanned photo to reflect how the sweater looks on me. Or I can send out an intelligent agent that can find me a white Lacoste shirt for tennis with specifications, 100 percent cotton for under $50. Think about this: It would be wonderful to come home and have your groceries delivered or things you are looking for searched and found and delivered as well. That's what an intelligent agent inside the computer will be doing. You can pick an item and set parameters like, "I only want the tennis shirt if it's under $50 and if I can have it delivered within the next week." I pay for it on the computer with electronic money.

LK: Will we be making large purchases over the Internet?

YESIL: Once the trust issue is settled, we will. And that happens with digital ID, digital signatures, certificate authority, and third parties who are willing to intervene. Today when I use a Visa card, Visa is providing a service of trust. You know my card has validity when I present it to you. When I give you a dollar bill, the American government is taking the position of trust. When I write a check, my bank provides a certain amount of trust. In the electronic world, we're going to have the same need for trust as well, and I'd expect those to be the same entities that provide these functions in the physical world today, like the credit card association and banks.

LK: What will a bank look like when you walk into it?

YESIL: You probably won't.

LK: Won't what?

YESIL: You probably won't walk into one.

LK: So how am I going to go to the bank?

YESIL: I don't think there will be many brick and mortar banks. There might be a lot of bankers, but they'll come to you. I expect most of my communication with the bank will happen over the computer where I can balance my account, move funds around, send money to others, pay bills. My bank will be a collection of "smart bankers" who will come to my office or talk to me on my computer screen. The physical bank building is not going to be as important as it is today.

LK: But if you want hard cash, then what?

YESIL: You use the ATM machine, but it won't be at banks. It will be where the cash is needed, like shopping centers and grocery stores.

LK: The twenty-first century sounds like a good place to be if everybody is ordering things on-line and you run a delivery service.

YESIL: I think delivery services, especially UPS and FedEx, are going to be big winners out of the information superhighway revolution.

ALFRED BERKELEY
PRESIDENT, NASDAQ

Get very very smart about something specific as opposed to smatterings of this and that.

LK: What are the significant changes in the next twenty years in the stock market?

BERKELEY: I think, at least from the standpoint of NASDAQ, that the market is going to become more accessible to ordinary mortals than ever before. There's going to be a huge amount of information on the World Wide Web about how the market works. Prices are available with a fifteen-minute delay, and I would expect that to become real time in the next century.

LK: This suggests a lot of trading can be done from home?

BERKELEY: It's already true and it's going to become all the more true in the next century. But let's not denigrate the role of knowledgeable brokers because their role is changing. It will no longer be value-added to call him or her up at lunch and get quotes because you'll be doing that on your PC. Brokers in the future are going to become more specialized, and I think that's a good thing.

LK: What will this do to Wall Street?

BERKELEY: The geographic denominator will be obliterated. There will be an anonymity and distance. The trick will be to have a basis of trust upon which transactions are done. The very impetus that may make you want to hold your cards close to the chest and be in a different place physically is the same set of information another guy will want to have. When you play poker you want to look the other guys in the eye. So to the extent we have markets that are geographically removed, we need more news about what cards are showing. That's why there will be more forcing of information disclosure of the professionals from the amateurs. That's why markets now have to report trades within ninety seconds of when they actually occur. That's valuable information and it used to be information used by one party as an advantage over another party.

LK: What does that do to those who make a living on Wall Street?

BERKELEY: What it means is, it doesn't matter where they physically live. It's going to mean those who make the higher value-added functions, like actually making the decision of where to put the investments, are going to be more valuable, and those who merely carry the information from one part of the organization or one part of the world to another will disappear.

LK: Half the population has stocks now. What does that mean?

BERKELEY: It means we're starting to accept the fact we have to take care of ourselves and we shouldn't rely on the government for retirement and a standard of living that is acceptable to middle-income people. Government will provide the minimum of a safety net for the poorest of people and the reason for that is these deficits we're dealing with—or at least trying to deal with.

LK: Are you worried about the huge amounts of money in mutual funds creating a leverage in the market?

BERKELEY: Of course. You have exactly the same issues that were involved in the consolidation of this market that you've had in every market before. Concentration in America causes suspicion. It's a cultural dimension here.

LK: Should people worry if there isn't a balanced budget in the year 2002?

BERKELEY: I think it is terribly important because we pile up that burden on our children and our children's children.

LK: Well, how comfortable are you it will be done in the year 2002?

BERKELEY: I think it will take an extraordinary will on the part of people who are elected on two-year cycles (congressmen) to overcome their propensity to enjoy today at the expense of tomorrow. I think it's a very tough problem for democracy. Entitlements are forcing us to transfer money from one part of the economy to another.

LK: What will the market be like in the next century?

BERKELEY: I think it will be open twenty-four hours within the next twenty years. We already have near–twenty-four-hour trading in liquid securities. The book will roll with the sun so when one person comes to work, another is leaving and files will be transferred to different markets around the world. If there's news about a stock, that stock will continue to trade in world markets after our markets close.

LK: Do you think there will be a need for a market like NASDAQ in another fifty or sixty years?

BERKELEY: Markets are going to be more important than they are now. Understand this: The primary purpose of a market like the NASDAQ is not the secondary trading that goes on in issued shares but to allow companies to get capital and then build factories and create jobs. They can't get that money in unless there's a subsequent market where their shares can be traded.

LK: Who will be issuers on NASDAQ in another fifty years?

BERKELEY: Right now it's computer technology and health care technology that are the areas to be in. But we're the Ellis Island of capitalism. I think you'll continue to see privatization of government all around the world. Garbage collection might be privatized in the future. You could see that business on the market.

LK: What will the Dow Jones be like in another twenty years?

BERKELEY: I think it needs to be more representative than it is. There's no technology sector in it right now. And there's not a single NASDAQ stock in the Dow. They are going to have to change the index to reflect some of these other industries. Something is going to happen. It has to. I find it difficult to understand how the thirty stocks in the Dow can represent an economy as large as ours. I think one hundred stocks is better.

LK: Are we going to carry money in the future?

BERKELEY: I think it will be a handprint or something like that which is easier than carrying a card of some sort. But until we get to that point you'll be using the smart cards. I do see people in the future putting their hand on a scanner and then typing in a PIN to pay for a meal in a restaurant.

LK: How will we buy stocks in the next century?

BERKELEY: First of all, I think mutual funds are a better investment for the vast majority of people. Stock picking is a very tricky game, and even though I'm running a stock market, I think it's prudent that people be aware stocks aren't for the faint of heart or the casual observer. Buying stocks and buying mutual funds will be done on the World Wide Web or something like that. And by the way, this proves the need for brokers all the more. There will be those who look at a particular plan with investments within particular industries. But the growth in choices increases the need for somebody to come in and thoughtfully consider those choices. They do it now for institutions but someone will find a way to bridge the gap so individuals can be included. It's going to be easier to buy a stock whether you know a damn thing about it or not.

LK: Will markets continue to be affected by emotion?

BERKELEY: Yes.

LK: Will there be any way to avoid that?

BERKELEY: Maybe someone will invent computer software that will jump in and tell the user he is becoming emotional but a person's fear and greed will overcome it.

LK: If the Dow drops one hundred points in a day ten years from now will that mean the market isn't doing well?

BERKELEY: Not necessarily. In some cases you have great waves of people trying to create a sensation that things aren't going well. We have day traders in the market and they gang up on a stock and try to sell. They can force panics and force prices down after selling at the top. Then they buy it at a lower price.

LK: Well, it seems logical you ought to be able to stop that.

BERKELEY: The Securities and Exchange Commission makes it easier for these short-term speculators to continue to increase their business by allowing them to increase the rapidity with which they can trade.

LK: What scares you about the new century?

BERKELEY: We're not educating our young people. We don't have an ethic of education and we don't have an ethic of savings. In this global economy we're doing business with those who have a reverence for education as well as saving, so we're on the verge of being beholden to people, and that will ratchet down our standard of living.

LK: How do we educate our children to save when it hasn't been done for generations?

BERKELEY: The message we are influencing people with in this country is one of consumption. It could be a message of savings. It begins from the top down.

LK: Are people saving now?

BERKELEY: We landed on the shores in America and the food was free for the picking. If you didn't like your neighbor you could move West. We are adjusting as a country now to crowds. The population is starting to reach a state of panic. I'm fifty-two, and all my contemporaries are feeling their mortality and realizing that Social Security being there for them is a hollow promise and they have to provide for their own retirement. So we are now seeing an incredible rate of savings among baby boomers. And it is transferring to people just coming out of college. I suspect we saw tremendous savings, but from a different base, when immigrants arrived. They worked their butts off and saved but it was for a better house and then a series of better houses and then it was a car and then two cars. It wasn't until we got this saturation of mass manufacturing and all this consumer plastic stuff that people have had a backlash. We are saving in cash forms now and that's new.

LK: Why?

BERKELEY: I think it's for security. The fast pace of change causes instability. People don't know what's going to happen to them. No longer can you work for a company all your life and put your faith in it as well.

LK: Will there be a crash in the next century?

BERKELEY: There probably will be as long as we have all these human beings acting like lemmings and fear grips them. The market shuts down because of circuit breakers which kick in after a drop of 250 points. That used to be a lot but the market is higher now. I think the breakers should be expanded to 500 points.

LK: Give me some advice for good places to put money in the next century.

BERKELEY: It depends on where you look in the world. Coal-fired plants are being built in South America right now but they aren't a growth business in this country. So it's simplistic to say there are "old" industries and there are "new" industries. But if you want to stay close to home, the most exciting developments with worldwide potential are in biomedicine as we get genetic cures for diseases. The second major area is information, particularly content. You are going to see tremendous emphasis on the value of databases of all types. Communications services will be a valuable growth area. I think you are going to see distribution businesses being set up all over the world to bring the low-cost distribution we have in the United States to other countries. Keep an eye on a company called Corporate Express, which is going global with a combination of Domino's pizza delivery methodology and yellow pads or whatever you want for your desk. You type into your computer you want two pencils and a yellow pad and it will be shrink-wrapped on your desk the next morning.

LK: Speed is attractive now, isn't it?

BERKELEY: It is very important now in almost every industry. People pay for convenience and immediacy. It lowers inventory costs. You have a faster response to your customers, and it's a better way to do business.

LK: How do you feel about the next century?

BERKELEY: I was talking to a fellow in his eighties who said at the end of World War II there were 50 million to 75 million people in the United States and about the same number in Western Europe living in freedom, and all kinds of totalitarianism all over the world. Now there are a billion people living in freedom and they all want to improve their standard of living and they all want to work hard. It's risky to bet against all these people trying to do better. The coming down of the Berlin Wall is as important as anything in history. Setting so many people on a course that provides access to information and capital could be something really dramatic. I think about that a lot today.

Sports

In the year 2062, although it could be as early as 2057, two guys will be standing around arguing with each other about last night's ball game. Neither will be able to afford to actually go to the game, but both will have watched it on their home entertainment centers. And though each will know you always take two and then hit to right on a bunt and both will disagree about whether Sol Tuck is really worth $422 million a year, they'll probably be having the argument somewhere in Katmandu. I have no doubt in either year, 2057 or 2062, there will be a bunch of side bets at the beginning of each season about whether this is the year the Cubs go to the World Series. I think it will happen in the twenty-first century but I can't get any closer than that.

Sports has always been, and will continue to be, common ground. We will always argue about the runner being safe at second or if a field goal should have been kicked with four minutes remaining and a touchdown was needed or if the game has been taken over by those who care only about the numbers on a bottom line instead of on a scoreboard. Diverse opinions and backgrounds will always come together because of The Game as long as change is minimal.

You are going to hear from three people who go to the arena or ballpark or stadium from three very different perspectives and with three very different jobs. But each of them loves The Game.

Bob Costas has called NBC games for Major League Baseball, the

National Football League, and the NBA, as well as many college basketball rivalries. He has been a part of coverage for the big games too: Super Bowls, World Series, and the Olympics. From 1988 to 1994 he was host of the popular and Emmy Award–winning *Later with Bob Costas* on NBC. He's had a front-row seat and sees the big picture.

Bud Selig owns the Milwaukee Brewers but since 1992 has been the acting commissioner of Major League Baseball. He is known for an ability to build consensus, and when you consider that the owners of Major League Baseball teams can't sit in the same room without arguing, it becomes obvious what a tough job Bud Selig has had for the past few years. But it's been a tough few years for The Game as well. Because of labor disagreements the entire 1994 World Series was canceled. Both Selig and the owners and the Players Association know that can never happen again without The Game going right down the tubes. Bud and I spoke during a Brewers' game in the seventh inning. He may have been looking on the field but he can see the big picture.

David Falk is an attorney with treetop-level offices just beyond Georgetown in Washington, D.C. The walls where he works are filled with cereal boxes with Michael Jordan's picture. There's a baseball bat signed by Jordan and there's a director's chair in the corner with Falk's name embroidered on the back. All of that, as well as the basketballs and shoes, is the work of David Falk—and, of course, that other guy too.

BOB COSTAS
NBC SPORTS

In the first few months of the year 2000, be extra careful not to misdate those checks.

LK: It's 2010. What are we watching on television?

COSTAS: We're watching more and more of what the viewer specifically wants to see when he or she wants to see it. There will be some technology which the networks will probably cringe at that will allow you to receive and store and file shows on some kind of disk. So if you want a separate disk that has every *Seinfeld* on it, whatever the equivalent of *Seinfeld* is in 2010, you wouldn't necessarily have to watch it at the time it comes down the line. You just receive it and file it and watch it whenever you feel like it in a less-cumbersome way than taping shows now.

LK: So I could receive and store the entire 2010 Orioles' season?

COSTAS: That's right.

LK: Will I ever be able to direct myself? Will I ever be in the hockey goal and choose from what camera angle I watch the game or parts of the game?

COSTAS: I think for an extra price you will be able to tap into technology that says if you want to watch the entire game or any portion of the game that you wish from the goalie's perspective only, you'll be able to do it. You will be in the arcade.

LK: Will I be able to see anything I want? If I'm in Washington or you're in St. Louis will we be able to see every baseball game and every NFL game?

COSTAS: We're pretty close to that now with direct TV for baseball and basketball. And where it's going to be a boon is to the NFL because they play the fewest games so those games are more at a premium. You'll be able to add it to what people already have without taking anything away. You'll still get the two or three games every Sunday from free TV but if you're a 49ers fan in Boston and you just want to tap into every 49ers' game, they'll charge you ten bucks or whatever and boom.

If you're in Washington, D.C., and they're getting two or three NFL games on a Sunday but not the 49ers game, you can pay a fee and get that specific game.

LK: With this kind of concept, nobody's going to get huge shares anymore.

COSTAS: But what I think is going to remain a constant is the networks, or whatever the equivalents of the networks are, will pay a premium for this—an even greater premium than they pay today. Major sports events will become even more valuable because they'll cut through the clutter. So the old game of the week concept won't mean much anymore because there will be so many games available for a given regular season. Meanwhile, the Super Bowl will cut through everything. The World Series, the Olympics will cut through everything because, unlike this five-hundred-channel universe, it'll be the one place where you can watch a major thing while it's happening live. Cable will be the home of the regular season products.

LK: Will broadcasting change?

COSTAS: I don't think you're going to find Vin Scullys or Jack Bucks or Ernie Harwells. I think a guy like Jon Miller (the San Francisco Giants radio announcer) is a young version of the last generation. The whole idea of a local broadcast will become less and less important because people have access to so many different things that it will dilute the importance and the specialness of "our guy." As a result, there will be more broadcasters known by people in all parts of the country. Now, this doesn't mean they will truly be nationally known. Instead, with more games available, the broadcaster of the Seattle Mariners or the Colorado Rockies will be seen and heard while you are sitting in Rhode Island. Real sports fans, then, are going to know the names of more broadcasters than they used to and have some familiarity with their work. The Al Michaelses and Dick Enbergs and those people handling the biggest events will still have a national following but it won't be the impact that Curt Gowdy once had. It's a numbers game. There are more games on so there are more broadcasters to be heard. Many will be on stage for a while but not as many get center stage for as long as they used to. I think if Red Barber (long-time voice of the Brooklyn Dodgers and the first television announcer of a baseball game, August 26, 1939) started today he'd be an exceptionally talented broadcaster but there'd be no way he could have the effect on his audience that he once had. You can't replicate the circumstances of radio, of the Dodgers, of Brooklyn.

LK: Will we have a dugout camera? Will we have players wearing microphones?

COSTAS: Yes. I think the sense of distance and mystery will be reduced more and more. As young people seem to be drawn to technology and things with lots of bells and whistles, if it's a Nintendo generation, then we'll put cameras everywhere we can, give them point of view every place we can, we'll do everything that seems quicker and faster-paced until some significant portion of the audience reacts the other way. The tendency of television is if you have a gadget, use it. Restrained is not exactly our hallmark. You might have a market for people who feel they are experiencing sensory overload. And in the face of all this, an afternoon at Wrigley Field, or whatever the equivalent of Wrigley Field is, may seem all the more appealing, not just on its own merits but as an antidote to what's mostly out there. So maybe there'll be a reaction to it the way people move away from cities and live on a mountaintop.

LK: Will this help or hurt baseball?

COSTAS: You know, the best days of baseball may be past for a variety of reasons. Baseball is probably better on the radio than it is on television. Baseball on television is best when it isn't too intrusive and where the game's pace and rhythm are respected. Baseball is not an in-your-face spectacle. It's designed to be a leisurely pastime. So, in the sense that television always imposes its sensibility on baseball, it's always a bad fit. If you use the cameras so the drama of the game is captured, great! But this isn't a game where you force in five replays between pitches, and I don't think anything is gained by having a microphone at third base.

LK: Will this change the way a game is called?

COSTAS: In theory a guy calling the Texas Rangers game could think he's being seen on the satellite by someone in New York but he shouldn't be. On network television, a good broadcaster is going to have to have a grasp of some of the peripheral issues like legal issues, the economics of stadiums being built for teams, the threat of moving from city to city, the conflict of Players Association and management. The announcers are going to have to include those business understandings along with their understanding of the infield fly rule. Also, the guy calling a big game is crazy to think of himself as the center of the universe because all the rosters have been dissected and the game has been fully talked about and it's on the Internet and who knows whatever sources of information there will be. But he is the only voice being heard as it's happening. Announcers have to learn to be less heavy on raw information because the real fan has access to all of that information and, instead, emphasize more an engaging description of the game, have some give-and-take and opinion so that it doesn't duplicate the massive amount of information that's already out there from other sources. Stop thinking of yourself as The Source of information.

LK: Will a woman become the voice of a particular team?

COSTAS: Yes, it's coming and it's only a matter of time. Unlike interviewers, hosts, reporters, and sideline reporters, the craft of play-by-play is one you have to go to the minor leagues or the college level to learn and even if the networks wanted to hire a female play-by-play announcer, there's no feeder system, no place to develop a pool of candidates.

LK: Will announcers be "homers" and constantly root for the home team?

COSTAS: The emphasis on being a homer will depend upon the management and ownership of the given teams. Some will prefer a more sophisticated approach while others are going to want something more obvious. It's a matter of taste and will never be an across-the-board standard. Now it can also be argued, with more games on television and even though fans root for and have an emotional fascination with their local team, they have a less parochial point of view than they used to have because now they are getting more national influences. That is going to diminish the need for an announcer to be a homer. The fans are little more sophisticated. Of course it can be argued, and

I'm not saying I buy into this, that you could make it an avidly pro-Orioles broadcast, for example, and that will distinguish it from everything else out there.

LK: Are you looking forward to covering games in the future?

COSTAS: Sure. These changes are interesting even if they're not always pleasing. Now that said, I wish I could have done games in the fifties and the sixties when the game was more center stage and where some of the romance of the game was still there.

LK: Are indoor stadiums going to change much, and what's going to happen to the ballpark?

COSTAS: All new arenas and stadiums have to have incredible modern amenities because the cost of running a franchise being what it is, you have to get a lot of money from the highest rollers and they're not coming to the game solely to watch the game or root for their team, they're coming as a social or business evening. They've got other reasons for being at the game besides the game and you have to give them their luxury boxes, you have to give them their special services, you have to give them places to entertain their clients and feel like big shots. In baseball, ballparks of the future will be a strange combination of the past and the future. They will all be made to look like baseball theme parks. They'll all look like their version of Ebbets Field or Wrigley Field, but at the same time, they'll all bear the name of some corporation that's willing to pony up the millions of dollars for the advertising, like the Transworld Dome in St. Louis. A professional baseball team, for example, actually talked to Ralph Lauren to see if he'd cough up $50 million over ten years and then they'd call the place "The Polo Grounds." That's an example of trying to capture nostalgia on one hand and modern marketing on the other. At parks like that you'd have a rustic setting along with the most expensive 15,000 seats in the place which are super high-tech, super luxury, where these people who are willing to pay not just the cost of the ticket but a seat license on top of that, will sit in seats that have small television screens and computer terminals. If you want to call up the statistics of a given pinch hitter versus a relief pitcher or you want to see what's happening in other places around the league, or watch a different game or see a replay of the play you just saw with your own eyes, boom, you punch it up. Then you punch to another channel and you'll beckon your seat-side waiter, so instead of your standing in line for a hotdog at the old ballpark, your seat-side waiter will come up to you with quiche and champagne if that's what you want.

LK: Is soccer going to get popular?

COSTAS: I think soccer won't get popular in the United States because the other sports have a foothold and there's no cultural tradition.

LK: NBA will continue to boom?

COSTAS: NBA will continue to boom, but well before 2010 it's going to level off because Michael Jordan drives the league like no individual has in team sports in our lifetime. When he retires, the NBA will take a dip in popularity. He's Babe Ruth. He is to NBC, on the night that he plays, what Jerry Seinfeld is to NBC on the nights when his show is on. The Bulls in a blowout get a higher rating than other teams playing a close game seven.

LK: International NBA?

COSTAS: Definitely. There's no question it will fly. The only problem is logistics. If they can work it out so they can give teams the equivalent of basketball charter flights that can travel like the Concorde, I think that's the only thing that separates the NBA from being in a half-dozen non-American cities.

LK: Major League Baseball in how many cities?

COSTAS: I think thirty-two. And they stop. And a real commissioner would say, "We have to stop right here." The talent is spread too thin. We don't even know who's on our own team, let alone all the other teams around the league. We've got to go to thirty-two, which is a workable number for scheduling, four four-team divisions per league with no wild cards and only the champions of the four divisions per league, and hold them there.

LK: More NFL teams?

COSTAS: The NFL can keep expanding, not because it would not dilute the style of play but because there are more and more cities that would support an NFL team. It's not necessary that you know and follow the players on other teams the way it is in other sports so I think the NFL could probably go to thirty-six teams.

LK: Will there be better players in 2010?

COSTAS: Absolutely. Will there be others who are as interesting as Michael Jordan? Absolutely. But: Will there be a confluence of events where you have a guy who (a) is electrifying, (b) is truly great, (c) is very handsome, (d) is very well spoken, (e) is very appealing to people of all races, age groups, sexes, and (f) is on a team that is good enough to go to the championship while putting him at center stage? Add to this the marketing of that guy at a time when people are becoming jaded by the marketing and the answer is I don't know. It's going to become tougher to accomplish in the future.

LK: Is the name of a team going to stay with the city?

COSTAS: I'll bet you there will be some attempts to make teams truly the Cleveland Browns the way the Green Bay Packers are truly their city's team. Why would New York lay out a billion dollars to build a new stadium for the Yankees when the whole franchise is worth, at maximum, $250 million? Why not just buy the franchise?

LK: So we're going to see city-owned teams?

COSTAS: A few. Then the only problem is, who runs the team? And would the city elect its general manager? Would you have a referendum on trades?

LK: Are uniforms going to be wilder?

COSTAS: As long as the merchandising continues to work you'll see teams, except for the most traditional teams like the Cubs and the Yankees, change uniforms every three or four years because if they can make a few changes in the uniform then they reap profits on the merchandising. Expansion teams, even without a following, are always near the top in souvenir sales. Collectors want the first edition of uniforms. The Houston Rockets changed their uniforms to the crazy ones they're wearing now: Guaranteed they sell five times as many souvenirs as they sold a year earlier.

LK: Will sports be as important?

COSTAS: I think it will be even more important economically but it'll be less important for people emotionally. People won't feel about their team the way you felt about the Dodgers or I felt about the Yankees or my cousin felt about the Giants. Too much of the innocence is lost. You still have excitement about sports but the affection people feel for it has been diminished, and those are two very different things. It won't kill the game but it will change the way we relate to the game. When people like me talk about the fondness and connection they feel to baseball, they're really remembering what they used to feel and not describing what they still feel.

LK: Rule changes in baseball: What will happen?

COSTAS: Uniform rule on the designated hitter. Either both leagues with or both leagues without. I think it will be eliminated. The mound is going to be raised because the hitters are running rampant. They've got to level it off. So they'll split the difference from where it was in '68 before they lowered it and where it is now. And, eventually, they'll dump the wild card concept because they'll realize it dilutes the feeling of what a pennant race is and the importance of finishing first.

LK: Will seasons last as long as they do now?

COSTAS: I think they'll cut back to a 154-game season if they can get the Players Association to agree to it. They already have another round of playoffs and it's supposed to be an outdoor game, and they're pushing pretty close to November with an extra round of playoffs and 162 games. So cut it to 154 because you still have historical validity, which is what all the teams played prior to '61.

LK: Is hockey ever going to be a success on television?

COSTAS: I think it can be a success but it's never going to crack the top three. It's not part of the background and childhood memories of enough Americans.

LK: How about fines for players who fight or benches that clear?

COSTAS: If it keeps going the way it was starting to go in 1996 in the NBA, I think we'll realize that even a substantial fine of $30,000 or $40,000 doesn't mean much to a guy making $2 million or $3 million. You have to cost them and their team by sitting them out of games. And if need be, sit them out of playoff games where it would have the biggest effect.

LK: So it's going to be done by sitting out a game or two or three?

COSTAS: Sitting out games that matter. It would have more of an impact if, in the middle of the season Dennis Rodman headbutts somebody, the league says, "We're going to dock him so much money right now and he's going to sit out the first playoff game or the first two play-off games."

LK: How come the behavior on the field or the court or the rink is so bad?

COSTAS: There's a tone of belligerence in sports in general. It's anti-sportsmanship that now goes beyond toughness or competitiveness and it's occurred within the last five years. I think, to a certain extent, television has encouraged it. Look at the way NFL games are promoted, or NBA games. They aren't passionate competition but, rather, all-out wars and battles. It's the collisions and the injuries and the violent moments that we tend to focus on in the highlights. There's almost a reward in terms of attention. Look at Dennis Rodman, who is a very very good basketball player. The reason he's a celebrity doesn't have anything to do with his quality as a basketball player because, if that were the case, Karl Malone would be ten times the celebrity Dennis Rodman is. Players being harder to control isn't necessarily a bad thing because you wouldn't want it to be the way it used to be when they were completely under the owner's control, but there should be a happy medium. In team sports, to say that a player is analogous to Barbra Streisand or Michael Jackson is wrong because team sports count on a certain amount of stability for their appeal. Until the sports culture stops rewarding people for being jerks, what keeps them from acting like jerks?

LK: Instant replay going to make a comeback?

COSTAS: It will be used in a limited basis in football but it will never be part of baseball or basketball. In basketball it could be used for timing things—did the shot take place before the buzzer, or was the foot on the line or not on the three-point shot? But it won't be used to determine charge or goal tending because that'll slow the game up. In baseball, I think the tradition with the umpire makes it impractical. Football will use it for possession calls only, touchdown or not, in bounds or not, and they'll limit the number of times the opposing coach can challenge to maybe three times a half so they won't have as many slowdowns in play.

LK: There going to be domed stadiums everywhere?

COSTAS: Nope. I think there will be fewer and fewer of them, especially in baseball because the whole appeal of the sport is retro. As they modernize with all the amenities in the new stadiums the atmosphere has to remain old-time. The whole movement is back to the ballparks rather than impersonal and cold multipurpose stadiums. The move is toward parks like Camden Yards. When the Cubs need a new ballpark, it's going to be a new Wrigley Field. When the Red Sox need a new ballpark, it's going to be a new Fenway Park. I wouldn't be surprised if they take the Green Monster itself and transplant it in the new place. That's the whole appeal of baseball. The only places where you'll see domed stadiums in baseball are those places where the weather makes it absolutely necessary. It rains too much in Seattle. It's too damn hot and humid in Houston. But the new domed stadiums will be retractable, not just a little slit that you have at the Skydome where only a third of the field would be awash in sunlight if you opened it, but one where it would retract virtually all the way. You could put it up if it's raining or cold but if it's a nice day you give the fans a feeling of being outdoors, which is what the game is about. As we talk about sports becoming more and more modern and more and more overwhelmed by technology, it might be one of the places where people retreat from that. They retreat from the world where everyone's connected by the Word Wide Web and five hundred channels and the classic books on disks and computers. Sports might go back to something simpler and less technological where people could sit in the afternoon sun and not have their senses assaulted. It could be to baseball's advantage that instead of trying to be more like the fast-paced society the appeal will be to be less like it.

LK: You sound like there's a future for natural grass.

COSTAS: Definitely. I don't think you will see, other than in domed stadiums, another ballpark in our lifetime built with artificial turf. Most of the artificial turf places like Riverfront and Three Rivers are going to natural grass.

BUD SELIG

OWNER, MILWAUKEE BREWERS;

CHAIRMAN, MAJOR LEAGUE BASEBALL EXECUTIVE COUNSEL;

ACTING COMMISSIONER OF BASEBALL

Go to the ballpark for the day. You will feel better.

LK: Okay, let's say it's the year 2015—

SELIG: That's going to make me seventy-five years old.

LK: You and me both. Will baseball be in Cuba? Mexico?

SELIG: Well, one thing is for sure: I'm not going to be running it. Baseball will have gone international by this time. And it will be very aggressive internationally. I really believe by that time we'll be in a true World Series. If we recognize Cuba by that time, it will be in the league. Mexico too. Japan also.

LK: In other words, the Chicago Cubs could make a road trip that includes Japan?

SELIG: Sure. I think baseball's greatest strength will be in its ability to go international and to transcend things that you or I couldn't conceive of.

LK: Will baseball keep its American quotient even if it becomes international? Or is that important?

SELIG: We have much to explore and much to adjust to. It will enhance baseball, and the international element won't take away anything at all. The world loves baseball. Why shouldn't we develop the proper relationship between American and international baseball? It's waiting for everyone's advantage. The fact it's baseball is enough to keep its American flavor.

LK: Will most parks be baseball-only parks?

SELIG: Absolutely. That's the best way to present the game and it makes the most economic and social and psychological sense. Keep in mind, baseball is a game that must be played in the most intimate surroundings, and in my judgment, it should be played on grass. It needs to be played the way it has been played for the past 125 to 150 years. As a result, baseball needs to be played in ballparks whose seating capacity is less than the multipurpose stadiums have.

LK: Baseball parks need to maintain nostalgia, regardless of how modern they are, correct?

SELIG: Parks should look older, and at all times we should be governed by our history and tradition, but not to the extent of hurting ourselves in making some changes, but we have to be very careful about how we do it. New ballparks need to look old. Camden Yards (new park built in Baltimore) is the way to go.

LK: Where will the Jackie Robinson Stadium be built?

SELIG: I hope there will be one built. It's up to an individual club somewhere down the line. It's the most powerful and proudest moment in our history.

LK: What will the baseball commissioner's office be like?

SELIG: It's going to be much different. There's been an interesting evolution even now from Kenesaw Mountain Landis, who changed the office dramatically in the thirties, and by the time we got to Happy Chandler, they changed it some more. By the time we got to Ford Frick the office was changed even more. If one reads Ford's farewell speech in 1965 in Phoenix, you sense all the frustration and agony I catch today. This has been going on thirty-forty-fifty-sixty years, and people don't seem to understand it. More changed when Bill Eckert came in but it really started to change with Marvin Miller and the Players Association under Bowie Kuhn. So in my judgment, say in 2010, if we have done all our work properly and we have a labor agreement that's still in effect and one in which we are really partners with labor as we should have been all along, the commissioner will have a sport that is not only international but whose tentacles go everywhere in the world. While it's important that the commissioner is a figure perceived by the public as attendant to the game, and this includes matters of discipline, the job will be to take the game continually to different heights but with the understanding that there's an enormous amount of competition. There wasn't any in 1949.

LK: The job of the commissioner will change in what way or ways?

SELIG: Given the aggressiveness of the Players Association and given how life has changed, the job of the commissioner is to build consensus. I think the tough work has been done in terms of revenue sharing and labor peace and now we need a person who can take the game to new heights and not be encumbered by the internal economic wars that we had for three to four decades.

LK: Will there ever be another acting commissioner?

SELIG: For baseball's sake, I hope not.

LK: The relationship between commissioner and owners will change?

SELIG: The relationship between the owners and the commissioner has been changing since 1921. Look at the various commissioners: Chandler got fired, Eckert got fired, Bowie Kuhn in essence got fired, others resigned before they got fired. And the Players Association, as it got stronger, clearly doesn't care what the commissioner thinks. You can't govern a sport without a permanent commissioner and the fact of the matter is, you are going to need to make sure the commissioner can take this group of thirty disparate enterprises and move them around to get things done.

LK: So he will be a marketing kind of person?

SELIG: I hope it isn't the only thrust but marketing is going to be a very important part of the job. Pushing the game into new heights will certainly be determined by marketing skills and if the commissioner doesn't have those skills the people around him or her certainly will have them.

LK: Future issues will be what?

SELIG: I don't know they will be any different than they are now. You are going to have to have cost restraining issues in terms of salaries, no doubt about that. There will always be a relationship between revenues and salaries whether you call it a salary cap or not. Disparity in the markets and small markets versus large markets will continue to be issues.

LK: Future talk between labor and management should keep what in mind?

SELIG: One of the things we learned in 1994 was we were headed for a strike and we can't have that anymore. We had seven work stoppages. Never again. The American public is fed up with all that. We've gone over the wall this time and I have every confidence we will be able to do it in the future. Everyone learned.

LK: Future owners should remember what from this century?

SELIG: Keep the game in focus rather than their personal or individual interests. That's as important fifty years from now as it was fifty years ago and it's one of the problems in the game today.

LK: Do you envision a $50 million contract for a player or is it going to level off?

SELIG: Well, I think things will level off, but as we grow, certainly the players' salaries will continue to be the major cost item. We now have the top four of the top five payroll teams in the playoffs. That isn't by accident. What you've got right now is the guys who can spend the most are the guys who are going to win. Spending doesn't guarantee you anything but if you don't spend, you no longer have any chance to win.

LK: We've had coverage of the playoffs with two networks. What will television be doing with baseball?

SELIG: Multi networks will cover baseball in the next century.

LK: Pay-per-view?

SELIG: I don't think so. A lot of people would disagree with me but I don't think baseball should ever have any of its key games on pay-per-view. Now you could make a lot of money but it would be an extremely short-term thing. What you will find as you expand to having an international World Series, you may have all the networks involved.

LK: Will players move around as much as they do now?

SELIG: I hope not. As we change the economics of the game internally so that the Pittsburghs and the Twin Cities and the Seattles and so forth can compete, I think you'll see less of it. Everybody has begun to understand that while we can recreate the old days, it is terribly important that the premier players and the star players stay where they are if at all possible. The stability factor is helpful to baseball.

LK: Hockey has fighting and players are thrown out of the game. Two technical fouls in the NBA and you're thrown out. Specific penalties for specific things. What about baseball?

SELIG: Yes, there will be a code of conduct. We can't leave it subjective as it's been. This is in nobody's best interest. This game needs specific discipline. There will be a specific penalty for a specific infraction.

LK: Tell me about attendance.

SELIG: I believe if we do things right—marketing, keeping the game moving, having an enlightened television policy, and going international—baseball will enter another golden era. By 2010 you and I will be stunned at the popularity. It is also imperative that we keep baseball the lowest-priced of the major sports. It's going to have family prices and there will be a lot of discounting.

LK: Will there be a designated hitter rule in one league and not a designated hitter rule in the other?

SELIG: I'd say yes. Both leagues are firm on their positions and it will probably run through the entire twenty-first century. People have said to me, and I tend to agree, that a little controversy between the leagues isn't bad. We'll argue forever about it and that's okay.

LK: So the National League will be the only baseball league in the world without the DH rule?

SELIG: It sure looks that way.

LK: Will seasons be shorter?

SELIG: I hope so. We need to get back to 154 games. We're trying to play too many games now and we have too many weather problems in April. We demean ourselves and the game by playing in weather we shouldn't be playing in. The season should start about the twelfth of April, no earlier. And we need to keep it at seven games for the first playoff round and keep the rest of them the same. World Series stays in October.

LK: Not in November?

SELIG: Under no circumstances.

LK: You going to keep it at four balls and three strikes?

SELIG: We're not going to tamper with that at all.

LK: Orange baseballs?

SELIG: We're not going to tamper with that either.

LK: Will there be advertising at first base?

SELIG: Not at first base but there will be ads all along the infield as we're starting to see now.

LK: Are we going to see more field seats like at dugout level?

SELIG: The answer is yes. We even have a few in Milwaukee, and the Dodgers have it too.

LK: What scares you about the game? What is the worst-case scenario which could happen but you aren't predicting will happen?

SELIG: A war could change the game. An economic crisis in the country could change it. We need to understand the need for labor peace and we need to change the way we do business with each other in this game. Greed could kill us. It's done so in the past.

LK: What will a sky box of the future be like inside?

SELIG: It will have all the things that it has today. Corporations will design their own and decorate them the way they want. I don't anticipate private entrances from the parking lot if that's what you're asking.

LK: Will we see more blacks in ballparks?

SELIG: Baseball needs to reach out much more than it has. I can remember sitting in the upper deck at Wrigley Field with a cousin of mine in May 1947. We were the only whites in the upper deck. Jackie Robinson turned the game around. I'd like to see a ball park named after him. Kenesaw Mountain Landis (baseball's first commissioner) was one of the worst bigots of all time. I've gone through documents from all the commissioners and I found a letter he wrote I've not shown to anyone, and he speaks of hating blacks, Jews, and Catholics. If he knew there was a Jew sitting as acting baseball commissioner right now he'd be spinning over and over in his grave.

LK: What needs to be done to ensure minority ownership and management?

SELIG: We need to have more minorities in what I call the "pipeline" so when general manager jobs come available you will have people who are trained and are ready. The pipeline will have minorities, and when the farm jobs and the marketing jobs and player development jobs come available those people can slide right into them.

LK: How do you see the licensing issue in baseball being solved?

SELIG: Those revenues have to be shared throughout the league in order for us to survive. It can't be given just to one team.

LK: Will it be sportswear or could it be a car or a phone company?

SELIG: Could be everything. All of it has to be shared equally. It could mean every player wears the same emblem or logo on his uniform. That's reality.

DAVID FALK

CHAIRMAN, FAME;

LAWYER FOR MICHAEL JORDAN, PATRICK EWING,

CHRIS DOLEMAN, AND JUWAN HOWARD, AMONG OTHERS

There's an explosion of change. The pace is changing. Some people are threatened by the technology. The things we were brought up with and learned to fear, such as Big Brother watching or the information age or even the computer, are the things we can use as tools.

LK: Let's say it's 2016. Will an athlete be making $50 million in one year?

FALK: Yes. I think the star system is going to continue to evolve, where teams and players recognize there are superstars who create a market for television, stadium attendance, marketing, signage, and sponsorships. It will be similar to music in the sixties, where groups like the Supremes became Diana Ross and the Supremes. In football, basketball, and so on you will continue to have "Michael Jordan and the Chicago Bulls," "Shaquille O'Neal and the LA Lakers," or "Ken Griffey and the Seattle Mariners." Those players will continue to have a disproportionate value.

LK: What will that do to a team?

FALK: As television and marketing become more important to the business, and let's understand that sports is now entertainment, there will be a difference between the pure sports element of the teams which want more cohesiveness salary-wise and that basic economic reality of running a team that requires an inventory of stars and not twelve interchangeable players. Look, a movie needs a Schwarzenegger, a Pacino, a De Niro, a Michelle Pfeiffer, or a Demi Moore to be successful. Those names are starting to cost $20 million and by the year 2016, they'll cost $50 million.

LK: Will a team seek out a player who is a good gate and secondly a good rebounder?

FALK: Absolutely. When Indiana hires Larry Bird to coach, the hiring is more for marquee value at the box office.

LK: Is that dangerous?

FALK: It potentially could be dangerous. You need a balance between the entertainment value and the inherent quality of the product. If Dennis Rodman couldn't play as well as he does, nobody would put up with the histrionics, but he happens to be a very good player. That's the balance.

LK: So if you're paying $50 million a year, will there still be a salary cap?

FALK: There's always going to be some kind of revenue sharing system. I think the salary cap has always been a little bit of an anomaly because there are exceptions to the cap that allow teams to keep their own star players, and I think that ability is incredibly important for the identity of the team. You want to know you can protect your asset. The purists already challenging this structure are suggesting this issue has come about because people in my position are stretching the envelope because we want to protect our fees. I argued against this bifurcated system last year because it was going to affect salaries at the expense of the middle-class players. Having negotiated four of the five highest contracts in the history of professional sports, I'm not very concerned about my fee structure. In another twenty years there will be five or six marginally talented players at the minimum, which might be $500,000 or $600,000, and there will be one or two players making megabucks, and there will be others in a transitional period to determine if they'll become a mega-player or a functional player.

LK: Contracts will be shorter?

FALK: I don't think so. They'll be longer for the stars because teams will be afraid of losing them to their competitors, but they'll probably be shorter for the functional players because those folks will be more interchangeable. Those contracts will run from one to three years. Teams won't want to commit resources any longer than that because it's a risk.

LK: More free agency?

FALK: Yes, more free agency. But teams need rules, similar to those in football and basketball, where they can pay significant amounts of money to protect star players. The issue is not the amount of money they get paid but, rather, protecting the longevity of the asset because it creates identity for the franchise.

LK: How about team loyalty? More or less of it in sports?

FALK: If the rules aren't protecting the owners as the century turns, and as a result don't protect their franchise assets, there's going to be more and more free agency and less identity to the team. The current rule only allows teams to extend the contracts of players when they become free agents. Once you get to the threshold of free agency where a lot of teams are bidding on you, you're naturally going to want to know your market value. If there's an ability early on to get security, you're more likely to bargain away some of your market value for a "bird in the hand" today. Take away that ability for teams to do it early, then you're forcing players to become free agents.

LK: What will happen when a high school athlete comes to your office and says he wants to turn pro?

FALK: I've always said while these players are ready physically, they aren't necessarily ready emotionally or socially. It's a very difficult transition. I've looked at players at the college level and then seen them a few years later ready to come into the league and have noticed the greater level of maturity. Antitrust laws prevent the league from keeping high school players out. I think you're going to see players in the next century try to get into the league before they even finish high school. I'm against it because it changes the role of people like myself.

LK: What do you mean?

FALK: There are roles to be business advisers or personal advisers and the kind of attention someone needs when he is twenty-two years old, and the kind of attention someone needs when he is sixteen is a little different. I think you have to be much more physically present with someone much younger. It's going from the business role toward being a parent. It's a question of where do you want to spend your resources? The entry of so many young players who want to come in from college is the biggest threat to the game right now. The NCAA Finals is the single most important factor responsible for the success of basketball over the past fifteen years. You get to see most of today's stars starting out on television. As players leave college earlier or don't even go to college, they may be very talented but the fans don't know who they are. There's a reason why people go to college and grow up, and we're thrusting very young people into a game in the same way you see it happening in tennis.

LK: Should there be an age limit?

FALK: Maybe Congress could amend the antitrust laws, although it's unlikely since they haven't amended it for baseball. It's a very serious problem. I think the allure of the money is forcing people to make bad career and life decisions.

LK: Will you accept young players as clients?

FALK: On a case-by-case basis. I tease Michael Jordan his son may be the first to leave elementary school to go straight into the pros.

LK: Will college players be paid?

FALK: Difficult question. People want to pay these players to reduce the inducement of renegade agents who flout the rules. Unfortunately, I don't think you can legislate morality. If you pay a player $10,000 who really wants to make $20,000, then someone is going to step into the backroom and supplement his income. These players create tremendous value for the schools in television dollars, and when teams are successful, admissions increase. A lot of these players aren't economically prepared to even live on a campus; they don't have the right clothes, they don't have a car, and they aren't allowed to work. So there will be some kind of stipend that will differ by division. Some may find the whole idea distasteful and not participate at all. And if men are going to get paid, women athletes in college will be paid as well.

LK: Tell me about your vision of endorsements. What will change?

FALK: Companies are going to become even more sophisticated. They'll realize one Michael Jordan or one Allen Iverson is worth more than fifty other players. It's a personality issue. Basketball is becoming like Hollywood. You sign one blockbuster guy with supporting members. It's never been that way in sports but the league is starting to market the teams that way. Therefore, when companies go to promote the players, the tendency will be to spend more dollars on the "impact players," if you will. I'm not so sure you won't be seeing down the road the "Sony Lakers" or the "Paramount Knicks," and all the players will be used to promote the corporate product, even to the extent of wearing the corporate logo on their uniforms. The mentality in America is to be less overtly commercial but as the price of the players continues to escalate and gets beyond the ability of all but the most wealthy individuals, corporations will seek to leverage their identity more through the teams than they do now.

LK: What will the superstar in the next century need to survive?

FALK: I think they are going to be increasingly young and as a result they will have to understand their conduct at a young age is going to dictate over a ten- or fifteen-year period what their level of success is going to be. Michael Jordan evolved into it gradually because nobody knew those kinds of opportunities even existed. That's changed now and the young athletes are going to have to know that how they interact with the media and how they give back to the community and how they conduct themselves despite tremendous pressures will dictate how successful they become.

LK: Will major markets continue to get the best players?

FALK: As corporate owners come in I think we could balance it. Individual owners in smaller markets don't have the wherewithal to compete with the Chicagos, New Yorks. and LAs but corporations could.

LK: Athletes are role models. Will leagues, regardless of the sport, become tougher about conduct on the field or court or arena or rink?

FALK: Unfortunately, I don't think so. I think the leagues are always concerned that they will diminish their product by strictly disciplining the players. In the long run it works but very few people have the patience in the short run to suspend or harshly discipline a player because it takes away from the product. There's always discussion in sports about getting quality people and building for the long term but the pressures are so enormous to win in the short term that it doesn't afford the people managing those businesses the luxury of long-term decisions.

LK: So if a future player hauls off and smacks another future player, nothing will happen, correct?

FALK: I think there will be discipline but it won't be commensurate with the need for discipline. No immediate suspension. Maybe a hearing at another time.

LK: Will contracts contain a clause saying if this player acts improperly on the field this monetary penalty will apply or this discipline will occur?

FALK: It's difficult to predict every contingency but if you step off the playing field it would seem that kind of conduct would be detrimental to a player's image in a marketing sense. There are Dennis Rodman, Charles Barkley, and John McEnroe who are known as bad boys, and the public likes to see this Peck's Bad Boy syndrome. Strange at it seems, this is very marketable. Remember Derrick Coleman, who, when told there was a dress code, responded with, "Well, let me write you a check." So the big-salaries-carry-the-big-fines way of doing things comes down to the question: Is the fine significant enough to change behavior? Only time will tell. I think for the players that need it the most, it probably has the least impact. Future fines will go to a charity determined by the league as it is done now. Right now fines are proportionate but the question is: Will we fine a higher-paid player more than one game when the lower-paid players are fined only one game? I think that is something people will look at and it's likely to happen. Will this change behavior? I think it will be difficult to do.

LK: Drug tests for all players?

FALK: The balance of personal liberties and the integrity of the leagues and the increased knowledge of the health of the players will move toward more testing. For their own good, certain players need to be tested. Twenty years ago I thought it was an incursion on civil liberties but after watching players die of AIDS and seek drug rehabilitation, I think the time has come to recognize they are very young and subject to a lot of difficult influences and they need protection, in some cases from themselves.

LK: Will a drug test be given weekly, before each game, how often?

FALK: Daily is too much. Some diseases aren't detectable for a while but I think it will be weekly or monthly.

LK: The NBA commissioner, David Stern, says sports must raise issues in society. Do you agree, and how will this be done after the year 2000?

FALK: I agree to a certain extent. People tend to listen to athletes and celebrities more than they do teachers. At the same time, athletes thrust into being role models are sometimes asked to comment on issues they simply are not knowledgeable about. When Charles Barkley did his famous commercial saying he wasn't a role model, I think there was a lot of truth in that. He is a role model in certain situations but you can't start asking him about issues, get a response off the top of his head, and then have young people follow that lead as fact. I think sports is going to continue to be a vehicle for the promotion of social messages but as the age of the players declines, and they are a lot less sophisticated, that credibility is going to be severely tested in a lot of different areas.

LK: Let's talk about basketball. More games in a season?

FALK: I think there will be fewer games in a season. By the end of the first decade of the new century you will find basketball, baseball, and maybe football played on an international basis. You'll see an American venue where basketball operates from the end of the Super Bowl to June or July covering sixty games and then the venue will switch to Europe or Asia where there will be a separate league. Players will decide if they want to play just the American circuit or the European one as well. This will bring a new infrastructure of television and cable to promote and carry the European circuit.

LK: So basketball might be played year-round?

FALK: Yes, I think so. But it can't always go head to head with other sports in that venue. In America it will be played after the Super Bowl but before the World Series. In Europe it might be after Wimbledon but before Formula One. It will be more coordinated but there will be fewer games in each venue. Players will decide how much money they want to make and if they want to play year-round.

LK: Where will the NBA expand?

FALK: St. Louis, Mexico City, Cincinnati, Baltimore. With fewer games, smaller cities will be able to draw fans but I don't think there will be that many more cities in America. Buenos Aires will have a team. No more Canadian teams in the NBA. With these new cities, the NBA's going to have to be realigned because it's not practical to travel from Vancouver to Buenos Aires unless we're going to have SSTs on a regular basis, and that's why we'll get into segmented venues. There will be a South American venue and at some point there will be a true world's champion from playoffs with the European League and the Asian League and the Oceanic League and Australia. You'll see American players sprinkled throughout all these teams.

LK: Will some teams get out of the NBA?

FALK: I think by the year 2016, ownership is going to be largely corporate and they are going to look at the bottom line in a different way. Teams will be content-delivery systems for massive entertainment empires. You'll look at COMSATS and Comcasts and ITT not necessarily saying, "How do I turn a profit?" but rather, "How do I use my sports division to create content for my movie division or my Internet division or my television division?" You are going to have two corporations that battle each other every day in the marketplace now battling each other in the sports arena.

LK: Cities will own teams?

FALK: I don't think they'll be able to afford it. It's going to be private ownership by large international corporations.

LK: Then who builds the facilities for these teams?

FALK: It will be partnerships between corporations and city governments. The cities will demand concessions from companies in terms of building not only sports facilities but plants and manufacturing facilities, corporate headquarters, and the result will be more integration of identity. It may be that ITT's world headquarters will be in New York and they'll own the Knicks and the Garden and the Rangers, and they may have to put up a cultural center or something like it in the city as a cost of doing business and having the franchise and the building.

LK: Are we going to see the day when center court has the Golden Arches?

FALK: I think you are going to see it with all kinds of products. I think you'll see players wearing a shoe with the Golden Arches and it'll be available in stores as well. What you're going to have much more of is the development of electronic signage where you may watch a game in the stadium that has a certain signage for the people there, and for the people watching television there will be different signage superimposed onto the field or onto the court that will be local. If you're watching a World Cup Match from Europe and BNP, which is the Bank National de Paris, is sponsoring the event in the stadium, in America you might see signs for Citibank. It's happening in the NBA where local teams have signage but for the nationally telecast games the NBA doesn't allow the signage to be shown because, otherwise, you're getting national coverage at a local rate. So while they've yet to change the electronic signs they are forcing the teams to change the billboards. You are going to see a lot more of that.

LK: What about uniforms?

FALK: I hope it doesn't become like race car drivers. I hope it stays modest. You will see players wear a Nike shoe or even a Swissair shoe as long as the colors stay consistent. But if twelve players wear different logos, it will create a circuslike environment.

LK: There is talk about sports being out of the reach of common people. The NBA playoffs, for example, began at nine P.M., when children couldn't stay up to watch Michael Jordan. Will this change?

FALK: Absolutely. You will see more and more attention paid to that. All the predictions in the past have been leading up to sports becoming a studio sport. Only the elite will be able to go and watch the games in person, but on television, it will have to be accessible to be watched by the masses. Despite threats from time to time, I don't think there will be a lot of pay-per-view in sports. I think the legislature is going to demand that it be available on a broadcasting basis.

LK: Ticket prices have gone up 36 percent over five years in the NBA and even more so in football and baseball. Is that trend going to continue?

FALK: I think it's going to have to continue to fund the salaries of the players.

LK: So all of this is your fault.

FALK: I think prices for actors go up and you pay more money at the theater and the price of lumber goes up and you pay more money for your house, and we ought to get used to paying increased prices for increased services.

LK: This suggests people will watch the NBA at home and a special occasion or an "event" will take them to the stadium.

FALK: I think there will be a hard core of really avid fans like you see in hockey right now, and I think it's going to become increasingly difficult for the average fan to take a family of four to the games because the price is going to be so high. Those in the seats will be a lot more corporate.

LK: More sky boxes?

FALK: More sky boxes. More corporate season tickets to use as an entertainment vehicle. I think it's important we find some way other than Juwan Howard buying a block of tickets for underprivileged kids to go to the game, that the average fan has the ability to go to the game. But it is going to be more and more difficult.

LK: So how will the average fan get inside the stadium?

FALK: Could be done by subsidy. Could be done by corporations buying tickets and then making them available. Teams might do it. I see sales promotions and contests, but it's becoming increasingly out of the reach of the average person to do. And this is no different than any other form of entertainment.

LK: Will agents become involved in policymaking as they begin to control more of the superstar players and salaries?

FALK: I think they should become more involved. The players' union represents the players collectively and we represent the players individually, so those who are in the trenches every day should have a voice on behalf of our clients. This is a partnership, but people view all your interest as being just you when we need to be mutually supportive.

LK: What policy should be changed in the next century?

FALK: I think the way the money is distributed among the players can be improved. The salary cap rules benefit the superstars. I'd like to see the marketing changed because I'm not a big fan of the league having so much control over the licensing of the players. I think it's inimical to the owners to have some movement of the superstars. At the end of three years a star after evolving his niche with that team can get up and leave and go wherever he wants with no protection by the team that has him. I like it but I think for an owner it's too risky if there's too much movement because it will dilute the identity of the teams, which is what is happening in baseball. There's an ebb and flow in the negotiations for these types of policies that requires what each side really needs. In the last round of collective bargaining, I don't think either side got what it really needed because the people who did the deal for the players weren't sophisticated enough to understand the inherent horse trades. There is a set length on contracts but at the end of those contracts, the players become free agents, which I like. But as an owner, I wouldn't like that.

LK: Are we moving toward a time when an owner will say, "I can't pay you the dollars you're worth but I can make you part owner of the team"?

FALK: I think it would be terrific. It used to be available. I'd like to see players become equity participants and share the upsides and the downsides. And I see it coming.

LK: What scares you about the time after January 1, 2000?

FALK: It's what scares me about the game itself. The age of the participants.

LK: Tell me about going to a basketball game twenty years from now.

FALK: There will be television screens in every seat. There will be interactive capability so you can do your banking during half-time. You'll be able to turn on the Jacuzzi in your house from the seat. Check in with your personal computer at the office to see if there's anything going on while you've been gone or make different flight arrangements. There will be dramatically enhanced customer service, especially in food. There will be less fast food and more ethnic food. Two people might look at the same billboard inside the stadium and see different signage. The game won't change that much, although I'd like to see more zone defenses so the smaller teams without dominating big men can make up for it.

The Arts

Talking about the arts is talking about us. It has to do with how a paint-brush crosses the canvas or where the chisel slams against the surface of the marble or the pen against paper, as well as why the two surfaces are together in the first place. Since cave dwellers were writing on walls 25,000 years ago it's a safe bet this need to pull ideas from somewhere inside (be it the soul, the truth, the center, the spirit, or the demon) and display them somewhere outside suggests that this is the way human beings operate, and don't expect any changes anytime soon. At least not in the next century.

I was sitting in my condo that January day watching Maya Angelou read her incredible poem "On the Pulse of the Morning" during President Clinton's 1993 Inauguration ceremony. And then she hit that last line and said "good morning." Something snapped inside me, and since that moment, more than one person has said the same thing. This interview, I believe, explains what happened that cold January after-noon. Maya Angelou has written ten best-selling books, including four collections of poetry. She wrote and scored an original screenplay called *Georgia, Georgia* and was the creative force behind a ten-part television series on African traditions in America. In the sixties she worked with Dr. Martin Luther King as the northern coordinator for the Southern Christian Leadership Conference. She currently teaches, and of course writes, at Wake Forest University in North Carolina.

Peter Max in person is like Peter Max on canvas: colorful, opinionated, and most notable of all, in motion. I have always wondered if that's an artistic technique or simply a result of the time he spent in Brooklyn. Regardless of the reason, he is considered this country's "painter laureate," and in the past four decades has been a teacher to all of us about the movement of color. I interviewed him in a phone call early one morning while he worked in his studio. I haven't any idea of what Peter Max was painting at the time, but his picture of the future is pretty exciting.

You are also about to meet five people whose careers depend on how you spend your downtime, those all-too-few moments away from a boss or a household when you, rather than someone else, can choose the routine. Downtime is the time when we do something for ourselves. It's not selfishness, it's survival. And it is going to be just as important, if not more so, one hundred years from today, in the many shapes it will take during the next 36,525 days we call the twenty-first century (yeah, the math is accurate).

One shape will be a screen and it's going to get larger and larger as well as closer and closer. You are about to meet three people whose careers depend on how you spend your downtime in front of a television or a movie. Each of these people has listened to experts say, "It can't be done," and then gone out and done it.

Lucie Salhany is a former chief executive officer of UPN Television, a former chairman of Fox Broadcasting, and president of Paramount Domestic Television, where she developed programs like *Hard Copy* and *Entertainment Tonight*. In 1997 she became president and CEO of JH Media, her own industry consulting business, located just outside Boston. Salhany has been in the front lines of framing UPN around a specific audience (in this case young urban viewers), which is an example of the phenomenon called narrowcasting.

Stephen J. Cannell has been writing and producing television programs for years, including *The Rockford Files, Silk Stalkings, 21 Jump Street, Wise Guy,* and *The A-Team.* Aside from that, the guy hasn't done a damn thing.

Sherry Lansing is going to tell us about the movies. As chairman of Paramount Pictures, she is in constant motion but was kind enough to talk with me about movies nobody has even heard of yet. She produced *Indecent Proposal* and *Racing with the Moon*, coproduced *Fatal Attraction*, and backed the script that became a movie called *First Wives Club*. Success is nothing new for Sherry Lansing, but she has maintained something rare in Hollywood: modesty. She became the first woman studio head to receive a star on the Hollywood Walk of Fame (and if you go looking for it, check out number 2092, which belongs to a talk show host you might know).

Regardless of the century, we have always worried about what to wear and how we feel when we wear whatever it is we worried about. And so it will be in the twenty-first century. Isaac Mizrahi lets loose about what we will wear after the year 2000 and he makes headlines in his predictions (braces are still going to be worn whether Isaac says so or not). He is known for saying Jackie Kennedy and Mary Tyler Moore had the most profound impact on fashion in this century. He flat-out refused to tell me who will have that role in the next century, saying he isn't there yet. Still, he is one of the more creative thinkers I've come across, and already is looking at what we will wear in the years ahead. He has a Ouija board in his office, but I believe his predictions are more Isaac than Ouija.

MAYA ANGELOU

REYNOLDS PROFESSOR AT WAKE FOREST UNIVERSITY;

AUTHOR OF *I KNOW WHY THE CAGED BIRD SINGS*

Read.

LK: What changes will we face in the next century?

ANGELOU: I would imagine the center of the human will not change. We have been dealing with selfishness, fear, hate, and betrayal for seven or eight centuries. We've been saying, "Don't kill each other" and "Don't be cruel" for centuries. I don't think it's going to change. In another thousand years, if we can stick around, we might make some quantum leaps and care for each other a little more.

LK: Who are we right now?

ANGELOU: We are fearful children right now standing around a nature-set fire. We like the fire and we like each other but we're afraid of each other. Because we don't trust ourselves we find it impossible to trust each other. So what we use more often than not is might to protect our fear. We use our power. We are duped sometimes because we live such short lives and it's over so soon. We can't see much positive change for our positive acts, and as a result, we become disheartened and cynical.

LK: We don't have hope?

ANGELOU: Oh, we have hope, but if it remains targeted to things, then we are lost. If we can aim it at sensitivity and humanitarianism, then we're going to be fine. I know this sounds awfully soft but that's what we've got to do.

LK: So how are you going to do that?

ANGELOU: It's a combination of church and state and academia and personal. It's unique and it's general and it's complex and it's simple. I don't think any portion of society can be less a participant than another. I would like very much to have every politician and lobbyist reread the Preamble to the Constitution and hear the dream of those men two hundred years ago.

LK: Are you optimistic that in another one hundred years when somebody is writing a book about the twenty-second century, they will look back at the twenty-first and say, "They did okay"?

ANGELOU: Yes. But I have to realize two hundred years ago, the people who wrote "We the people" had the incredible gall to own other individuals. Look at how we have changed! Even the idea is unacceptable and incomprehensible. At the same time they wanted to "ensure domestic tranquillity" and they wanted to "provide for the common good." So I can look back two hundred years and admire those men. So in the twenty-first century, I hope people will look back at us and say, "Gee, they rioted in the streets and there was vulgarity in the neighborhoods and communication and they abused children and they were cruel to women and had restrictions against people of different color, and yet they actually tried to stop war. One country which had absolutely nothing to do with another country tried to stop the killing." That is optimistic.

LK: Were you thinking about the next century when you wrote "On the Pulse of Morning," which you read at the 1993 Inauguration?

ANGELOU: I think about the future all the time. I think about what we can be. I have a great respect for clichés, and the early bird still does catch the worm.

LK: So "On the Pulse of Morning" was a variation on a cliché.

ANGELOU: It was a variation on many clichés. The main one was that he or she who does not count on victory is doomed to defeat. So I try not to ignore the past—

LK: Because, otherwise, you are doomed to repeat it?

ANGELOU: Something like that.

LK: Well, if you were asked to write a poem about the twenty-first century, what would it say?

ANGELOU: I would hope that our fascination with technology does not separate us from our souls. I would hope that CD-ROMs and Web pages don't separate us from our respect of each other. I don't know if that could be said in a poem, though. My office is replete with computers but I still write on long yellow pads. I have three in front of me right now.

LK: What scares you about the next century?

ANGELOU: Isolation. We are a people, we are a school, we are a group. And we are weakened when we are separated. But there's a uniqueness in each one of us. However, all together is when we are at our best and our strongest, and you can see that when we have a crisis. Something pushes us to each other when there's a hurricane or a fire. I hate the crisis but I love to turn on the television and hear that fire-fighters have gone from Nebraska to California to help.

LK: What would you say to high school students in the year 2009 who, this evening, have been assigned to read a poem but are leaning toward turning on the television or hanging out with friends someplace?

ANGELOU: My first encouragement is to read it aloud. And read it to someone else. There's nothing so wonderful as having help in a required endeavor. We run together. We jog together. We walk together. High school students will be amazed to hear their voices read those words written by someone else, maybe two years or two hundred years earlier. When you read to someone else you are doing the read-ing but you are also doing the listening.

LK: And the English teacher should also read aloud to the class?

ANGELOU: Yes, it's the same thing. I read to my students and I can see them physically begin to relax. Teachers have become, I'm sorry to say, superficially sophisticated, that we don't read to students.

LK: Is the role of the artist going to change in the next century?

ANGELOU: I think the poet and the painter and the choreogra-pher are all reaching for the same thing they've always reached for.

LK: Do they ever grab hold of it?

ANGELOU: On occasion. Michelangelo got it when he did the *Pieta*.

LK: Did you ever get it?

ANGELOU: Only in a line or two.

LK: So the role remains the same?

ANGELOU: I think so. The artist is always trying to show the truth of our experience, not necessarily the facts. Sometimes the facts obscure the truth because there are so many facts. But if you hit the truth you know it whether it's Confucius or Martin Luther King. You know the truth whether it is spoken to you or you hear it in a piece of music. Haydn got it and so did Ray Charles.

LK: Are you glad the human condition is such that we were never told the truth from the get-go and instead we have to rely on poets and the arts and religion and ourselves to determine what it might be?

ANGELOU: Sometimes I am. But sometimes I ask the Lord, "Why can't you be a little clearer?" But having not been given it, I'm glad to have the right of first refusal.

LK: But you're a little ticked at the Lord, aren't you?

ANGELOU: Sometimes, yes, I think it could have been made a little more plain than it has been.

LK: More and more programs are being moved from the federal government to the States in an effort to let the people make decisions rather than Washington, D.C. Do you think the federal role in the arts is going to change?

ANGELOU: It will have to. When politicians begin to siphon off the money for the arts, it really frightens me. The first thing to go in the school system is the arts. Children have lots of energy and curiosity, and when there's no band and no class and no art they run into the streets.

LK: Well, some would say if the federal government isn't going to do it the burden falls on the local community, the village, to do it.

ANGELOU: The local village is a part of the larger village. The larger village has to take responsibility to protect our egress and ingress.

LK: Are you saying the federal government will devote more to the arts?

ANGELOU: I hope so. But I hope the next generation will insist upon it. We need an introduction to the arts in grade school so that something will reach the ear by the time the student gets to high school. They might say, "I like the tuba," though I don't know why anyone would like the tuba.

LK: So you want federal dollars for elementary school art education, and then the local contribution kicks in in the higher grades?

ANGELOU: Both. Look, I want to see a return to band practice. The instruments weren't all that great in high school but they made the sound and they could be tuned and children had the chance to do some decent music. If you have success in one thing, it spills over and pumps you and prepares you for success in the next thing. So if the junior high school student is able to play that tuba and get through a piece of music, whether it's Grieg or Stevie Wonder, you can see the shoulders straighten up. Children are the ones who buy music. Shouldn't that tell us something?

LK: If someone on a school board in the next century is reading these words right now, and he faces cutting arts out of the school budget, what do you say to that person?

ANGELOU: It should be the last thing to cut back. We are forever talking about protecting the life of the environment but we never talk about protecting the life of the soul.

LK: There is talk about business funding arts projects throughout communities and concern that, for example, the art exhibit will have ads for the corporation throughout the gallery. Are you worried about that?

ANGELOU: The corporation should get something back. Doesn't bother me.

LK: What will the next century offer to artists?

ANGELOU: I don't know. But having flown across this country many times and looked down on a clear day at the farms and the fields below, I've always wondered what Van Gogh would have done had he been able to see those patterns. I think particularity will change. Brush and oil will give way to something else, but what the artist is trying to find and illuminate will not change.

Maya Angelou's required reading for the next century:

1. The Bible

2. *Hamlet*

3. Charles Dickens

4. James Baldwin

5. Edna St. Vincent Millay

PETER MAX

ARTIST

For those wanting to be in the arts: Keep on drawing with a pen even though you may end up using computers. The skill achieved with a pen on paper is very important, so learn structure drawing (the hand, the face) and learn fantasy to stimulate your creativity.

LK: We are entering what has been described as the information age or the communication age. How will that change how we look and learn and feel about art?

MAX: The information age is connecting every point on the globe with every other point. Before, we used to have certain connecting cities like Atlanta or Houston or Denver. But with the Internet we have a transportation vehicle of data and pictures and information and television and music and movies, and now you will be able to ship it from one place to another, any place in the world in the same amount of time, instantly.

LK: Does this mean more people will see and experience art, or does it mean there are more opportunities to see and experience art?

MAX: It will be available to everybody. A child in Zaire is going to have as much opportunity to study Van Gogh or Rembrandt or, I hope, Peter Max as a kid at Harvard.

LK: And the result will be what?

MAX: The result is the world becoming unified in similar thinking, civil ideas, and I think there will be a paradigm shift in education. Intelligent people who aren't being educated will now have the opportunity to be given something to read or to access. For instance, I love astronomy. I will be able to access one hundred different sites and get information. Or if I love a particular actor, I'll be able to see all his films.

LK: We could look at the moon without going outside.

MAX: That's correct.

LK: How will art classes change?

MAX: Art is going to be affected in a very big way because what is traditionally known as "art," which used to be a life drawing of nudes and figures and perspectives and stuff like that, is now so available on computers that people won't be going to class anymore to study it academically. Art is going to become an aspect of creativity; you'll be able to combine and create things that are in the computer and make new things out of them, rather than start from scratch on a white canvas.

LK: So there won't be a blank canvas on an easel?

MAX: Less and less. What happens today is when a mother or father sees the child has talent, the first thing they get him or her is a computer. So the child doesn't get to have that skill anymore. The skill is lost. I'll give you an example: There are beautiful sculptures in Paris and Milan and Rome and there are some in Central Park that are stone, and in the whole world today there's not a handful of people who know how to do that anymore. Just a hundred years ago there were tens of thousands of stone sculptors that knew how to make that. You know the realist kind of paintings like Velázquez and John Singer Sargent did, people who used to paint like photographs? There are very few of those around. It's becoming a lost art. I just finished a portrait of you, Larry. I used a photograph. I didn't need to paint you from the start. I made a half-tone and then a silk screen and then I color-enhanced it. I used my creativity rather than slave over painting every aspect of the face.

LK: Painting my face can be tough.

MAX: It's not as bad as others.

LK: Why does not working from the real thing bother me?

MAX: Well, you'll be able to manipulate images and landscapes. You will take a gazebo out of India and put it in Egypt and take a sunset from Maui and a waterfall from another island and a rainstorm from upstate New York, all from photographs, and combine them so it looks like it's all happening in one place.

LK: Why would I want to do that?

MAX: Because you are creating interesting images. What always makes art interesting for the viewer is to hear something or see something that is new. We discovered rock and roll and like it better than the classics because it was brand-new with a new beat and rhythm and different kinds of words. The art created in *Toy Story*, the movie, is computer-generated. Artists who normally would have been painters are instead creating animated characters on computers and making them walk and talk and have personality, and as a result, giving the audience a brand-new experience. This is just the beginning, but in the future James Dean will reappear as lifelike as you can imagine. He will act in a film and you could put Marilyn Monroe and Cary Grant in there as well. Your voice will be electronically enhanced to sound like Cary Grant. It's a scary thing to think about but it will be done.

LK: So what you're saying is, I will be able to paint when I actually can't paint?

MAX: There are programs right now where somebody with a little bit of skill can paint with a brush but the strokes come out the way Van Gogh would do them.

LK: Well, here we go again. That bothers me. You're taking something that's already been created and just putting a different name on it. There's no blank canvas.

MAX: I know, in the beginning it sounds like "My God, this takes away from Van Gogh," but I'm just giving you examples of what's possible. And these possibilities are increasing 10,000-fold. It's not doubling or tripling. Look at the Model T Ford from the 1920s. I don't know how many were made in the first year, but we have that many makes of cars today. What all of this means is we will be able to do more things in less time, and I think that's equivalent to living longer. In the past twenty-four hours I went to San Francisco, did a hundred phone calls from the plane, made 150 drawings on the plane, had a meal, had a conversation with a fellow I traveled with, had a meeting, talked to the folks at The Sharper Image about a project, had dinner with friends, got on the plane at ten o'clock, and was back in my apartment twenty-three hours later.

LK: Are we going to define "art" differently?

MAX: Yes. It's changing a lot. History of art is still the history of art. A Picasso is still a Picasso. But creativity will change because the options for an artist will be much greater.

LK: Will the role government plays in the arts change in the next century?

MAX: Art and government go in cycles. It's like life: Certain things are taken away and certain things come in play. So if the government doesn't supply art schools with money anymore, at the same time there's stuff available on the Internet that the government had a role in making happen. Things aren't taken away as much as they change form.

LK: Will it be taught in schools?

MAX: I think it will be the same for right now. People will still study the violin or the accordion, but when they get older they'll get an electronic keyboard. They will start with conventional instruments but it doesn't last long.

LK: You've talked a lot about computers and technology. Are you worried there are suddenly going to be a lot of Peter Max originals hanging on walls that aren't originals at all but are the result of a laser printer and a good computer?

MAX: No. They can't do it because of the copyright.

LK: Well, are you worried someone will have a Peter Max hanging on the wall and will double click it with their computer and suddenly another Peter Max painting shows up?

MAX: I'd rather be clicked off and on in a couple hundred countries than never be clicked on and off at all.

LK: The thing I'm driving at is technology could inspire imitations. You could be plagiarized.

MAX: Imitations happen all the time.

LK: Are you worried people are going to say, "That's not art" in the future?

MAX: They've been saying it for hundreds of years. Every time a new medium comes out, when it goes from oil to acrylic or to the video screen, there will always be a critic to say, "It's *not* art." But art is what the artist thinks it is, it's not so much what the viewer thinks it is. It's what the artist wants to do. If the artist likes it, usually there's a following.

LK: Will we have new colors in the future or have we seen them all?

MAX: I think there are always new colors being invented. That's a nice question because I'm always looking for new colors. Sometimes there are colors that look like new colors but they're just sped up and they look like a third color. When you have a shiny shell from the ocean, sometimes it has an iridescent color. So we might get colors like that; sort of in-between colors.

LK: So that's good for the artist?

MAX: The world is good for the artist and the artist is good for the world. The artist creates new ideas for people to enjoy. The new set on *Larry King Live* is created by an artist, or the new logo is created by an artist, or new art in products or animation or advertising. So artists color the world for the people to live in it.

LK: And the result is?

MAX: It uplifts the soul. The viewer sees something new. It would be boring to constantly look at everything the same way. It stimulates the interest in the people who have an intellect which is visual or science or just stuff. We are filling our world with culture. We take in more in a single day than people a century ago did in a year.

LK: Are we going to go to art galleries by staying at home?

MAX: Absolutely. There might be an opening in both Milan and Paris. On my computer I'll be able to view live the gallery in Milan and tape the opening in Paris and come back to it later.

LK: But it's still not as good as being there.

MAX: It's not as good as being there. But with virtual perception you'll put earphones on and it will almost be like being there. It might even be more fun because you could be at the pyramids for fifteen minutes and then go to the Louvre for twenty minutes and then you could come over here to my studio for twenty minutes and you haven't left your house!

LK: How would you draw the next century?

MAX: It's going to be faster. It's like a sped-up film. You will see things at high speeds. Take someone from a hundred years ago and let him spend a day with you or me. He wouldn't believe what we go through or what we do. How we walk into a room and lights go on or off. The movies. The channels. The perceptions. Everything is busy,

busy, busy. Cabs are going. Elevators are going one hundred stories high. He'd just shake his head in disbelief. In the same way, we'll shake our heads just thirty years from now. We are going to be everybody while we are us.

LK: It's going to be tough being a human being.

MAX: We're going to evolve into a new species. We're going to become like a matzo pie! I'm drawing with one hand, listening to you with earphones on, but I'm also making another phone call and listening to that with the other ear, I got a friend next to me watching a movie, and I'm glancing at the film while I'm ordering food! I got six or eight things going on at the same time and I love it!

LUCIE SALHANY

FORMER PRESIDENT AND CHIEF EXECUTIVE OFFICER,
UPN TELEVISION

The ability to get information from the Internet and to communicate with people from all over the world in just seconds is very exciting. The twenty-first century is going to be a wonderful time to be alive. You will actually be able to control your own entertainment.

LK: Do you think networks are going to exist in the next century?

SALHANY: (Long silence on the phone.)

LK: Okay, let's try the question this way: Will networks do news in the next century?

SALHANY: Probably. Some networks will do news. In general, there are going to be so many choices, and so much competition, that it's going to be difficult to produce good strong programming without a dual revenue stream (advertisements and subscription fees). I think one of the Big Three will get out of news if it has a cable news channel or it may just pick up the feed from that channel. The cost of doing news is very high.

LK: Networks will become narrower and narrower in their approaches to an audience?

SALHANY: Everyone is going to become narrower and narrower. Cable television came in and made small audiences legitimate by saying, "We're going for this niche." The advertiser felt this was a way to create competition to the Big Three; hence, niche programming was born. Their cost per thousand wasn't that high and they were able to reach an audience large enough to support the program. We're all doing niche programming now. Another word for it is counterprogramming. Networks will become more defined and unique in order to survive in the next century. They are going to have to try and relate to the lifestyle of the audience they are trying to reach. In fact, we're already seeing "branding." CBS decided to go back to older-skewing programs, NBC is the younger, hipper, urban network, and ABC has no definition. Fox was the upstart.

LK: There will be more networks in the future?

SALHANY: Sure. They'll be more defined and focused but they won't get as narrow as radio. They can't do that and survive.

LK: How important will it be for networks to carry sports programming?

SALHANY: Critical. You cannot duplicate the NFL, you cannot duplicate the NBA, you can't duplicate the Red Sox or the Pistons. This is one of the foundations of broadcast television. We say to our affiliates, "We hate being preempted but we love the idea you do sports." Local sports shows a commitment to the local community. There will be network sports as well, though. The country cannot let sports go to pay because it will grow the gap between the haves and the have-nots. I think you'll see soccer on TV.

LK: How are we even going to watch television in the future?

SALHANY: Well, I'll probably be sitting in a rocking chair at the Former Television Network Presidents Home, going on about what I did so many years earlier. But the TV in the future will be bigger and it will be integrated with the computer. Television as we know it will not be what it looks like now. It will have a mouse or a remote control that won't have wires attached. You will have the ability to interact. You will be able to control your house with this device. There will be TVs in everybody's room so you can become more narrow and program them the way you want, and now that I think about it, I don't even know if we'll call them TVs. It will have another name, personal entertainment unit, or something like that.

LK: By the year 2006 all televisions, or whatever you call them, will be digital. What happens after that?

SALHANY: The next step will be when we implant those chips in our heads and we don't even see it on TV, we'll just imagine it!

LK: Will there be a day when there is no free television?

SALHANY: The Supreme Court went a long way when it continued the must-carry rule, which said we want to keep over-the-air free television alive (must-carry requires cable systems to carry free TV signals). But I also think free TV will remain so, if we can find other sources of revenue. Those sources will not interfere with your high-definition picture but will allow you to have text. You will be able to have local interaction as a result.

LK: Will there be an FCC?

SALHANY: I don't think we'll call it the FCC. It will be some sort of a government oversight agency since, in the future, it will be impossible to separate businesses. While the FCC focuses on rulemaking now, Congress is going to try to control more of the content. For many years they have tried to influence content and they have made inroads. The V-chip is an example of that. How it's used and if it's used is the question. But it will be a fact shortly: either in the remote control or surgically inserted into the heads of all the television entertainment executives in Hollywood. I'm not sure which.

LK: The V-chip will do what?

SALHANY: Placate a couple of politicians.

LK: But there will still be violence on television in the next century.

SALHANY: Well, there's not much violence on broadcast television now. But we get painted with a very broad brush because most politicians don't separate cable from broadcast when they talk about violence. When Bart Simpson does something physical, like pushing his sister, and somebody says that's an act of violence equal to an act of violence on pay-per-view where somebody's head is blown off, well, I worry about our country. When I hear people say they are worried about our show *Star Trek Voyager* but they are not worried about handguns on the street, then this country is in trouble. The folks in Washington aren't differentiating, they just complain because the entertainment industry and the networks are easy targets.

LK: When a program comes on television in the future, will it be preceded by a slide saying, "This program contains nudity" or "adult themes," or will the V-chip do it for me?

SALHANY: You have to disclaim the show, V-chip or no V-chip. But do I think the current rating system will be different than we have now? Probably not. This isn't to say in the next century there won't be pressure to change it. Understand, I don't believe in any rating system because we shouldn't put labels on what we see. That means the government is affecting the content even if we self-regulate it. And when you label subject matter as "nudity," kids run to it, especially teenagers, and I know because I have one. People should monitor what their children watch and deal with that.

LK: Will these ratings only be seen at certain times of the evening?

SALHANY: No, although certain members of Congress would like nothing better than to bring back the family hour. Still, I'm the one who never thought we'd ever see the V-chip happen. Television is rapidly changing because those in broadcasting now are businesses and no longer individuals. The days are gone when stations are run by a mom and pop from Pittsburgh with a commitment to their community. There's no question television isn't as good as a result.

LK: Will sponsors shy away from a program that receives an R rating?

SALHANY: Well, some people say as long as there's a V-chip, advertisers can say the people at home have the opportunity to block it. But I think the minute you put an R or an X on a television show, you are going to have advertiser issues.

LK: So the R or the X on television will be an unsponsored show?

SALHANY: I don't think it will be unsponsored because I don't even think it will be on.

LK: This would suggest that all broadcast programs are going to be watered down.

SALHANY: *NYPD Blue* still has advertiser issues, but let me tell you something, once you put a rating on a show, not just a disclaimer as is done now, at what point does an advertiser start saying, "I won't be a part of any program with an R rating." I think that's something we're all going to be concerned with in this business. We already are losing business just by talking about the system.

LK: We tend to click out commercials now. How will commercials be seen in the future?

SALHANY: In some cases the commercials are better than the show. But I do think you will see integration of commercials into the content of the program. We may be moving away from commercials and find other ways of bringing in the advertiser. For instance, if you do a show for teen women then you might go to Sears and offer that all the women will wear Sears clothing and here's what it will cost. That's product placement. Now, during the show we can somehow inform the viewers they can order this dress or that pair of jeans by going to our Web site, where they'll be sent into the local market, and the Sears closest to them will take the order and the viewers can have the clothing the very next day. The way a commercial is presented will have to change in the next century. And while we're on commercials I will say they will be less than fifteen seconds in length. The attention span is so limited now and the competition for it is so great that the message must be very short and very focused.

LK: What do you see for cable television?

SALHANY: I think it faces some very strong competition from satellites.

LK: So there won't be five hundred channels?

SALHANY: We won't call them channels the way we do now. I think you'll go to one number and use a navigator of some sort and pick things out, For instance the UPN affiliate might be Channel 9, but Channel 9 will have different subchannels. Channel 9A, for example, might be a text provider, Channel 9B could be a news channel, and Channel 9C is a movie channel, maybe with a subscription fee. You then take our programming and time-shift it down to one of these other channels. You may be able to take all the movies being run in a given period of time and put them on your own movie channel. I think once you can bring your local station into that mix using satellites, it's going to be very difficult for cable to continue. It's too early to know the end game.

LK: The government wants three hours a week for educational programming.

SALHANY: And for the time being it will remain three hours a week unless it starts to become tougher for a politician to get elected. That's when it will become four or more hours a week. It's beyond me how this is the country with public television and here is the perfect place for educational programming but the country won't support public TV. Instead, the government goes after us. If you put chocolate ice cream on a plate, I totally buy into the idea the child will go for that rather than the peas and carrots on another plate. But if you put vegetables on that are well prepared and say, "This is good but it's also very interesting," they'll eat that. The problem is putting up the three hours and mandating it has to be interesting, because that doesn't get the audience to view it.

LK: Will public television exist?

SALHANY: Does it exist now? Have we as a nation put enough resources into it? I would hope that it will exist in some form but I hope it will be much more viable. It serves a very narrow audience now, not that I expect it to reach a broad audience. But I look at public television as unique and I think we as a people are a little apathetic about it.

LK: Will it have more blatant ads than it does now?

SALHANY: I'd have no problem with that but I also think we need to contribute more money toward public television. I do think public television needs to get a tiny bit more commercial. I don't agree bringing British television shows to this country is all they should be doing. I hope we'll see more local events from public TV in all cities across the country and even do some in concert with a commercial station. Some of us here made a suggestion to the FCC about children's television, saying, "Let us pool our money and get the very best programming on public TV. Let them produce it and put it on and we will run it also or take parts from some of it and support it." Didn't happen.

LK: Will topics of television shows push the envelope in the next century?

SALHANY: It depends on the advertiser. Generally, I think content will get softer as a result. So then you take that program to pay-per-view and again we have the two-class society I was talking about earlier. You will have those who can afford all the entertainment and information and the have-nots. As broadcast television gets weaker, the have-nots become all the more disenfranchised.

LK: You were involved in the creation of shows like *Entertainment Tonight* and *Hard Copy*. Will our fascination continue with celebrities?

SALHANY: There's never been a time in our history when we haven't been fascinated with celebrities.

LK: How about tabloid television?

SALHANY: It's becoming less fashionable. I think we're going into a more conservative period but I think it's cyclical. Hedda Hopper did gossip in the thirties, and we saw it again in the eighties and nineties.

LK: Will daytime television talk shows of the future continue to focus as they have on dysfunctional people?

SALHANY: I think we're always fascinated with another view of life. When we talk about dysfunctional people, I remember growing up and watching *Queen for a Day* where people had no money, they needed operations, people were out of work and everyone was suffering. And I remember *Joe Pine What's on Your Mind*, which was brutal. Talk shows have always existed. They came from radio. They'll never go away. I don't think looking at different kinds of people, as we call them dysfunctional, will go away. It will change. It will become less important and then it will come back. All of these things are cyclical.

LK: In this world we are about to enter with the five hundred channels and such, are you worried people in the next century won't pick up a book and read?

SALHANY: Well, I ask this question: Does that mean actually reading a book, or can you get that information a different way? When I wanted information I used to go to the dictionary or the encyclopedia and pull out the resource material. Now I go to my computer and I get it much more quickly. Some people get the book from their computers. Others get it driving to work and listening to an audio version. It is just about getting information and entertainment and how you get that doesn't matter as long as you get it.

STEPHEN J. CANNELL

CHAIRMAN, CANNELL ENTERTAINMENT;

EMMY AWARD—WINNING WRITER AND PRODUCER OF

MORE THAN THIRTY-FIVE TELEVISION SHOWS;

AUTHOR OF THE BESTSELLING POLITICAL THRILLER *THE PLAN*

My dad once told me if you took everything away from everybody as you drove down the street, their cars, their house, their bank accounts, and we're all standing in the park with just our underwear and we're told, "Okay, new world, start again," in ten years the same guys will have all the money. The rules don't change. Work hard.

LK: What are we going to see when we turn on television in the future?

CANNELL: I think we're going to have a much different menu or programming in that we'll all have entertainment rooms. We are a video-intense society, and I only see it getting more so with interactive capability. You'll have wall-size televisions and will be able to pick up a programming guide and order programs to come to your home either through telephone systems or satellite. There will be an entertainment bullet stored in your set, and you can watch it whenever you want. What might happen is instead of people making pilots for television shows, they might produce a trailer like you see in the movie theater and you can tune in the trailer channel or whatever it will be called to choose the product that way. Whether or not that program comes to you depends upon how many other orders there are. It will be demand-driven. Because of improved production techniques and the movement toward narrowcasting, some music fans will literally have the Boston Pops in their living rooms.

LK: Do you envision television being interactive?

CANNELL: I'm not one who believes interactivity is going to take over entertainment television, and the reason is that I don't think most people want to work that hard when they're watching television. I don't think people want to sit in their living rooms and vote on how the plot of the story is going to be told. There's too much of a relaxation that goes with watching television. Interactive will be part of the whole picture but it will in no way be overwhelming. Now, that said, sporting events will have interactive television. You will be able to choose if you want to see the football play from the quarterback's perspective or from the defensive end's perspective. Or you can isolate the bench. You'll have a remote with a button for each camera angle.

LK: Will this be all pay-per-view or will there be networks?

CANNELL: As a supplier I'd like to get the middleman out. As we're getting toward a situation where we are all so vertically integrated in this business, at some point it may be the same person making that decision. I really think this idea of trying to be home on Thursday night to watch *Seinfeld* is going to be a thing of the past. It will either have commercial breaks in it as we have now or it will be a sponsored event but it wouldn't air in a designated time slot. I tend to think there will not be networks. As you watch the audience continue to fragment and the network shares dropping and the fact they continue to make ten clones of a hit show as a way to chase demographics and the fact we're getting more and more channels for a narrower audience, networks haven't found a way to solve the problem. The way to solve the problem is to take a chance. They don't do that.

LK: Programs will be hour long or half-hour?

CANNELL: Well, if you're not dealing with a strict television schedule it's not going to matter. An hour program won't have to be forty-seven minutes, fifty-three seconds long as it is now.

LK: Will we still have the black slate before certain programs advising parents the program they are about to watch may not be suitable for children?

CANNELL: It's going to come to pass. But it's a political football, and until the American public realizes that's all it is, it will continue.

LK: But we will have a V-chip to keep adult themes from being shown to children?

CANNELL: The V-chip is one of the real loony ideas. To expect all these fifty-year-old guys who still can't get the number "12:00" to stop flashing on their video recorders to now install a V-chip or, if it's already installed, make its blocking code kick in, is bullshit and it's never going to happen.

LK: So the only way a parent in the year 2020 will have control is by the graphic or the slide which precedes the program, correct?

CANNELL: I believe television which comes from the result of what you've ordered is already going to have the benefit of being pre-censored by the adults. Or you might be able to order the adult themes to the one set where you as a parent normally watch.

LK: Do you expect future programs to push the envelope with themes, be it profanity or nudity or violent acts?

CANNELL: There will always be an attempt by the artistic community to push back what it considers to be boundaries. I'm not terribly interested in that struggle. That shouldn't be the goal for television. But there will be backlashes if it goes too far.

LK: In the year 2017 we'll still be watching cop shows?

CANNELL: Yes. But those shows will reflect the current morals or whatever the values of that time are. If you go back and look at the cop shows from the Elizabethan time, they dealt with the same thing. *Macbeth* was about murder, so was *Hamlet*, but they were dealing with the idiom and emotional relationships which were part of that period. The good stuff today is doing the same thing. Shakespeare wrote in five acts, Ibsen wrote in three, Bochco and Cannell write in four but commercials make it three.

LK: So future cop shows will follow the same structure today's cop shows follow?

CANNELL: If not the same steps it'll be pretty close to what has been done all along. Today act one defines the problem and you meet all the central characters. Act two complicates the problem and ends with the hero at the lowest point. Act three is the solution. The structure will remain but the subjects and themes will change.

LK: We're done with Westerns though, right?

CANNELL: Wrong. Westerns are morality plays. *Star Trek* is a Western. It's just the location is outer space instead of Dodge City. I did a show called *Renegade* and that was a Western. You had Jack Palance sitting in a bar swilling whiskey and wearing a black hat while shooting people's dogs, and into town rides Shane on a white horse with a white hat, throwing his past away, trying to lead a good life, and these two guys meet. That's a Western. Today some of us try to deal with the moral dilemma of life, and in a Western you just shoot the guy because he's an asshole. That story began on the walls of caves and continues today.

LK: Violence will continue to be an issue in the future?

CANNELL: It will be an issue because the argument of those wanting to curtail violence contains enough credibility that it needs to be looked at. There is graphic violence and there is cartoon violence. In the latter, the Road Runner throws Wile E. Coyote off the cliff as a solution and people say that trivializes violence and this is being taught to children. Then there is graphic violence which desensitizes the viewer. My opinion is, the argument against graphic violence carries the most weight.

LK: So will the issue of graphic violence be resolved?

CANNELL: The only way to do it is be responsible. Now some will say, "Go fuck yourself" and do what they want to do and they will be under fire. Then the issue becomes will it create enough of a media stir to make more people watch it. We are still going to slow down to look at a car wreck. People are people. But there will always be pressure on those who manufacture this material to keep it down, and I don't think that's wrong.

LK: Television has to provide three hours a week of children's programming. Will this eventually become ten hours a week?

CANNELL: You're not going to get *Sesame Street* every time you do an hour of children's TV. Instead you get a purple dinosaur or a mindless cartoon show, so we aren't going to educate our children with television. It isn't being used as an educational tool. It will be financially driven and an entertainment medium. It might be three hours a week one year and four hours a week another year. It will come and go.

LK: What will happen to the evening hours now called prime time?

CANNELL: I may be dead wrong but if we order programs into our entertainment center, then, no, there won't be prime time anymore.

You will choose your own prime time. If there are still networks, there will still be a grid, a schedule of programs.

LK: What scares you?

CANNELL: I can't think of anything. I try not to live my life worrying about getting washed out with the next tide.

Stephen Cannell's choices of five television shows which will never be topped in the next century:

1. *I Love Lucy*

2. *The Dick Van Dyke Show*

3. *Star Trek*

4. *All in the Family*

5. *Hill Street Blues*

SHERRY LANSING

CHAIRMAN, MOTION PICTURE GROUP, PARAMOUNT PICTURES

Technological advances are wonderful but the single most important thing in anyone's life is human intimacy. Find somebody to love and love what you are doing. All the technology in the world isn't going to bring you any happiness.

LK: What do you think the movie theater of the future will be like, and maybe even more important, do you think we'll go to a movie theater to see a film?

LANSING: The only thing I know for sure is that, no matter what the century, we're going to need movies and more movies than ever. It is encouraging that, as people debate the issues whether or not films will be on tape or will theaters be eliminated, there is still a primal need to hear stories whether you are watching a movie at your house or in a multiscreen facility. I think that need will continue and there will be more of it for all kinds of audiences. The form in which you'll see it is clearly going to be available to you by choice. We already can get movies by demand on television, and within the next decade there will be home viewing units available. These will be mini screens for people to have in their homes. Now that brings us to the question you asked about even going to a movie theater. I think you still will because we want a community experience and see a movie in a crowd the same way we go to a rock concert even though we have the band's record at home. The movies will have to continue to be seen in safe urban centers, otherwise nobody's going to take the risk of being a victim of violence. My optimistic view is that crime will not get out of control. If I'm wrong and violence continues to grow, people will retreat more and more into their kind of futuristic world inside their houses.

LK: So violence, not technology, will keep people out of a movie theater?

LANSING: That's the way I feel, yes. Now, having said that, I'm in the business of making movies. Someone else decides where to put them. I've watched movies in the Paramount screening room, on television, on tape, and sometimes in the screening room I used to have in my house, and nothing ever took the place of going to a nice theater, buying my box of popcorn, experiencing that community feeling where everybody laughs and cries or boos. It's a great experience to see a movie with a couple hundred people as compared to just yourself. It's not the same laughter when you laugh alone.

LK: Will movie theaters turn cold when the scene on the screen shifts to Antarctica, or will our chairs lean back when we watch a jet taking off?

LANSING: We have been experimenting and trying to push the envelope to make the experience more and more realistic and interesting. Way back it was 3-D so yes, it is all possible. But it's what's on that screen, so if you smell it or you don't smell it or it's cold or it's hot, you'd better like that story.

LK: Will the trend of adapting books to screen continue?

LANSING: Anybody with a good story, and if it's a good story in a book, we will continue to use it. Books are a rich source of material. Novelists have been very good at telling a good story. Now reading it isn't enough. We want to see it.

LK: You speak of the primal need to hear stories. Do you think those stories will be different?

LANSING: The stories will be different in the sense they will adapt to the world. Stories about women are different today than they were in the past because women have emerged with careers. But people will always continue to explore certain relationships and movies will continue to expand those stories. Now, what I will say is we are not just doing special effects movies; there's an idea out there that those are the only kind that will ever work so we're only going to have technological movies and not character movies. I disagree with that. We will have technological movies that will do things we've never seen before, but I think more and more people are going to yearn for human beings that they can relate to. We'll have explosions and special effects but we also have to have people you care about.

LK: *Toy Story* is not necessarily the movie of the future then.

LANSING: There are going to be so many choices. When I started in this business people were saying you can only make movies for kids. Today we're making movies just for people over sixty. We did *First Wives Club* targeted for women.

LK: It is technically possible for a dead person to show up in a film, as we saw with one of your movies (*Forrest Gump*), and that brings us to the issue of a future movie with an all-dead cast or at least a costar who is dead. Possible?

LANSING: The technology is moving so fast that I wonder if we'll have actors who aren't really actors but are animated or digitized. It does make me wonder if the time is going to come when we won't use people anymore.

LK: Do you think that is possible?

LANSING: Anything is possible, but keep in mind I'm technologically impaired. A whole movie starring Humphrey Bogart I think would be eerie, but without knowing the plot or what the movie is about I have to say anything is possible.

LK: The industry has been putting out more movies than ever before and we've seen any number of four- or five- or six-release Fridays. Does this mean the movie-going public will become more and more narrow and movies will be specifically designed for a demographic?

LANSING: I do believe in the next century everyone will have his own screening room, and these will be affordable and as simple to purchase as a television set. You will watch those movies for your demo at home or you'll watch them with your family and friends. But you'll go out for "event" movies in the same way you'll go out for a concert because you want to be with people. The public will become more and more selective. I think there will be fewer theaters and there won't be the need for the small theater because you'll have it in your home. There's no doubt the Hollywood screening room will become as simple as a television set and new movies will be available by demand or cassette or through some kind of telephone line or whatever the equivalent is going to be. And maybe only six people will fit into the room. But you will go out and see the bigger movies because of this primal sense of community I mentioned earlier. Now the winner in all of this is the filmmaker because we used to bitch and moan about having to make movies for just people age twenty-five or I can only make this particular kind. And now, with all the Gramercys and Miramaxes and so on, the filmmaker can make movies he wants to make. There are so many movies and so many choices. And that is not only good, it's wonderful. In the short term, we will make fewer movies but if the ancillary markets grow and if I get to make movies for a more and more segmented audience, my choice of movies will expand and my revenue streams will be much bigger.

LK: More movies suggests the chance of more failures, doesn't it?

LANSING: Not necessarily. Remember, there's an increase in the access to these films. I might make a movie for $3 million and make it available only to your home, and that movie might have a much narrower audience than the ones we'd put in the theaters. You will eventually be able to see that kind of picture in your home but it might be two years before that happens.

LK: Do you think movie studios will make educational movies and sell them to schools?

LANSING: Yes. It will grow and grow.

LK: *Star Wars* was rereleased. Will we see more of that?

LANSING: You are going to be seeing what you think is more of "that" but it really isn't. We've always mined our libraries for what we can rerelease but it is usually done nicely and with a return on investment but never done the way *Star Wars* was done. There are very few movies that are the phenomenon in that way where the parents saw it and wanted to show it to their children and not only relive their memories but pass them on. We were always rereleasing *Godfather* on the twenty-fifth anniversary but only in ten or twenty markets because there wasn't an audience for anything more. There are very few pictures that will translate like that.

LK: Will there be sequels?

LANSING: Oh sure. Remember, it's becoming, even now, more and more of a target demo business.

LK: Will there still be a video after films have had their run in the theater?

LANSING: Absolutely, or something like it. I think there will be lots of choices. But the window for the release will depend on how big the picture is. It may be longer for the major ones. I do think we will see more ancillary markets (videos, CDs, computer disks) opening up for pictures. One may only be seen on CD-ROM or whatever the medium happens to be. It may go direct to cable or direct to television. We don't know.

LK: Will we pay attention to film critics in the next century as much as we do now (and that presumes we do pay attention)?

LANSING: Well, if there's more access from your house, you will be making your own choices. But I think the film critics will still have a role and will be one of the components of whether or not you go out to see a movie.

LK: How about ratings? Will there be more or fewer?

LANSING: Well, if the film is in your home, you'll probably know the rating but you'll make the choice yourself. I don't think we need more ratings, but we need to have more information. For instance, something like, "We have given this an R not because of sex but because of violence." When you see the R you're not sure what it means. As a parent, you might not object to your child seeing two people making love but you wouldn't want your child to see someone being beheaded. So I don't think more information is going to hurt anyone and it will allow people to be more individualistic in their choices.

LK: In 1996 politicians went after Hollywood and I'm wondering if this is something we can look forward to every four years or if you see a change of some sort occurring?

LANSING: I feel very strongly that Hollywood has become a whipping dog for the ills of society. I think movies have an obligation to show you all sides of society and there are going to be stories in which people don't have a good end. The movies are showing you a slice of life. To not show you that slice of life, to not show you that people are on drugs is, in a funny way, immoral. To paint a rose-colored garden is silly and, as a result, I do think we need violence in films and sex in films and to show the real world. We would eliminate classic films like *Boyz in the 'Hood* if we decided we didn't want to see violence.

LK: So will you and others have more face-offs with Congress?

LANSING: Again, as it becomes more of something you see in your own home, I don't think there will be a way for Congress or anyone else to have influence over you. There may be a discussion about so-and-so doesn't want you to see this picture and another so-and-so likes the picture and here's what the critics say and you'll say, "Forget them, I'm going to watch what I want to see." Nobody is going to be able to tell me what I can and can't watch in my home. I'm a big believer in the community and I know we are becoming more and more isolationist and living in our own little worlds. I think that is very sad, but the interesting thing is I'm watching whatever I want to watch. Now, to go out to a theater and see such and such a film is more of a statement. Still, I don't think interest groups or Congress or whatever will be able to chip away at artistic freedom. There will be more labeling but I don't think they will be able to control the content.

LK: Do you think Hollywood will continue to be the film center?

LANSING: The center will be Hollywood because there will need to be a place where the studios are. The only other place I think it could go would be a warm climate and that's just because of the nature of how you can shoot a scene. It's conceivable studios will have off-shoots in places like Florida but it's more climate control than anything else.

LK: Will there continue to be mergers of Hollywood studios and companies buying Hollywood studios?

LANSING: I really think we've merged-out for a while. I don't think bigger is necessarily better.

LK: You are a successful woman in a business that has not always been kind to women, not that there are that many that have been, but do you think the glass ceiling will continue to be around?

LANSING: It will totally disappear. Women are slowly but surely being accepted in all areas of any business. We entered the workforce late. For a long time we couldn't even vote, and I think we are making remarkable progress. I think the movie business is one of the least prejudiced. Ten or fifteen years into the next century, there will still be some barriers but they are disappearing very fast every day. The glass ceiling will shatter by the middle of the next century.

LK: Will we continue to see sweatshirts, caps, toys, and so on associated with movies?

LANSING: The marketing of a movie is becoming as important as, if not more important than, the movie. It used to be the word-of-mouth was the single most important thing in a movie's success. Today the marketing and publicity are more important. An inferior movie with an extraordinary marketing campaign can be successful. There will be more products specifically tied to a demographic as home viewing increases.

LK: How about movie lengths? I've heard that an audience is content for ninety minutes but after that, they're ready to leave.

LANSING: Not true. Good is good. *Forrest Gump* was longer, as was *Braveheart*. It's not about how long it is but about how long it should be. What's appropriate for the story.

LK: What scares you about the twenty-first century?

LANSING: My biggest fear is the isolation. I get scared violence will so envelop our streets we won't go out. And then there will be no theaters. And then we'll live in our little pod pressing buttons, with the kids in one room and the parents in another room. Right now the technology is so good people do sit in their home and watch a video. Imagine if there were a wide screen with the same quality as a movie theater in their home? I don't know how many people would leave their house and drive to a theater and experience urban violence for the experience. Now what saddens me is you'll be seeing it with maybe just ten people.

LK: The role of a movie star is going to be more and more important in selling a movie?

LANSING: The single most important thing is the story. If you have that, it's a bonus to have a good star. The economics of this business have become horrifying. The fact is if you have a great story you can make it without a star but in today's marketplace there are more and more pictures, and so you need to distinguish yourself from the others. That can be done with special effects and sometimes you do it with a name. There are fewer than ten people today who have a name. Now if you have a really good movie without any names in it, word-of-mouth is required. Unfortunately, we're losing word-of-mouth in our business because of too many movies, too much competition, and too much competitive marketplace. *Shine, Secrets and Lies, Slingblade* were word-of-mouth pictures. I think we will see fewer pictures being made in the near future and I think we will see fewer $100 million budgets for movies. The burn on a picture like that is so enormous that it will force studios to try and tighten their belts more.

LK: Would you like to run a movie studio in the next century?

LANSING: I think the more choices you have in making movies the more creative opportunities become available. But to answer your question, I just hope I'm alive.

LK: One more question about the twenty-first century: Do you think the Oscars will be shown on TV in less than three hours, or are we going to have to wait until the twenty-second for that?

LANSING: I sure hope so. Everybody would like it to be shorter but with all these existing categories and the new technology for animation and digitization, a trend could develop making even more categories. But I don't think anyone wants it to be any longer.

ISAAC MIZRAHI
FASHION DESIGNER

Buy something because you love it, not because you think it's going to change your life or because you think your mother or your husband or your wife is going to love it. Enjoy clothes the way you enjoy food.

LK: What might we find hanging in the closets of a professional man and woman in the twenty-first century?

MIZRAHI: Knits. Tailored jersey suits. Those would be the perfect fiber and the perfect weight. It might be a lightweight knit suit or even a jumpsuit or a dress that is worn with a jacket. Men will still have the classic gray slacks and blue blazer, though. I don't think men will choose between single-breasted or double-breasted suits. I really see office workers wearing something simple like a one- or two-piece jumpsuit.

LK: Here's one of the most important questions in this entire book: Will men still wear a long tie?

MIZRAHI: No. In 2097? I don't think so. It was the twentieth century when the long tie was invented. No ties at all now that I think about it. Men won't wear anything at all around the collar because what we wear in the future is going to be really easy.

LK: Isaac, you're going to be the headline in this book.

MIZRAHI: In the next one hundred years people are going to be into all sorts of different things. For executives and working people I think it's going to be about cleanliness. It will be pared down. Very few details. There will be few colors and few things going on. It's going to be like a jumpsuit of one color or something. It's going to be made of some incredible knit, something that breathes. Now outside of the office, it will be very eclectic and very mixed up and artful and beautiful. It will be an event. I think we'll see an extreme version of what's going on now.

LK: We are going through something called dress-down Friday in the office. Do you think we'll have a dress-down Thursday?

MIZRAHI: It's going to become dress-down always. There won't be a dress-up thing anymore. I think it's going to be out of choice and people will want to look different than just wearing jeans and a T-shirt to the office. Denim will still be around, though it will be a transmuted version of what we see now.

LK: Where do you see this heading, then?

MIZRAHI: You know I tend to think the big thing that's going to happen is men will start dressing up. Now, having said that, I'm not sure exactly what that means until I get there but the roles are going to change. Women are going to be in the workplace so much more and men are going to be in the home so much more, and it's the men who are beginning to look at themselves and say, "Hey, I'm good-looking, I'm not just the breadwinner, I'm not just supporting a family, I'm also an object of desire." So we're moving from men as the subjects to men as objects. Through the last two centuries it was the women who were objects and men were the subjects. So once men discover themselves as objects of desire, they're going to start responding to themselves by dyeing their hair, tweezing their eyebrows, makeup and fancy dress and so on.

LK: Men are going to wear makeup?

MIZRAHI: A bit of makeup, yes. It won't be artificial eyeliner or colorful but it might be a brow or a contour of the cheek. It could even be a lipstick or a gloss. They did it in the seventeenth century and the eighteenth century.

LK: Everyone I've talked to regarding politics is saying while they can't pinpoint events, they are absolutely positive a woman will occupy the Oval Office—

MIZRAHI: I'm not going to be the exception to that rule.

LK: Can you tell me what she would wear at work in the White House?

MIZRAHI: Maybe it would be like sort of a sleek jumpsuit of some sort. It's something not so much implying her sex and not so much implying her position. My theory of the workplace is it's going to be some kind of uniform. What I'm observing about culture is that political correctness is getting more and more heavy. We're at the point where we don't want to look rich or like a smoker or like a straight man or a gay man, but rather this weird generic kind of thing. Now that's troubling but I think that's what's going on. So I hope this uniform will bring out individuals. It will be the standard.

LK: We will wear the uniform to work?

MIZRAHI: That's right. They won't be exactly alike. I mean the government's not going to issue them or anything like that. The past fifteen years has seen a uniform for women in the office and that's been Giorgio Armani: three pockets, one button, dark suit, crepe wool worn with a T-shirt or a little silk blouse in either a dark color or a taupe or a khaki. So it could be a jumpsuit if we can figure out how to go to the bathroom easily with something like that.

LK: Gender lines will blur in what we wear. Correct?

MIZRAHI: That's accurate. Shakespeare always wrote that the minute you have a villain you have a honey of a guy as well. Somewhere he is evil but somewhere he is goodness. Everything that takes place also takes place in exact opposition. So we may be wearing a uniform or it may seem we are dressing the same but suddenly people will become flamboyant as a result to emphasize they are a separate kind of person. This will occur outside of work.

LK: Some fashion designers are saying too much was done in the eighties and the nineties and things moved much too fast. You agree?

MIZRAHI: Everybody, collectively, did that. It wasn't just fashion designers. I don't see that as a criticism as much as it's an observation. Things are going to speed up even more. Fashion is going to become a museum with no curator and it's because of the speed of communication. Look, everything is speeding up. This is what will kill the human race, not nuclear holocaust but the stress of living with speed and the stress of knowing you can move so fast. I go through stress going from here to Paris in an afternoon. They didn't have to worry about that in the eighteenth century.

LK: Well, this is the perfect place to ask what scares you about the next century?

MIZRAHI: The pace. Individuals are the only ones who can say they want to slow down but as a group we aren't going to do it.

LK: Will a size six in 2020 be the same as a size six today?

MIZRAHI: Fashion changes. But I would say it is very specific to the piece of clothing that you are talking about. A size six always had a certain waist measurement but a woman might want a size smaller in a big full trouser because she likes it snug, whereas if it's a skinny pant she might take a size bigger because she likes that a little looser. If anything, sizes might get a bit smaller because people are smaller than they were forty years ago.

LK: Do you think we'll buy clothing with specific labels indicating the particular product was not made by children or something like that?

MIZRAHI: I think by the next century it's going to be a given. I think in the future people are going to take this more seriously. People in the future are going to say to themselves, "I've got to be more careful." Now, will there be a specific label saying, "Not made by child labor"? No. I do think we may see labels indicating the amount of UV rays the clothing absorbs or something like that. You will see more scientific information on labels. There might be some kind of a federal agency assembled to ensure human rights violations, like child labor, aren't involved in the product whatever it may be. That's what it sounds like to me.

LK: Do you think models who wear the clothes you design are not going to be so beautiful and sleek and perfect as they are now and will instead look like women on Main Street America?

MIZRAHI: No. I tried really hard to show clothes on real women and it works to an extent but it doesn't have the same kind of appeal as does a really perfect example. Perhaps mass-produced clothes will use real women more and more but in terms of fashion, the ideal body is the one you will always get the best results from. Now people always say, "Oh we want to see that dress on a real woman," but it's not true because when they do, they're not as interested.

LK: They don't buy the dress?

MIZRAHI: They don't feel they need it. It doesn't have the same kind of sexy edge to it. It's weird because this is something women ask for and they get it and they don't want it.

LK: New fabrics?

MIZRAHI: There are already some incredible synthetics that don't wrinkle and don't need to be dry cleaned as often as what we have today. Tensel is such a fabric. You'll be hearing about it. On the flip side, precious things are an extreme commodity now, like fine woolens and silks and cashmeres. But of course a fraction of that is sold as compared to the rayons and polyesters and gray cottons.

LK: What else will change in what we wear?

MIZRAHI: Underwear. It's going to be more scientific. For instance, Japan has pantyhose that moisturizes the legs. So I think there will be some incredible discovery made about how to wear something underneath your clothes that is good for the skin and keeps you at exactly the right temperature. As a result, what goes on the outside isn't as important as it is now. I also think men are going to decide, on their days off, which ruffled shirt to wear with which brocade suit.

LK: Men are going to be thinking about that?

MIZRAHI: I think so. They did in the eighteenth century. But women will dress up too; however it will be from choice. That's what I try to stress: Choice is the important factor. It won't be mandatory. For instance, in the next century, skirt lengths will go up and down in the same season. It won't be one length for one year only.

LK: Will women still wear heels and pumps in the next century?

MIZRAHI: Yes. Vanity will do it. Nothing does for a leg what a high heel does for a leg. Nothing does for height what a high heel does for height. Comfort is relative. When you feel beautiful then you feel comfortable. A woman can feel like a queen when she puts on high heels (I know I feel like a queen when I put on high heels). And I think men will start wearing them too. Smaller men will be the first and it will catch on. Tall is a great thing. Women love being tall unless their husbands are small, which is why I think heels are such a fantastic thing.

LK: Will New York and Paris remain the centers of fashion, or do you think there will be another city, like Danbury, Connecticut?

MIZRAHI: I can assure you Danbury, Connecticut, will not. I think centers of fashion will be Paris, Milan, London, and New York.

New York is taking on a greater bit of importance because fashion, while becoming more global, is also becoming more American in its outlook. Milan is also becoming an important fashion capital because it's the most realistic of the European fashion capitals while Paris is more flamboyant. In fact, Paris is the fashion show capital but it's not a fashion capital any longer. In New York you will see a more diverse look, more difference between designers who work there. The difference between designers is what makes the clothes sell, not the sameness. That will be a change.

LK: What do you mean by fashion becoming "more American"?

MIZRAHI: It's the way people need to dress every day. It's not as obsessed with flamboyance and fashion as it is obsessed with quality and propriety and being functional. Now people say I'm flamboyant—

LK: I've heard that.

MIZRAHI: But I'm witty and that's all. My clothes are just a bit more good humored.

Spirit

As I looked at the thousands of words about what we might accomplish and what we might confront, I wondered where God was going to be in all of these expectations. And if not God, how are we going to feel about our place in, to use the oft-used phrase, "the larger scheme of things"? Technology, by its nature, allows us to extend physical and cosmic property lines and, consequently, as the lot becomes larger the domain of things spiritual, the untouchable becomes smaller.

My search brought me to three individuals, each of whom has spent most of his or her life in pursuit of explaining that which can be sometimes seen and many times felt but continues to lie just outside the ability to be defined. My interviews were to have been about that larger scheme in the next century but settled, instead, on us. I'm beginning to think there's a connection here.

Whenever the Dalai Lama comes to America, Robert Thurman is usually at his side. He teaches Buddhism at Columbia University and promotes Buddhism from the New York City-based Tibet House. *Time* named him one of its 25 Most Influential People in America in 1997. He is a former monk who gave up that calling so that he could marry (actress Uma Thurman is his daughter) and make a living in academia.

Elaine Pagels is well known for her popular books *The Gnostic Gospels* and *The Origin of Satan*, as well as her Princeton University classes on religion, which continue to be SRO. That says a lot about what she has to say, just as it says a lot about those who want to listen.

She is a chronicler of religions and spirituality and a participant in the exploration of, to use her words, "invisible beings."

Appointed archbishop in 1980, Oscar Lipscomb oversees more than two hundred thousand Roman Catholics in a two-state area, with his base in Mobile, Alabama. He has worked with the national conference of Catholic Bishops as chairman of their Committee on Doctrine (1988-91) and as chairman of their Committee on Ecumenical Affairs (1993-96). In addition, since 1995 he has worked on their Subcommittee for the Celebration of the Millennium.

ROBERT THURMAN

PROFESSOR OF INDO-TIBETAN BUDDHIST STUDIES,
COLUMBIA UNIVERSITY

Cultivate your tolerance. Use the Internet and the schools to understand the world better. Don't just be angry and don't accept slogans. Never follow anybody who tries to get you to scapegoat a weaker person.

LK: What would you suggest we be doing today to prepare spiritually for this new century?

THURMAN: You have to look at where we are now. The faith in materialistic progress has declined. We've all kind of given up on what they might have thought of in the fifties, such as: Medical science will make a heart designed so people will live practically forever, everything in our body can be replaced, all health problems will be solved, engineering will fix all the poverty and famine, and psychological engineering will fix criminality and any other mental problems. None of these things has happened. As a result, religions are coming back as offering some kind of solace to us in our present situation. But with the return of religions as serious worldviews, we have the danger of extreme fundamentalism, intolerance, and even fanaticism. So I think in the twenty-first century the big spiritual or religious difficulty is the old religious worldviews coming back and bringing with them new sources of conflict between people. To avoid that, we're going to have to educate ourselves religiously. We'll have to learn about others' religions and develop tolerance about others' religions and try to come to a sort of middle way. If we're trying to recover from the extreme materialism that characterized the nineteenth and twentieth centuries, we shouldn't go into a fanatic spiritualism where we end up in new religious wars. We need to discover a spirituality that enables us to get along on a smaller planet where people are very much up against one another. Bosnia is a religious war. The Serbs are orthodox Christians, the Croatians are Roman Catholic Christians and many of the Bosnians are Muslim. The difference in their three identities is religion. Their treatment of each other is an example of the religious intolerance I was talking about.

LK: So in the next century if somebody has a disagreement about the way another sees religion, he should do what?

THURMAN: Learn about the other way and develop tolerance for it. Whether you say "God," "Yahweh," or "Allah," for example, the difference between Christianity, Judaism, and Islam is really very small. People might think Buddhists are atheistic because they don't believe the version of God that is taught in Genesis, but if they look closely, they'll learn Buddhists basically believe in the goodness of the universe and the providence of Divine Intelligence, but they don't have the same story. Same with the Hindus. Same with most of the Chinese. So I think if people look past some of the surface differences they will find the commonality. That's how you develop tolerance of the differences.

LK: This is being called the information age and there's a Buddhist site on the Internet as well as a Catholic site and a Judaic site, and I'm curious about how this will make us feel about ourselves and if it can change our relationship with God or a God king or some central entity?

THURMAN: I think the information age is a good thing that can give us hope for the new century. Because of the much larger spread of information, people can fairly easily learn about each other's ways of life and worldviews, and different races can get more used to each other. There's more imagery about people from other nations, races, and cultures. People can become familiar with different languages. We can overcome these causes of great conflict and senses of alienation in the past. So the information age can help the new century to be a peaceful one, which means a tolerant one.

LK: And that means our relationship with God, or whatever we call it, will change?

THURMAN: I hope so. In the past, religious attitudes were manipulated by governments to make people feel a sense of difference between themselves and others so they could mobilize them to fight, like in a Crusade type of thing. Governments didn't want people to feel and develop a common identity with people on the other side of borders because they wanted their people to fight. Today governments realize there's not much profit to be made by taking away people's territory or oppressing other people. The way wealth is created and the way that people prosper is by learning to get along with other people. You approach them as a market and as consumers. You want them to do well so they can buy your things. We now have a stake in creating some degree of planetary citizenship. The spiritual identity is crucial in that. We don't want to develop versions of God or faith that make it necessary to destroy other people who don't share that version. Rather, we have to develop versions that find something in common with other people. This is going to be the big difference in the next century.

LK: And what might that be?

THURMAN: Well, I don't believe it should be one religion. I closely agree with the Dalai Lama, who has this metaphor: Imagine if we have food that was the same for breakfast, lunch, and dinner everywhere in the world. People would get sick of it and we'd have malnutrition or bulimia or something because it would be so boring to eat the same thing. Different kinds of people have different tastes. So once we become convinced that everyone shares certain positive ethical outlooks and a certain sense of respect for each other, then we should be delighted there is a variety of stories and myths of the way we look at spiritual force. The key thing that all religions share in common is that they basically give people a feeling about the goodness of the universe, that there is something worthwhile about living. There is evil. There is stupidity. There is hurtfulness in the world. But stronger than the hurtfulness is a sort of benevolence and a well-wishing. That's crucial because that gives people the security to behave well themselves. It prevents them from becoming cynical. In fact, we could say that even secular humanism itself is a very important world religion, in which people who don't follow rigidly any particular religion hold this sense about the value of humanity. They feel the world is a good place, and human goodness has some value and meaning, and this is what has to be held in common. What can be different is you can call God "Allah" or "Rama" or "Buddha" or just "Love." Whatever you want.

LK: In order for a religion or spirituality to do well in the next century, it has to say, "I'm not the only game in town, and if I'm right for you it doesn't mean everybody else is wrong." Correct?

THURMAN: That's right. That is a Rubicon that more fundamentalist varieties of all religions will have to deal with, and I include Buddhism and Hinduism in that. Everyone should develop the ability to think, "My religion is true and right *for me*." This means we can say another religion can be true and right for someone else. In the past there's been too much of "My religion is true and right so I have to shove it down everyone else's throat." The result is a Crusade or a Holy War, and that's the one we have to draw the line on, and religions in the next century are going to have to restrain themselves. My friend Jim Morton, who is dean of the Episcopal St. John the Divine Church in New York, always says we have to have the faith that God is wiser than any of his religions.

LK: So just to be clear here: It's your feeling religions after the year 2000 will understand there are other ways of looking at the same thing?

THURMAN: Yes. Some religions have the idea that God spoke only in the Koran or the Bible, or that some ultimate being stated some ultimate text. But followers of those religions have to understand that people wrote them down and people translated them into different languages. The word "God" is a human word, and God might have a different name for himself. Who are we to say?

LK: Clashes of religion and politics will continue, and if so, where will the clashes occur?

THURMAN: The usual clash is precisely where particular religious institutions decide they want to take over a political system and enforce their ideology upon a society of beings, and that's where the intolerance comes in that I mentioned. Here something that America invented is very valuable, and we have exported it around the world, namely the separation of church and state.

LK: The countries where religions are taking over politics are?

THURMAN: Well, Iran of course. There's a danger in Saudi Arabia.

LK: What about the Christian Coalition in the United States?

THURMAN: Exactly. We should be alert to attempts by Christian fundamentalists to take over things like school boards, county councils, and state positions. Our Founding Fathers very carefully put in the Constitution that no religious group should run the state.

LK: Well, the Christian Coalition isn't going away. How does this play out?

THURMAN: I think they are going to become more moderate. I think our people are too pluralistic and we have too many different religious minorities who would be afraid to be dominated by a certain version of Protestantism. This country was founded by people escaping religious persecution in Europe. Fundamentalists are having a certain type of reaction against the extreme secularism and for that I applaud them. I think they should challenge the orthodoxy of materialism in our country, the religion of those who insist there can be no soul and that all religions are superstition and that sort of thing—we can call it the scientific orthodoxy. They are right to challenge that ideologically, but when they carry that challenge so far that they want to get into the government and start legislating that people pray a certain way and adopt certain vows of allegiance, then that's going too far.

LK: What scares you about the coming century?

THURMAN: The persistence of nineteenth- and twentieth-century habits into the twenty-first century that could cause it to be a century of even worse devastation than we've experienced. The twentieth century was one of world wars and many other proxy wars, the Cold War, and it has been a very violent century. Stalin has about 40 million dead on his record. Mao Zedong has 60 million. Hitler has about 25 million. And there are a lot of other people killed in smaller conflicts. We still see on our planet that the major expenditure of government money in all of the countries goes into military budgets. The militarism of the planet is really excessive. At the end of the Cold War we had the possibility of reducing nuclear weapons and reducing conventional forces all around but we have not done so. In a way you can say the Cold War has not completely ended. So we are all keeping up these old habits and there's no enemy. Our real enemy is our own selfishness, which creates the millions of poverty-stricken people on inner city streets, drug addicts, criminals, and people without jobs. Our enemy is this internal problem. My fear, then, is people with a certain definition of defense—weapons to kill external enemies—won't adapt quickly enough to recognize the real enemy is a certain type of internal confusion and stupidity and greed.

LK: Do you think they will adapt?

THURMAN: Well, I'm not sure. I have a basic feeling they will and that faith is backed up by the way that we can understand the information revolution, the computerization of learning. But sometimes when I'm a little bit depressed, I'm just not sure.

LK: There is excitement about the possibility life existed or exists on Mars. What does this do to those who are spiritual as well as those who follow a specific religion?

THURMAN: Well, spiritual people have always felt that there are many other life forms in the universe and not just the human one on this planet. Ancient Christianity had all kinds of angels and also had the idea, and still does, that God is omnipotent and can create anything that he wants. So why would an omnipotent God be satisfied with one dinky little planet? Ancient Christians, Muslims, Sufis, Buddhists, and Hindus all have the idea of a universe as a much richer place filled with life forms than the modern materialistic worldview where we think we're the one people sitting on this one little rock. So this will only confirm the faith in the infinite life-giving power at the heart of the universe.

LK: So this is okay for those who are spiritual, but those who are religious may have a problem with the discovery?

THURMAN: I can't make a blanket statement on that, but remember when Galileo was muzzled for saying the Earth goes around the sun? Well, particular narrow versions of religions will probably have trouble with this. The spiritual people who follow religions will have to appeal to those with a narrow view inside their own religions and handle it that way.

LK: Technology can keep us alive longer. What does that do to our religious and spiritual perspective?

THURMAN: Science and technology are, in a way, keeping us alive longer. They are lowering the rates of infant mortality around the world very drastically. On the other hand, the overpopulation caused by this is a problem that science and technology cannot, alone, solve. So when religious institutions won't change rigid attitudes about birth control and we see the world under this terrible overpopulation danger, then those old-fashioned attitudes are not adapting to current reality and they become part of the danger. All religions will agree abortions are unhealthy and could be seen as close to killing and should not be used as a method of birth control. But contraception has nothing "killing" about it. You are preventing a life from happening. You are not taking a life. If this method were used to balance the overpopulation caused by those other scientific breakthroughs, I think religions shouldn't complain. In fact, they should foster it. The overpopulation of the planet is resulting in a living death for so many people. I think religious institutions are going to have to become partners with science because this could make the twenty-first century viable.

LK: How could that happen?

THURMAN: Well, I was at a conference near the Aegean Sea hosted by the Christian Greek Orthodox Church, where environmentalists were brought together with monks, lay people, and religious people, and they exchanged information about the environment. The patriarchs of the Orthodox Church do not accept the Augustinian interpretation of the Book of Revelation where it argues that the world will be destroyed in the battle between Christ and the Devil—Armageddon—and after that God will make a new world. Well, there's another interpretation that the new world is this planet if used intelligently. Those who interpret the Book of Revelation according to Augustine will say, "Well, God put resources here for humans to use so let's use them all up." If religions could change those interpretations then environmentalism could be taught from the pulpit and in Sunday school and not just in the public schools or the college graduate schools. In Islamic countries the mullahs could teach environmentalism in the mosque. Contraception could be taught in churches and temples. The churches, then, could work with science to keep the planet viable. Imagine if world religions could take an educational role that fit with the reality of today and there was a partnership with science instead of being the enemy of science.

LK: How likely is this?

THURMAN: I think it is likely after all because the final motive in all the world religions is to help life on earth. Religions which preach some extreme thing, like everyone should jump off a cliff at midnight on a full moon, well, they haven't lasted very long. So in a reality where we soon will have a world with 20 billion people, religions harp on the same old doctrines that were appropriate centuries earlier when a woman would have ten children and six of them died. Here you have a religion saying it's helpful to be harmful. I don't think people will tolerate it. So, yes, it will change. The next pope is very likely to be much more modern in his outlook with regard to science as well as other religions. Pope John Paul II was a big factor in getting his country, Poland, free of the Communist oppression of Catholicism and he was a great champion of the freedom of religion. Now that most religions are free, the danger is mutual intolerance among religions and mutual intolerance between religion and science. If they don't do something new, they are going to lose their followers again and they'll destroy themselves.

LK: How would you describe where we are in the big picture and where might we be in another twenty-five years?

THURMAN: Different Buddhists have different visions of the big picture. Those from Sri Lanka see us in a decline which is going to get quite a bit worse. It won't go into total destruction. Then things will begin to improve when another Buddha appears. The Tibetan Buddhists, on the other hand, see things now as close to a time called Shambhala. They are vague as to whether it is in twenty years or fifty years or one hundred years, but within the next century. When it arrives there will be no more world wars and people will take the effort previously put into militarism and put it into making a good quality of life. It will be a great era of world peace and enlightenment. Some Tibetans see the small wars which have occurred in all different parts of the planet after the great world wars of this century as the final war that was referred to in the Prophecy. And they understand with the advent of nuclear weapons the impossibility of world war because nobody can win one anymore. Others think we still have to wait, and the two places they fear are China and the Islamic world because both societies have the ability to create fear of others in their own citizens.

LK: We will know Shambhala is coming when what happens?

THURMAN: We knew it was coming when the Russians gave up their empire and their Cold War.

LK: How would you describe all of us today?

THURMAN: I think our society is simply more open about its feelings than others. We go on about how frustrated we are and this and that and we get up and say, "I'm mad," and we go to talk shows as a way to get it all off our chests. We air our frustrations, and that's a healthy sign. The danger, on the other hand, is that members of the elite, the wealthy are thinking everyone is frustrated and everything is bad and they are taking their money out to Switzerland and moving their factories to places where they can have underpaid workers. The poverty people face creates an added frustration.

LK: Is it going to be tougher or easier to live in the next century?

THURMAN: It will be easier. Imagine how tough it was for those who had to go out and fight World War I and World War II. It was terrible. Same with the Vietnam War. Same with those who had to fight on the streets during the civil rights movement. The twentieth century has been very rough, but the twenty-first century could see us in a much better position.

LK: More people will have the ability to touch their insides in the twenty-first century?

THURMAN: Yes. If you believe your deeper, innermost heart is naturally in touch with the good of the universe, be it a God or Enlightenment or Ozone Energy or whatever you call it, then you'll feel that things will work out okay.

ELAINE PAGELS

HARRINGTON SPEAR PAINE PROFESSOR OF RELIGION,
PRINCETON UNIVERSITY

Remain open to the possibility of a spiritual dimension in human life.

LK: We seem to be traveling faster, we are learning so much, everyone says there's going to be change-change-change, and I'm wondering what this is going to do to God.

PAGELS: You're talking about quantitative changes: changes in speed, medical advances, travel, communications, and the like. They've changed our lives. But they have also pressed with urgency the kinds of questions religion involves: What does it mean, and what do we think about living and dying, and what is it for? I work on a bioethics committee at a hospital where medical technology raises the questions about values of life in a very radical and practical way. These questions are becoming all the more acute.

LK: Well, this is an appropriate place to ask the cloning question. If a human being is formed in the laboratory, which is cloning in its most basic definition, is there a soul?

PAGELS: That reminds me of a conversation between my late husband and the Dalai Lama about whether artificial intelligence could have a soul or a spiritual element. It's a question many people are already talking about. The approaches of science and spirit are quite different because one talks about how it happens while the other talks about whether it has any meaning and if there's a purpose to it. Science can't answer those questions because they aren't scientific questions.

LK: So advances in science are forcing answers?

PAGELS: No, they are forcing questions that may be becoming more urgent than before. These are questions about what we ultimately value and what we find worthwhile about human beings.

LK: Are we starting on a road of having a different perception of a divine presence? On other pages there's talk of going to Mars. Does that change the idea of God, or is God static?

PAGELS: People used to locate God in the corners of their ignorance, you know, "This is what we don't know so that belongs to God." That is, I hope, no longer going to be the case. Certainly our perceptions are changing. The enormous awareness from communications and cultural transformations is making people aware of other cultures. Buddhists don't talk about God in the way Westerners do and yet they engage in issues involving the spiritual dimension of life, and that is going to come to the fore. The question of how one perceives a spiritual life is as powerful as ever. People are now thinking of God as "divine" and "good" and not as some kind of supernatural polarity.

LK: Okay, if our idea of a God is changing, one can presume our idea of Satan is changing also.

PAGELS: Well, the people who have taken Satan seriously have tried to account for certain things that have happened, certain atrocities of human violence to the extent of being astonishing. They are beyond what people ordinarily conceive, such as the Holocaust or some kind of slaughter or genocide. I think fewer people today think they have to invoke a supernatural presence to account for this. Instead, many people are suggesting that human nature and human culture has enough depth, weirdness, and mystery in it to account for these things. People talk about a supernatural reality but they're also talking about other people in that. I see the reality of evil not necessarily embodied in some supernatural person. It has been viewed, for instance, as being a part of disease. I also think many people are no longer seeing that God, or whatever we mean, is not opposed by some supernatural presence of evil.

LK: You are saying then that having ten pounds of "good" on one side doesn't require having ten pounds of "evil" on the other side?

PAGELS: My perception is evil can be accounted for by human beings quite well. If there's a reality out there that we call "God," that could be the source of solace but not malevolence.

LK: Death. How is our perception changing, and where do you see it moving?

PAGELS: I think of Walt Whitman's comment that death is different than what we supposed and luckier. People are now looking at the possibility that near-death experiences, be they actual or simply a chemical change in the brain, are a window to visions of angels. I thought we would have more confidence in the possibility of other realities and more awareness of the limits of our rational moments, and that, while it doesn't tell us everything, does tell us a great deal. Now people are aware that scientific answers have limits and that we are not going to learn everything from them.

LK: What happens if we have technology to put our personality and opinion on a computer disk, which then gives us the ability to interact with others after we are dead?

PAGELS: That's a very interesting question. I don't know how you'd feel about it but it would strike me as a little less adequate than our present existence. But does it change the notion of death? It could.

LK: We label ourselves as "Irish Catholic" or "Russian Jew" or "WASP." That going to continue?

PAGELS: Those religion labels resurfaced after nationalism broke out in Eastern Europe. You saw it in the former Yugoslavia as people identified themselves not as "Yugoslavs" but as "Catholic" or "Jew" or "Muslim" or "orthodox." So, surprisingly, these people went back to an archaic way of identifying themselves when more modern forms of political identification dissolved. I think these labels will become very important as we become more aware of how different we are in society. It's a way of recognizing that one's own opinion or viewpoint is shaped by social factors, and it has a great deal to do with gender, class, and so forth. So these labels may actually be very important in a society that is increasingly pluralistic as a way of qualifying our viewpoints. It helps us talk about who we are, and I think it could continue into the next century.

LK: Will there be more religions?

PAGELS: I would guess the answer is yes, but what they will look like, I don't know. Certainly the groups that exist are often breaking into different variations, and there may be others that join as a result. But I do think there will be new religions and quite new perceptions. There are already when you get studies of brain waves and states of consciousness and neurophysiology that may change the way we think about religions. I suspect we may learn quite a bit about what we call "religious states."

LK: What might some of these new beliefs be?

PAGELS: That would take a prophet.

LK: That's right. You just teach at Princeton. I forgot. Will religions become more tolerant of each other?

PAGELS: The only religions I know of that are genuinely intolerant are the three Western religions: Judaism, Christianity, and Islam. But we are going to see a borrowing from one for another, a mingling, and as a result, we will not see these as much as separate paths as we have seen in the past. Now, some people will say this waters one of them or all of them down. Some would even call it a betrayal. But I think people are going to move the boundaries in an attempt to become more open, and that will set in motion others who get nervous and, therefore, more and more rigid. The answer, then, is we'll probably see both. There is going to be a lot of discussion in the next century about this because people are becoming aware these traditions aren't just made in heaven, that they have their own depth, history, culture, and limits.

LK: What's going to happen to the established religions in the next century?

PAGELS: It seems many are losing members but groups like the Pentecostals are growing rapidly. These are religions which are much less intellectual; they are much more focused on an experiential sense of direct access to the divine. People are indeed moving away from these authoritarian religions, but we can also see many people moving toward them; groups like Promise Keepers, for example, or Louis Farrakhan and the Million Man March. These are not composed of a single denomination, but rather act as umbrella groups talking about values. Many people are looking for help in trying to act morally and so they are attracted to this clear-cut moral code.

LK: Is the Catholic Church going to have to change?

PAGELS: The pope's conviction is there may indeed be fewer members but these are the serious ones. Many Catholics I've talked to are convinced that after John Paul II there will be women priests as well as changes in sexual attitudes within the Church. Of course those predictions have been made before. But I am seeing many in the Catholic Church becoming much less rigid than they were before and they are open, for example, to Buddhist meditation techniques.

LK: Some would say these are all surface concerns.

PAGELS: Some would say that. But what we are seeing is that people are joining community religious groups rather than religious institutions. One reason has to do with the fact that we can talk on the Internet with people all over the world, but these are people you wouldn't invite to your wedding. Within communities or cities as people become more and more lonely and fragmented, the question becomes, "How do you affiliate with others?" One way is the community religious group which claims to be in touch with transcendental values.

LK: Christ has, for centuries, been personalized as a white man on a cross. Will this continue?

PAGELS: For many Western people, Christ has always been a living symbol of the self, and I think it's not that people change it to attract new members but people change it as they see themselves differently. There are quite a few images of an Afro-American Jesus, for example. The images of Jesus in Latin America look nothing like a white man. Instead you see a Hispanic man sitting around with his friends wearing a hat. More and more the pictures and features of Christ will resemble those that surround it. You'll be seeing pictures of a woman on the cross because in some places it's already been done.

LK: How are these larger denominations going to maintain their numbers?

PAGELS: I'm seeing a lot of people engaged in simultaneous exploration. While many belong to a synagogue or a church of whatever kind, they also are looking into Buddhism and other forms of religion and practice, even meditation techniques. What attracts many people is that they aren't being told what you have to do or what you can't do. In the West we've traditionally thought of religion as a set of questions and a set of answers (Do you believe in X or not? Can you do X or not?), but many more people are less concerned with that kind of question and answer than with a kind of a sense of their being, some access to the ability to center themselves and quiet the mind. Meditation is becoming increasingly important to many people. It's an experiential sense rather than a dogmatic one. Secondly, it's a group to which you can belong and refer and share a great deal of yourself on a level that has nothing to with money, social status, or profession.

LK: Eastern spirituality has attracted those in the West. That going to continue?

PAGELS: Absolutely. Westerners are going toward it not only to seek God but to help transform internal states; dealing with anger, loneliness, distress, and isolation. In this technological age people can be very lonely and very isolated and unhappy.

In meditation, solitude is seen as an illusion; we are, in fact, part of a living network of beings that extends throughout this universe. It's a sense of community and a sense of self in the universe. Look at the best-seller list: books about near-death experiences, angels, and so on. This shows that many people are becoming aware of levels of human experience that aren't explicable in scientific terms or psychological terms or reducible to those. I think many people are coming to the sense that there may be more.

LK: And we never thought about that until now?

PAGELS: Of course we did, but we always called it "religion." We don't yet have ways to integrate that to the kinds of scientific verifiability that other aspects of our society are. For example, ESP and psychic phenomena are things people experience, and people are going to be much more aware of this. While our medicine is extraordinary for healing, there is plenty that you can't do to save a human life, so we are faced with the same questions we had 120 years ago. The parameters have changed because we're talking about a longer lifespan and much healthier people. But the issues are essentially the same.

LK: Do you think churches are going to become more involved in police departments or with social workers in dealing with family violence?

PAGELS: There's a great deal of interest among psychologists and counselors in religious issues and practices. Although psychiatry was born as an atheistic practice, as Freud began it, today we are seeing an enormous explosion of therapeutic use of Buddhist techniques, meditation and so forth. We're learning more about the mind-body structure.

LK: Will that structure be different?

PAGELS: I think so. It's a way to look at the self which was probably born a couple thousand years ago in Greco-Roman philosophy. It's a traditional philosophical way of talking, now obsolete. Freud changed the language and made up an alternate model of the self. But when one takes seriously the implications of the interaction of energy and matter, these distinctions have to be seen more than ever as the metaphors they always were—crude metaphors at that. So I think definitely, with new understandings of the brain and consciousness and physiology, these will change. And it will be influenced by science as well as philosophical and religious reflection.

LK: Let's talk about the mix of religion and politics. We have the Christian Coalition and the Pat Robertsons and so on. Is this something new?

PAGELS: This is probably as ancient as religion itself. Several thousand years ago nobody separated religion and politics except Jews in the Roman Empire who didn't want to be discriminated against by Romans because they didn't believe in the Roman gods. They were the only ones in the ancient world who separated politics and religion. Later, following them, Christians did too; that was something new in the world. But the unity of religion and politics was otherwise taken for granted. So in a way I think we are realizing that if people have religious convictions then those convictions have practical implications that have to do with whether or not you can kill or commit suicide or perform an abortion. The interaction of religion and politics will increase in intensity in the next thirty or forty years.

LK: Is this clash of religion and politics driven by technology?

PAGELS: I don't think so. It's always been intensely engaged. New technology, instead of making religion irrelevant (which is what some people assumed before) in fact is raising the issues acutely. For example, now we can keep people alive who, five years ago, would have died. So the questions about termination of life are becoming increasingly acute because they seem to be much more in our hands. For instance, it is now legal in some cases to terminate pregnancy at a stage in which the fetus can be kept alive outside of the womb. So what do you do about it? Technologically you can support babies born very premature. Can you legally kill or abort them? These are fundamental questions about our values.

LK: We then are going to hear more from religious action groups like the Christian Coalition?

PAGELS: Absolutely. There are many people who see, first of all, how the world is changing and how technology is giving us so many more options, for example, to have a baby when you otherwise wouldn't have had a baby, or to prolong life in a very radical way. Those ethical questions are frightening and complex to many people who say, "Let's go back to the old answers because if it's good enough for Moses, it's good enough for me." But of course Moses, or Jesus or Paul or any of those traditional figures, did not face the world we live in. I'm not saying one can't look at Jewish or Christian tradition and deal with those questions, but we have to explore those issues in other ways as well.

LK: Will television continue to be the means to spread the word?

PAGELS: Yes. That's one way. The Internet is being used this way already; that's going to continue. Increasingly, many people are discussing issues involving religion and spirituality and exploring those in their own lives.

LK: Why do you think angels have become so popular?

PAGELS: Our science can no longer say, "This is ridiculous." For example, angels are a very ancient part of religion—invisible beings impinging on the visible. We are seeing the resurgence of the idea that human intelligence may not be the only intelligence in the universe. That's not provable by scientific means, but for many people it's more thinkable than it used to be. It may be that some people are tuned into levels of experience other than those they can articulate rationally.

THE MOST REVEREND
OSCAR LIPSCOMB

ARCHBISHOP OF MOBILE, ALABAMA

*Look at yourself and see how wonderfully you are made and
understand you didn't make yourself. Look at the world and see
the magnificent possibilities it possesses, and sometimes the
awful mess we have made of it, and ask yourself whence has the
wonder and the beauty come and where has the mess taken
place? That's where you will find God.*

LK: How might the Catholic Church change in the twenty-first
century?

LIPSCOMB: It's been changing in every century. But they are matters of style, matters of acceptability of the message in terms of the
medium, not just the language. But the message isn't going to change.

LK: What changes have we seen?

LIPSCOMB: Well, the Catholic Church built up a whole host of
pious practices that eventually acquired the status of law. When I was a
young man, eating meat on Friday was the same as standing up and
saying, "I abjure the Catholic faith." The Church decided doing without meat is not really relevant as imaging Christ in the Church of the
twentieth century.

LK: What do you want to see happen in the Church in the next
century?

LIPSCOMB: I want to see a deepening of personal and individual
spirituality that is the result of a reacquaintance with Scripture. It's
happening in small pockets throughout America. I want to see a deep
involvement with the Mass, homilies that tie in what is happening at
the altar with what is happening in people's lives so that it can be taken
home and put to work. I don't want people using it in the hunt for
something to do in order to pass time.

LK: What do you expect you will see?

LIPSCOMB: What I'm going to see is groups getting a lesser dimension of this, thirsting for it still because that is their precept, learning

with a charismatic (and that's not a bad word) influence which opens them up to accepting the Lord into their lives and trying to get him to other people. Some of it will occur under the guidance of the Catholic Church. Some of it will not.

LK: People with no formal church background will speak for it?

LIPSCOMB: Lay groups are doing it now. Lay people are recognizing their own capability for leadership and mediatorship between God and others simply because they have been given the gift that God is asking them to share. We have spiritual directors today who are guiding individuals into ways of sanctity that, in many cases, are better than priests could ever do.

LK: Priests will be stretched doing other things, and that's why the Church will use lay people?

LIPSCOMB: I think a little bit of both are at work there but more the latter. Can you imagine a pastor counting the Sunday collection? That was the occupation for Sunday afternoons for years. I know of no priest who does it today. There are whole areas of parish administration today which take care of things like this.

LK: How will religion and science get along?

LIPSCOMB: Technology does nothing to God. It might do something to our apprehension about God. There's never been any limitation with regard to God's capability to create or sustain. If we find life in other places, that's not going to change God. There might be a question as to how it would relate to the redemption of Christ, but for myself, it would not seem to have been touched at all by the redemption of Christ. Life on another planet will either be intelligent or unintelligent. If it's intelligent, that's a reflection of the Creator and it will have its own set of rules as to how it relates to him. Intelligence, after all, has a certain commonality with its identity, and so there would be a relationship to us as well. I would hope the Church would be interested in talking to another life form, though I'm not quite certain just how we would communicate. The Church will always be able to reflect upon the discovery of science. It will be slow sometimes in doing this but it will be very careful.

LK: What will be required of the pope in the next century?

LIPSCOMB: Probably his own airplane. We'll never have a pope who is isolated again. The effectiveness of the papal office is truly a worldwide charisma now. I scarcely think we'll be able to find someone like Pope John Paul II in the future, in that anyone who is chosen cannot just repudiate all that he has done, cannot go back to having people come to him all the time. The pope, in the future, will more and more be going to people.

LK: How about the Vatican? Will that remain the center of the Catholic Church?

LIPSCOMB: Not in the same way. The Holy Father will always be the center around which the Catholic world will revolve but it may have different radiuses. The pope has said we should get together and see if the way we do things now is the only way it can work. Let's talk about alternate forms of establishing a Christian community with the pope as the figurehead but not necessarily as the boss in the main office. He will continue to be a symbol of peace because he is the top guy in the Catholic Church.

LK: If there is another world war in the coming century, will the pope be a third party to keep the shooting at bay?

LIPSCOMB: I think the reasons that would lead to that kind of a conflict will have already discounted the pope. If people were going to have listened they would have done so before they got to that stage. I see him not as a player who could stop it but as a conservator who would have to pick up the pieces. In this century this gentleman has become more and more of a player and has had more of an impact on the fall of Communism, and I suspect even now, he is wondering if he did a good thing. He is finding the values, for example, in Poland which had shone bright and clear, are all of a sudden being eroded by what we have so much in abundance in the West: greed and selfishness and self-centeredness. I sometimes wonder if the pope says, "Have I taken away one master whom we recognize as cruel and oppressive to give another master whom they don't even recognize and who is capturing their hearts and their lives and they don't realize they're being had?" Read the annual statements of the bishops, and each one warns us of the fact we are being taken over by materialism. We are losing our sense of identity and are not becoming who we are but what we can get, what we possess, and what we want.

LK: And you see this continuing?

LIPSCOMB: I see no sign it's abating.

LK: Who will we be in the next century?

LIPSCOMB: If you give me twenty or thirty years down the road I see two, maybe three societies in the United States, all practically armed camps. I hope it won't happen but I find nothing that will reassure me.

LK: Who are the societies?

LIPSCOMB: The very affluent with vague protectors under the guise of the government, perhaps the government taking care of them. I see the have-nots on the other side, appealing to government but not trusting the government and forming their own sense of militia and their own sense of right. I'm not talking about the mountain men and those people that emerge as the far right because they're going to be in the third group. Those people will be out there to restore what we never ever really had.

LK: And this scenario is the result of what?

LIPSCOMB: Because the goods we consider to be the ends of our existence are being divided in our country. The Church doesn't have the means to compete with those who are holding the American spirit enthralled to materialism. Anybody who tells somebody what you have is more important than what you are, what you can get, what your bank account has, how much your Social Security check is, what you can buy on a commercial, whatever vision we throw up, be it printed or electronic, that is what is heard.

LK: So the Church has to be heard with ads, correct?

LIPSCOMB: The cost of one Super Bowl ad is the cost of an entire archdiocese public relations budget for a whole year!

LK: No ads for the Vatican on a Sunday in January?

LIPSCOMB: No, the Vatican can't compete either. Listen, what would the Vatican do buying time on a Super Bowl advertisement? What message could we put in a half-minute or even a minute? We buy better time when Cardinal Bernardin dies or when Mother Teresa dies or when a pope dies and another one is elected. People are caught up short to realize, here at least is another reality, here is a contrary view of life. People talk about women's issues, and here is the one woman the whole world celebrates: She is a poor, celibate, totally unselfish woman who gives her entire life for other people. There should be a little bit of Mother Teresa in all of us.

LK: Will there be women priests in the next century?

LIPSCOMB: I would say no. The priesthood is one of those things we can't change. This is not to say I wouldn't like to change it, nor am I unsympathetic to women wanting to do things, but in terms of theology rather than what people would like, I just don't see the grounds for admission of women to the priesthood. Maybe there's a mistake we've made about what makes priesthood so important. Mothers are more important than priests, both in the divine scheme and certainly in the scheme of our society. So my personal opinion is in another fifty years the question will be less agitated because the priesthood will come back to its celibate form. This isn't popular and it isn't what the media wants to hear.

LK: Will priests be married?

LIPSCOMB: It's possible, but I don't see it as an answer to our problems. It's happened. The Church could change it again. The Church would have to have compelling reason to say this is a necessity, but the lack of priests is not that kind of a compelling reason. There is a thrust for sacramental ministry as if the Eucharist, which is the heart and the center of priesthood, if denied, is a sufficient reason to change the discipline and even to change the parameters of the priesthood, so that women could become priests in order to ensure women could provide Eucharist. I'm not sure that is a valid assumption. Besides, the Church existed for years and years with people only going to Communion once a month. They survived.

LK: How will our perception of God change?

LIPSCOMB: We've already changed it quite a bit. God becomes as how we see him rather than how we see ourselves. I recall an essay years ago in one of the magazines, which asked "How do you feel about God?" As if that really matters, right? That's the wrong perspective.

LK: Well, how about Satan?

LIPSCOMB: Well, I think Satan exists. Evil is not just an embodiment. There's too much in our human experience not to believe.

LK: What would be an example of Satan in the twentieth century?

LIPSCOMB: Dachau.

LK: Will we go to Church on the Internet or through interactive television in the next century?

LIPSCOMB: No. The Internet and television can inspire us, but the interactive relationship with God is going to require a physical presence and a spiritual presence rather than the virtual image presence you find on the Internet. To the extent we depend upon gimmicks to preach, it will fall flat on its face.

LK: Will the Church change its stand on abortion?

LIPSCOMB: No. It's the direct taking of an innocent life.

LK: What scares you about the next century?

LIPSCOMB: I'm not frightened of it at all.

WILL WE STILL HAVE TO WORRY ABOUT . . . ?

OPEC?

Yeah, there's a commercial problem there with the supply of oil. The internal combustion engine will be around, and one of the fuels that you can use to drive it comes from oil. But pay attention to ethanol. It comes from corn, and there's no place that makes more corn than America. So in the short term we will be dependent to some degree on imports from OPEC.

> *Neil Ressler, vice president,*
> *Advanced Vehicle Technology,*
> *Ford Motor Company*

GETTING ASSIGNED THE MIDDLE SEAT ON AIRPLANES?

Yes. You are always going to have to worry about a middle seat in economy class. We think there is going to be a continued emphasis on economy of operation, and as long as that's a major driver in the design of airplanes, there's no way to avoid some middle seats.

John Hayhurst,
vice president, 747-500X Programs,
Boeing Corporation

LOW VOTER TURNOUT?

If we continue having several hoops to go through (having to register and so on), in today's spectator world it will be harder to get people to take the time to do it. Modern means will be figured out to make it easier. We'll have a means of communication allowing them to sit in their home and vote.

Doris Kearns Goodwin,
presidential historian;
panelist, Newshour with Jim Lehrer;
author of No Ordinary Time,
which won the 1995 Pulitzer Prize
for History

SEVEN-SECOND SOUND BITES?

Sure. But they are simply a peg to tell a fuller story. When I read a newspaper I'll look at a quote and time it. Invariably, it's always less than seven seconds. The way I view television in the twenty-first century is very much like the front page of the *New York Times*. You'll have the lead story on that page, the headline and the punchier quotes and the lead of the story. That will be what you see on the TV. The jump page will be in the Internet.

Tim Russert,
Washington Bureau chief,
NBC News; host, Meet the Press

NEWSPAPER INK COMING OFF ON OUR HANDS?

No. There's nonrub ink used now by most newspapers except for a few major circulation gray and dull newspapers that haven't yet figured out that you ought to dry the ink before you fold the paper and send it out to the consumer. [Those are papers in the northeast corridor?] You said that, not me.

> Al Neuharth,
> founder, USA Today;
> chairman, Freedom Forum

BLAMING THE MEDIA?

Yes. We will always blame the media. But first, here's a language lesson for the twenty-first century. Stop saying, "The media is." "Media" is plural, so start saying, "The media are." But by saying, "The media is," we are saying all media are the same and we all get the same media. The media aren't an "is." The media are an "are."

> Joe Turow,
> professor of communications,
> Annenberg School for
> Communications,
> University of Pennsylvania

STANDING IN FRONT OF A DESK LOOKING FOR A MEMO OR A PIECE OF PAPER?

It's a thing of the past. We'll have intelligent agents that live in docu-spaces and we'll have know-bots that can go out and find whatever it is that you've lost track of no matter how many years before. It will bring calmness to the office, and this buzzing confusion we now feel will, hopefully, come to an end.

> John Seely Brown,
> chief scientist, Xerox Corporation;
> director, Palo Alto Research Center

WHY JOHNNY CAN'T READ?

Yes. It has to do with the fact we view reading as the most important thing to do in school, but it's not the most important thing in life. Children with things on their mind, like abuse at home or "My dad drinks all the time," that kind of thing, well, you simply can't get to those children because learning to read for them is not as important as survival. We'll get better but there will always be children with this problem.

> Dr. Larry Smith, chair, Department
> of Elementary Education, Ball State
> Teachers College, Muncie, Indiana

IF THERE IS A GOD?

We'll be talking about a dimension of our experiences and God is a primary way to do this. We're becoming much more aware of the different ways of picturing God.

> Elaine Pagels, Harrington Spear
> Paine Professor of Religion, Princeton
> University

PHOTO OPPORTUNITIES?

Yes, if we don't grow up. If I announced right here I've got George Washington's identical twin to run on the Reform ticket, many people would think, "Gee, the guy doesn't have a chance because he's got wooden teeth." If I announced Winston Churchill's identical twin who was born in the United States and can be a candidate, well, the first reaction is, "He ought to lose sixty pounds and quit smoking." It has nothing to do with anything except theater and it does not produce results, and somehow we've got to get that over to the guy in the street.

> Ross Perot, chairman, Perot Reform
> Party; 1992 presidential candidate;
> chairman, Perot Systems, Dallas

SPENDING A MILLION DOLLARS TO FLY THE SPACE SHUTTLE FROM CALIFORNIA TO FLORIDA BECAUSE THE WEATHER IN FLORIDA WOULDN'T PERMIT THE SHUTTLE TO LAND THERE IN THE FIRST PLACE?

Oh, that's something you shouldn't have to worry about. Safety comes first. We've got to get beyond nits and gnats. I don't want to say people shouldn't hold NASA accountable for appropriately spending money. We have astronauts in the shuttle. We could let them hang in space for a few days if there's bad weather at Cape Kennedy. Hopefully, the next generation of vehicles can fly all-weather. Don't worry about the million dollars. We'll have a better machine in the twenty-first century.

Dan Goldin, administrator,
National Aeronautics and Space
Administration

ANTICS OF PLAYERS AFTER THEY MAKE A TOUCHDOWN?

I hope not. I hope that goes out of fashion. Somebody ought to come along who makes it cool again to act with dignity and class and restraint and to respect the game as well as your opponent. There are more than a few Cal Ripkens and Grant Hills and Emmet Smiths who conduct themselves like sportsmen. But in the next few years I hope we get tired of everyone acting like a ten-year-old and celebrating after a touchdown that doesn't have any effect on the outcome of a game or making a tackle in the first four minutes of the game and standing over your opponent like a Roman gladiator. I hope it dawns on these people that all the antics look the same.

Bob Costas, NBC Sports

WAITING IN THE CHECKOUT LINE WHILE SOMEONE LOOKS FOR LOOSE CHANGE?

I think there will always be problems like that. Or the guy standing in front of you making a big order while all you want to do is pay for a cup of coffee. We will, however, be able to do a lot of the boring habitual shopping in an on-line environment where things are automated. The cyberworld will be used for this.

Magdalena Yesil,
founder, MarketPay

UNION BOSSES?

You only hear that when an attempt is made to divide a union's membership. One year we're irrelevant and dinosaurs. Then, suddenly, we become big union bosses and public enemy number one. That means someone new has an ox that's getting gored. So the answer is yes. They'll still be calling us union bosses in another one hundred years!

Richard Trumka, secretary-treasurer,
AFL-CIO; former president,
United Mine Workers

HATE?

It's the result of ignorance. If you don't train yourself to see the good in people you won't see it. If you don't work to develop another person's goodness, it won't happen. Remember there are Five E's which affect our behavior: ego, environment, education, emotions, and experience.

Colman McCarthy, founder and
director, Center for Teaching Peace

PEOPLE LIKE SADDAM HUSSEIN OR MUAMMAR QADDAFI?

Absolutely. I think nothing in history shows we are entering an enlightened period where we will not have despots like that and we will not have people who will take advantage of weakened neighbors, people who are just downright cruel and mean and will do it for their own advantage. I think we will have to continue to worry about them. And what's dangerous, because of communications systems available to them, it will be easier for them to mesmerize their people and lead them in the wrong direction.

General John Shalikashvili,
chairman, Joint Chiefs of Staff,
1993–1997

ONE COMPUTER PROGRAM AND SEVENTEEN BOOKS TELLING US HOW TO RUN THE COMPUTER PROGRAM?

Computers are getting easier to use but they're also taking on more difficult challenges. We used to ship software programs with thick manuals, sometimes sets of thick manuals. Most people don't need so much paper documentation anymore because the basic functionality of well-designed software is getting fairly intuitive. But there will always be people who want in-depth information, so I expect there will be a healthy market for books about how to use the software programs.

Bill Gates, chairman,
Microsoft Corporation

PEOPLE INTERPRETING THE BIBLE AS BEING CONCRETE?

Yes. The more concretistic they are about their interpretation, the more they will tend to hate outsiders. They can stay locked in a room and as focused on the interpretation as they want as long as they don't run out and attack somebody. We should find interpretations, though, that make them less afraid of others, but we can tolerate them having their own interpretations.

Robert Thurman,
professor of Indo-Tibetan Buddhist
studies,
Columbia University

THE COMMON COLD?

Yes. We haven't found a way to deal with the ability of viruses to change, nor have we developed anything to confront them. Luckily, the common cold is mild enough so it doesn't do a lot of harm.

Dr. David Satcher, director,
National Centers for Disease
Control and Prevention

HAVING TO SIT THROUGH THREE PREVIEWS BEFORE WE SEE THE FEATURE PRESENTATION?

I hope not. There might be five hundred. But I think if you watch a movie from your home, you'll have the option of clicking on the previews or bypassing the whole thing and going right to the feature. But you will just as easily be able to block out all the marketing we do and just watch the movie. It will be your choice. In a movie theater, there will continue to be previews.

Sherry Lansing, chairman,
Paramount Pictures

BEING OUT OF STYLE?

Yes. There will always be fashion. But it's not fashion saying, "This is correct." That is passé. Things are not necessarily correct anymore but there are definitely things that are wrong. We will always feel wrong in the wrong thing but we don't have to know what is correct. That's the difference in the definition of fashion that is changing.

Isaac Mizrahi, fashion designer

PROFESSIONAL TEAMS GOING ON STRIKE?

Yes. It's a dynamic of our labor system in America. It's a good check and balance on one side having too much power.

David Falk, chairman, FAME;
lawyer for Michael Jordan, Patrick
Ewing, Chris Doleman, and Juwan
Howard, among others

MEN HOLDING THE REMOTE WHILE WATCHING TV?

Yeah. There's something about men that there's an impatience. I see it while testing audiences. Women will get into something with the plot and men go, "Okay, c'mon, let's move on with it already."

Stephen J. Cannell, chairman,
Cannell Entertainment; Emmy
Award–winning writer and producer
of more than thirty-five television
shows; author of the bestselling
political thriller The Plan

UNINTELLIGIBLE E-MAIL ADDRESSES WITH SEVENTEEN DOT COMS-SLASH-NET-WHATEVER?

No. We will have shorter e-mail addresses, names instead of numbers, and they will be easier to remember. That is the one problem we will be able to solve.

Esther Dyson, president, EDventure
Holdings; chairman, Electronic
Frontier Foundation

GENETICALLY TRANSMITTED HATRED?

Yes. If you are a Serb or a Jew or an Irish Catholic or a Protestant and you believe what happened to your people in generations past is a function of a certain ethnic or racial composition of the perpetrators, you have doomed yourself. The result is, history will will itself into repetition. Croats, Bosnians, Serbs lived in Ohio and came to Dayton during the peace talks. They didn't go around shooting each other in Dayton, and I made this point to the participants. Here we are on the eve of the twenty-first century and our greatest crisis may be the ethnic and racial hatred from within. It is obviously part of human nature to hate those who are different from us. France and Germany will never go to war again. Anti-Semitism exists, but we're not going to have another Holocaust. Egypt and Israel won't go to war against each other again. But now we have to teach people to respect differences.

Ambassador Richard C. Holbrooke

COMING HOME AND TURNING ON THE TV AND SAYING, "THERE'S NOTHING ON TONIGHT"?

Yes. There is no question in my mind, the more you have, the more you want. Until you have individual choice for everything or the ability to create your own programs, you are never going to please everybody. I face that now, and I have every signal coming in except for the police channel. This will continue until we have available to us every movie ever made, every book that has been printed, and every art form available to us, and that is going to be a long time. It's getting closer, though, but don't expect it for another twenty-five years, minimum.

Lucie Salhany,
former president and chief executive
officer, UPN Television

BANNING *TOM SAWYER* OR *HUCKLEBERRY FINN*?

Yes. People are always going to be nervous about a book being too frank in how it deals with religion or race or a girl coming of age. The problem is never teaching the controversial book as much as it is what you teach about the controversial book. You have to talk about why the book is great and about its history. You have to step outside the window of the book itself, and that will frighten people. Controversial books make people think the most.

Farai Chideya,
national affairs editor,
Vibe *magazine; editor of Pop &*
Politics Web site
(http://www.popandpolitics.com);
author of The Color of America

A FEW
THANK-YOUS

For most of us, talking about the future isn't an easy thing to do. Writing about it ain't exactly a walk in the park either. Neither could have been done without the help of these people, and to them we are grateful:

Larry's assistant, Judy Thomas, who has all of Larry's schedule for the twentieth and twenty-first centuries in her office.

Jean Mekkaoui at Bob Woolf Associates, who so proficiently handled all of Larry's business matters this century and, if she's up for it, can do it in the next one too.

If Pat ever gets a business deal, the first call goes to Jean.

Mauro DiPreta at HarperCollins, with whom we shared more of the twentieth century working on the twenty-first century than any of us expected. He is an editor and a genius, and that's a rare combination indeed, regardless of the century. His assistant, Molly Hennessey, was always there, and we know these pages are better as a result.

In the course of doing this book Larry King met the love of his life, Shawn Southwick, and married her. Larry thanks Mrs. King for teaching him about the importance of the present moment rather than all those in the future.

Larry King